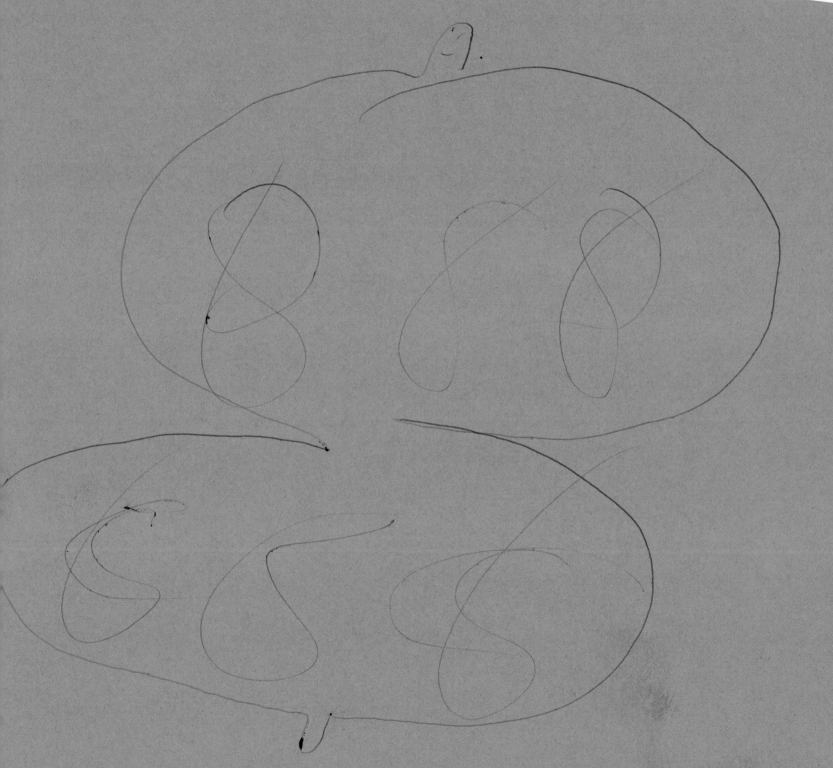

An American Perspective

Nineteenth-Century Art
from the collection of
Jo Ann & Julian Ganz, Jr.

Nineteenth-Century Art
from the collection of
Jo Ann & Julian Ganz, Jr.

An American Perspective

John Wilmerding   Linda Ayres   Earl A. Powell

National Gallery of Art
Washington

This catalogue was produced by the Editors Office, National Gallery of Art, Washington. Printed by Eastern Press, Inc., New Haven, Connecticut. The type is Palatino, set by Monotype Composition Inc., Baltimore, Maryland. The paper is Cameo Dull Text. Designed by Frances P. Smyth.

Exhibition dates:
National Gallery of Art, Washington October 4, 1981–January 31, 1982
Amon Carter Museum, Fort Worth March 19–May 23, 1982
Los Angeles County Museum of Art July 6–September 26, 1982

Cover: Sanford Robinson Gifford. *The Artist Sketching at Mount Desert, Maine*, 1864–1865. Detail, fig. 18.

Frontispiece: Samuel S. Carr. *The Beach at Coney Island*, c. 1879. Detail, fig. 48.

Library of Congress Cataloging in Publication Data

Main entry under title:
An American perspective.

"Catalogue. Biographies: John Lamb . . . [et al.] Entries: Stephen Edidin": p.
Includes bibliographical references.
1. Art, American—Exhibitions. 2. Art, Modern—19th century—United States—Exhibitions. 3. Ganz, Jo Ann—Art collections—Exhibitions. 4. Ganz, Julian—Art collections—Exhibitions. I. Wilmerding, John. II. Ayres, Linda, 1947– . III. Powell, Earl A. IV. Ganz, Jo Ann. V. Ganz, Julian. VI. National Gallery of Art (U.S.) VII. Title.
N6510.A64 759.13′074′0153 81–11092
ISBN 0-89468-002-1 AACR2
ISBN 0-87451-221-2 (cloth)

With the exception of the following, all photographs in this catalogue were taken by Larry Reynolds, Los Angeles County Museum of Art:

fig. 101, Christie's, New York; figs. 8, 9, 15, 24, 45, 51, 53, 57, 86, 89, 96, 97, 100, Helga Photo Studio; fig. 68, Joseph Szaszfai; and figs. 3, 17, 61, 74, Jann and John Thomson.

The hardcover edition of this catalogue is being distributed by the University Press of New England, 3 Lebanon Street, Hanover, New Hampshire 03755

This exhibition is supported by a generous contribution from Republic National Bank of New York; Trade Development Bank, Geneva; and Banco Safra, S.A., Brazil

Contents

Fig. 100
Martin Johnson Heade,
*Victorian Vase with Flowers
of Devotion*, c.1870–1875

Foreword

WITH MUCH PLEASURE AND GRATITUDE the National Gallery of Art, the Amon Carter Museum, and the Los Angeles County Museum of Art join in presenting *An American Perspective: Nineteenth-Century Art from the Collection of Jo Ann and Julian Ganz, Jr.* Exhibited publicly only twice before, and then in very different and more compact form, this collection brings together a remarkable group of American paintings, watercolors, and sculpture—distinguished by high quality and appealing subject matter. It is not ordinarily easy for private collectors to give up their cherished holdings to public showing for a long period of time. We are all therefore particularly grateful to these two astute and generous collectors, who have collaborated so closely in selecting their acquisitions, for making their collection available to our visitors over a year-long period. It is an especially happy and appropriate circumstance that this group of objects—vividly depicting aspects of nineteenth-century life and nature in America—can be seen by three different audiences across the country.

Any collection of art consciously formed by an individual or institution is bound to reflect the special tastes and interests of the owner. Jo Ann and Julian Ganz of Los Angeles have been collecting for less than twenty years. Since their first purchase in 1964 of a Robert Henri portrait, *Dutchman I,* 1907, they have reshaped the direction of their collecting interests dramatically and steadily raised the level of quality in the collection. The results of their passion, now graciously shared with others, offer a lesson in the connoisseurship of nineteenth-century American art, bringing to our attention outstanding examples by some of our foremost artists and by a number of long-neglected and little-known names.

We are indebted to Jo Ann and Julian Ganz for their kindness and helpfulness in providing scholarly information on their collection and in every way assisting us with the logistics of borrowing and installing the objects. Both graduates of Stanford University, the Ganzes are natives and long-time residents of California. In recent years he has served as a trustee and chairman of the Acquisitions Committee at the Los Angeles County Museum of Art, while together they founded the museum's American Art Council, an important and supportive group of area collectors.

We are also most grateful to Republic National Bank of New York, Trade Development Bank, Geneva, and Banco Safra, S.A., Brazil, for their generous contributions toward the costs of exhibiting the collection in Washington, Fort Worth, and Los Angeles.

This exhibition was initiated and organized by John Wilmerding, curator of American art and senior curator at the National Gallery. We are grateful to him and, for their assistance in coordination, to Carol Clark, curator of paintings at the Amon Carter Museum, and Michael Quick, curator of American paintings at the Los Angeles County Museum of Art. William H. Gerdts, executive officer at the Graduate Center of the City University of New York, was most helpful as an advisory consultant in the preparation of documentary material. To his graduate student at City University, Stephen Edidin, we express thanks for writing much of the catalogue information.

Others at the National Gallery who have played indispensable roles are Linda Ayres, assistant curator of American art, who contributed an essay and undertook many of the administrative details; Deborah Chotner, research assistant, and John

Lamb, a volunteer summer intern in 1979, who worked on preparation of the artists' biographies; Maria Mallus, who carried out clerical matters and manuscript preparation; Paula Smiley, who skillfully managed the editing; and Pamela Jenkinson in the Information Office, who coordinated publications on the Ganz collection elsewhere. Additionally, we wish to acknowledge with much appreciation the help of Larry Reynolds, head photographer at the Los Angeles County Museum of Art, who produced most of the impeccable prints reproduced here. An expression of gratitude is also due to Rose Schulter Donaldson, who has provided invaluable assistance to the Ganzes in compiling and transmitting information, records,

and photographs in conjunction with this exhibition, and to James L. Greaves, conservator of paintings at Los Angeles County Museum of Art, whose keen eye and hand have protected and enhanced a number of the works seen here.

The American art gathered by the Ganzes follows in the worthy tradition of such notable earlier collections assembled by Luman Reed and Robert Gilmor in the first half of the nineteenth century, Thomas Clarke at its end, and Maxim Karolik in the middle of the twentieth century. Now, Jo Ann and Julian Ganz allow us all to partake of their special perspective in collecting American art. We hope others will be equally delighted and informed by this distinctive experience.

J. CARTER BROWN
Director
National Gallery of Art, Washington

JAN MUHLERT
Director
Amon Carter Museum, Fort Worth

EARL A. POWELL
Director
Los Angeles County Museum of Art

Fig. 83   Roesen, *Flower Still-Life* (detail)

8

Preface

John Wilmerding

An *American Perspective: Nineteenth-Century Art from the Collection of Jo Ann and Julian Ganz, Jr.* brings to public view the finest private collection in the country of nineteenth-century American art. At the National Gallery it follows *American Light*, our large exhibition of luminist painting held in early 1980, as part of a continuing series devoted to significant aspects or figures in earlier American art. We have also drawn periodically from our own collections to put up smaller shows, such as the selections from the Garbisch group of American naive paintings shown in the summer of 1978 and the Indian pictures by George Catlin in the fall of 1980. Together these are intended to offer our public a cross-section and variety of American works of art held in both public and private hands.

The taste of the Ganzes is at once eclectic and coherent, far ranging and consistently focused, objective and personal. Their interests span a variety of subjects: principally still life, landscape, and genre. This last category is itself broad, extending from literal portraits to figures engaged in everyday activities both indoors and out. With a constant feeling for quality, they have acquired works in several different media: oil paintings and sketches, watercolors, pencil drawings, pastels, and some dozen sculptures in marble and bronze. While the collection is overwhelmingly nineteenth century in date and comprises objects from almost every decade, there are a few significant exceptions and some revealing concentrations.

Almost half of the one hundred works gathered and exhibited here date from the 1860s and seventies, approximately twenty-five from each decade. Smaller groups are spread out in the decades of the 1850s, eighties, and nineties. Only four of the Ganz pieces date from the forties, although Thomas Cole's important late landscape, *The Old Mill at Sunset*, anchors this decade. Just three paintings have earlier dates, but they are all major examples and have clear relevance in the collection as a whole. John Singleton Copley's *Sketch for "The Copley Family,"* 1776 (fig. 28), is the only eighteenth-century work here, though its informal domestic subject is a recurrent theme in later Ganz paintings. Just two works come from the entire first quarter of the nineteenth century—Raphaelle Peale's *A Dessert*, 1814 (fig. 77), and Thomas Sully's *Portrait of the Misses Mary & Emily McEuen*, 1823 (fig. 29)—yet they provide brilliant antecedents for the Ganzes' still-life and figural assemblages to follow. Likewise, there are only a handful of works dating from after the turn of the century, the latest being John Frederick Peto's *Old Companions*, 1904 (fig. 98), a summary work of the artist's career and of American trompe l'oeil painting.

At the heart of this chronology are two key groups: eight radiant landscape sketches by Sanford Gifford and a number of genre paintings by John George Brown and Seymour Guy. Most date from the sixties and seventies, exemplifying the Ganzes' penchant for freshness of subject and treatment in mid-nineteenth-century American painting, whether in plein-air oil sketches of the landscape or in direct and unpretentious scenes of youth. These pictures and the collection as a whole possess an aura of charm without being cloying, an emotional appeal without being sentimental. Save some half-dozen objects, the entire collection falls within the dates of Queen Victoria's reign (1837–1901), a fact which calls attention to the English academic background pervasive here and the nature of Victorian taste as it flourished in America.

The gentle and genteel images so prevalent in the Ganz

Fig. 29   Thomas Sully,
Portrait of the Misses Mary & Emily McEuen,
1823

collection give it this Victorian cast, which was neither a focus nor common denominator when they began collecting. Rather, their first acquisition of a Henri portrait initiated the gathering of examples in various media by other members of The Eight, including works by John Sloan and William Glackens. This in turn led them to a widening interest in the painterly realism of such late nineteenth-century artists as Edmund Tarbell, Thomas Anshutz, William Merritt Chase, Theodore Robinson, and John Singer Sargent. An early watershed in the collection came in 1969, when the Los Angeles County Museum of Art mounted a small exhibition of thirty-six works from this original core group. But now significantly added to the artists noted above was also a variety of earlier nineteenth-century figures, including Joshua Shaw, James Buttersworth, Edward Moran, Severin Roesen, John F. Kensett, Albert Bierstadt, Elihu Ved-

der, Alfred Thompson Bricher, and J. G. Brown. This exhibition and its catalogue were supervised by Larry J. Curry, then curator of American art at Los Angeles, and illustrated the broadening stylistic character of the Ganzes' acquisitions.

Inherent in this first formal assemblage was a sense of an aesthetic taste in transition, for from this period onward the Ganzes steadily expanded their holdings in the area of tightly painted yet lyrical works and eliminated almost all the examples of the later, more broadly painted aesthetic. This period was to mark the crucial beginning of their devotion to the art of Bierstadt, Kensett, Vedder, Roesen, Bricher, and Brown, all of whom would remain thereafter represented in the collection, though in all but a few instances with far superior works acquired subsequently. In this regard it is important to note that only two paintings exhibited in 1969—Kensett's *Lake*

Fig. 55 Joseph Mozier,
Undine, c.1867

George, 1858 (fig. 13), and Brown's *Children at the Gate*, 1872 (fig. 46)—remain in the collection today.

About the same time new scholarly publications and exhibitions in the nineteenth-century American field were stimulating fresh, serious interest, and the Ganz collection mirrors the impact of such influential events as the *19th Century America* exhibition and symposium at the Metropolitan Museum of Art in 1970 and the publication of *American Still-Life Painting* by William H. Gerdts and Russell Burke in 1971. The latter in particular sharpened the Ganzes' attention to still-life and trompe l'oeil subjects. Only two still lifes were included in the Los Angeles show, but over the next four years this group grew to almost two dozen, approximately the number presented here.

In 1973 Paul Mills, director of the Santa Barbara Museum,

organized a second exhibition of the Ganz collection, and again this was a revealing moment to take stock of the shape and dimensions of their collecting tastes. In the first place, this was a much larger and more ambitious undertaking, putting on display seventy-five objects. It included many of the well-known names associated with the collection today: Joseph Decker, Thomas Dewing, Sanford Gifford, George Lambdin, Jervis McEntee, Aaron Draper Shattuck, and John F. Peto. But again, from that exhibition only eighteen works still belong to the Ganzes today, as assiduous refining in terms of quality and significance took place. Perhaps most importantly, at this time works on paper were added in notable numbers. Since then further drawings and watercolors have been acquired, but in recent years the Ganzes have chosen to own only those which are fully realized statements, eliminating the small, slight, and more fragmentary works. Typical of this later focus are the impressive charcoal by William Trost Richards, *Landscape with Brook*, 1865 (fig. 4), and Homer's *Blackboard*, 1877 (fig. 58).

The third major phase of collecting by the Ganzes commenced after the Santa Barbara show with their first sculpture purchase in 1974, Joseph Mozier's neoclassic *Undine*, c. 1867 (fig. 55). This has been joined subsequently by nine other marbles and a bronze. From these emerged the development of what is almost a subcategory in the collection: late nineteenth-century paintings and watercolors with neoclassic subject matter. Also during the last few years leading up to the present exhibition the Ganzes have intentionally elected to own certain artists in depth, most notable being the works by Gifford, Guy, and J. G. Brown. We can also observe that, while there are a few large paintings and full-size sculptures here, the scale and feeling of these works collectively might be described as domestic. In addition, with the assistance of Stuart P. Feld, who has helped to shape the collection, the Ganzes have been notably successful in realizing their aim of displaying their paintings in appropriate period frames. This aspect is one often overlooked by collectors and museums today, but it is an aesthetic element which contributes importantly to our fuller understanding of taste in the nineteenth century. These factors serve to remind us of the individual nature of this collection, one in which selections have been a highly personal and collaborative process. Altogether, these are works of art acquired to be lived with, an aspect worth keeping in mind as a museum installation displays them in a fresh perspective.

An American Perspective: Nineteenth-Century Art from the Collection of Jo Ann and Julian Ganz, Jr. offers, then, a very different gathering from any of its earlier manifestations. Comprised of over one hundred objects, the collection offers a distinctive and unusual overview of American art through the last century. The Ganzes have deliberately not intended their collection to be a comprehensive survey; certain artists and styles are not represented here—for example, American impressionism—largely because they have not fit within the evolving aesthetic focus of the collection. The primary categories of subject matter here—landscape, genre, and still life—are the basis for the three respective essays which follow. While these discussions pursue generally chronological patterns and scrutinize the major works in the Ganz collection, the reader will find varying degrees of emphasis and occasionally overlapping commentaries. Not all objects are discussed at the same length, though each artist and work is fully documented in the catalogue section. Genre and figure subjects now constitute about half the total collection, with landscape and still lifes breaking down approximately into the other two quarters. From these numbers and from the images themselves we come away with a dominant sense of individuals, Americans from a past century, seen at ease indoors and out, surrounded by familiar things and a benign environment. From the vantage point of our own more troubled world, the American works of art in the Ganz collection provide a welcome opportunity for us to appreciate anew something of the optimism and promise of an earlier age.

Fig. 45   Brown, *Among the Trees* (detail)

Fig. 1   Thomas Cole, *The Old Mill at Sunset*, 1844

The American View: Landscape Paintings and Drawings

Earl A. Powell

Duringthe second half of the nineteenth century in America both the impetus to produce landscape art and the subject of landscape altered appreciably as the pressure of events surrounding the Civil War witnessed the emergence of a new national consciousness. It was a time when certain fundamental religious beliefs were assaulted by new scientific doctrines, most noticeable and influential among them the publication of Charles Darwin's *On the Origin of Species* in 1859, and when new critical writings, particularly those of John Ruskin, exercised an important influence on art. The landscape paintings from the Ganz collection provide an opportunity to examine the shifts in taste and the pluralities of style that characterized American landscape painting especially in the latter part of the century.

In the early years of the century American landscape was closely associated with the republican ideals of the new nation and took on significance in the popular imagination as a form of national propaganda. Landscape painting was conceived of as a vehicle for the articulation of the new republic's unique historical and moral position in world history. It was a position subscribed to by Thomas Cole, the dean of the Hudson River School, and was based on a religious interpretation of wilderness motifs. While the American concern for the founding of a school of historical landscape was most assertive in the first half of the century and is attested to in such grandly ambitious paintings as Cole's famous moral allegory depicting the *Course of Empire*,[1] interest in creating a national art based on American nature continued to influence the formal evolution of landscape painting.

As late as 1855 Asher B. Durand affirmed the importance of landscape as a forum for the expression of nationalistic sentiments. In the influential essays entitled "Letters on Landscape Painting" he commented,

I desire not to limit the universality of the Art, or require that the artist shall sacrifice aught to patriotism; but, untrammelled as he is, and free from academic or other restraints by virtue of his position, why should not the American landscape painter, in accordance with the principle of self-government, boldly originate a high and independent style, based on his native resources? ever cherishing an abiding faith that the time is not far remote when his beloved Art will stand out amid the scenery of his "own green forest land," wearing as fair a coronal as ever graced a brow "in that Old World beyond the deep."[2]

Landscape art prior to the advent of the war was influenced by a combination of patriotism and fundamental religious concerns which focused on millennialism and redemption in the wilderness landscape of the New World. As mid-century approached, however, the imperatives of landscape began to shift to reflect transcendentalist concerns for space and light painted in a tightly realistic mode of expression now called luminism. After 1865 painting styles became more diverse, paralleling the multiplicity of interests in a nation now given over to a certain introspection and concern at the same time it was expanding both its industrial capacity and consolidating its frontiers. Landscape painting in the second half of the nineteenth century changed as artists attempted to establish new ideals for American art that were less self-consciously and indigenously "American," in much the same sense as American literature experienced a profound change. Following the Civil War, as Howard Mumford Jones has pointed out,

We passed in literature from the standard classical American authors, mainly romantic, to another set of writers who afterward became standard—such as Henry James, William Dean Howells, and Mark Twain—men who as often "Europeanized" as not, who essentially abandoned the older doctrine that American writing should be unique and accepted the doctrine that American writing should study European theories.[3]

The plurality of painting styles that emerged in the latter half of the century underscored the difference between the two eras, as American artists sought to establish new ideals for American art. The wild landscape of the Catskill Mountains which inspired Thomas Cole's early landscape interpretations of American nature was replaced later in the century by a similar awe and wonder at the landscape of the American West, which was grandiosely interpreted by Albert Bierstadt and others. The heady optimism of the Jacksonian era gave way to the more introspective and private realism of Thomas Eakins and Winslow Homer. European academic standards fostered through the proliferating schools and academies in the United States had a transforming effect on American landscape art and exerted a strong dominance over American taste in general. Interest in European techniques and conceptions of style fascinated American artists who went abroad to study in Paris at the Ecole des Beaux-Arts or at the academy in Munich, and the darker chiaroscuro and academic realism of an older painting tradition contributed to the definition of this period as the Brown Decades. Indeed, by 1880 William C. Brownell was able to comment, "We are beginning to paint as other people paint."[4] A young generation of artists was now interested in relating the values of American painting to older European traditions and formal conventions in an attempt to identify American art with a broader tradition of the visual arts. The renewed interest in Europe paralleled continuing concern for a more purely indigenous landscape tradition, contributing to a rich profusion of landscape styles which in their diversity are a compelling visual index of a fascinating period in the history of landscape.

*   *   *

Thomas Cole completed *The Old Mill at Sunset* (fig. 1) as a commission from Mr. H. S. Mulligan in 1844, just four years before his early death, while he was in full maturity as an artist. It is the earliest picture in the landscape section of the exhibition and a magnificent example of the artist's late landscape style. Cole's biographer, Louis Legrand Noble, called *The Old Mill at Sunset*

. . . one of those rare creations of the pencil that touch the thoughtful beholder like a rich and tender melody. If the expression may be allowed, it is a pictured song; one of the finest of songs too, and most beautifully pictured. The manifold sounds and activities of the day are so far quieted that the cattle, ruminating or grazing in the luxuriant pasture, the children sporting on the flowery green, and the busy mill, are left as striking characteristics of the scene, and sing to the heart, while the rich vesture of the month, the glassy lake, reflecting the quiet beauty of the floating clouds, and all bathed in the day's last delicious light, fill the senses, and entrance the soul. For beauty of composition, fine colouring, graceful line and delicacy of touch, and that moist, living air, so peculiar to Cole, few of his pictures are superior to the "Mill at Sunset."[5]

This picture dates from a period in the artist's career when a concern for allegorical themes occupied much of his attention. In 1840–41 he had completed his famous series *The Voyage of Life*.[6] The idyllic representation of nature in *The Old Mill at Sunset*, which emphasizes light as a form of religious experience, can be interpreted as evolving within the framework of Cole's religious philosophy. This landscape is indicative of the general direction that the formal concerns of American landscape were developing as mid-century approached. Noble's references to the "glassy lake," the "quiet beauty," and the "moist, living air" of this late picture characterize an experience of nature very like that depicted in the work of the luminist painters Fitz Hugh Lane, John Frederick Kensett, Sanford Robinson Gifford, and others. The stilled realism and enveloping tinted light are expressive of a very different attitude toward nature than that depicted in Cole's early, wild landscapes. *The Old Mill at Sunset* is a provocative landscape; in its supreme distillation of a mood of nature it relates an experience of nature to which Cole often alluded in his writings but which did not attract his interest until late in his career when the wilderness landscape he so revered had, in his world of the Catskill Mountains and Hudson River Valley, become a nostalgic memory, under the impact of increasing settlement.

The Falls of Niagara attracted the interest of American artists early in the century and were viewed as the quintessential example of the sublime in American nature. The "feelings" inspired by Niagara were both patriotic and unambiguously romantic. A writer for the *North American Review* in 1816 responded in a characteristic way when confronted by the experience of Niagara:

When I found myself in this situation the roar deepened, the rock shook over my head, the earth trembled, with the sound and motion of an earthquake; the elevation of the fall increased; it seemed tumbling from the heavens: the foam rose in more fantastic shapes, and the whole assumed to my imagination an overwhelming aspect. It was sometime before I could command my pencil. I felt a sensation of awe which I would not long endure, and I hastened to return to a state of things more familiar, more on a level with myself. I rejoiced on arriving at the top, to find the rays of the sun once more falling on me. . . .[7]

Later in the century Niagara would continue to inspire the American imagination, as attested to by the brilliant success of Frederic Edwin Church's 1857 painting of the subject, which was exhibited to enthusiastic crowds in both Europe and America. Interest in Niagara was not limited to Church, however, although his picture received a number of accolades. Jasper Francis Cropsey, who became known as "the painter of the American autumn," was a follower of Cole and close adherent to his style of painting. He lived and worked in England from 1856 to 1863, where he painted several versions of Niagara from unique prospects based on oil sketches and drawings completed on an earlier visit to the falls. His first painting of the scene, *Niagara Falls from the Foot of Goat Island*,[8] completed in 1856, was an early composition which depicted the falls looking up the river from a position below the American Falls. A second version of the same view was finished in 1857. In both Cropsey emphasized the drama of the perspective in an effort to enhance the sublimity of the scene. He had first visited the cataract in 1852 and commented on the panorama of the scene in a letter written from Cataract House, "This sublime nature about me constantly moves my soul in admiration of its creator."[9] The Ganz painting, entitled *Niagara Falls* (fig. 2), was also painted in London and completed in 1860. It is interesting to compare this lovely canvas, which emphasizes how the falls appear to the two contemporary onlookers, with an earlier version of roughly the same scene painted by Thomas Cole during his visit to London in 1829 (The Art Institute of Chicago). Cole selected a slightly higher viewpoint and emphasized the horizontal panorama and natural grandeur of Niagara, without reference to contemporary civilization. The American Indians in Cole's picture share the spectacle of an untouched and cleansed wilderness view of nature following the passage of a storm. In Cropsey's later picture two lovers discourse on the beauty of the scene from a glade which overlooks a landscape transformed by successive generations of tourists; the scene now includes the observation tower and buildings on the far bank. The arch-topped composition of the Cropsey, popular in mid-century, is a framing device which organizes both the formal components of the scene and the viewer's relationship to it; it appears as if one were looking at nature through a cathedral window. This landscape has a grace and charm which can be associated with the picturesque sentimentality of the Victorian period, as opposed to the more vigorous early sublime interpretations of Niagara.

During the 1860s the ideas of John Ruskin, which particularly stressed technical proficiency in drawing from nature and accuracy in rendering details, influenced the development of a graphically accurate realist landscape style in both England and America. Asher B. Durand's "Letters on Landscape Painting" echoed Ruskin's principles, further inspiring many American landscape painters to work toward a precise recording of the specifics of nature, for instance the bark of trees and the corruscated surface of interesting rock formations. Writing in *The Crayon* in 1855 Durand underscored the importance of drawing in the creative process: "A moment's reflection will convince you of the vital importance of drawing, and the continual demand for its exercise in the practice of outline, before you begin to paint."[10]

David Johnson, a second generation Hudson River School painter, was an artist whose style clearly corresponded with the philosophy of Ruskin and Durand and whose work enjoyed considerable popularity in the 1860s and seventies. Johnson's formal training was limited to a few lessons from Cropsey, and his style developed in the artistic ferment of New York City. He never visited Europe, and the primary focus of his vision was directed toward the landscape of upstate New York and New England. He was elected a member of the National Academy of Design in 1861.

Consistent with the nationalist impulse which inspired earlier American landscapists such as Cole, Church, and Cropsey, Johnson also manifested an interest in natural phenomena which had strong associative connections with the sublime. Niagara had long been regarded as the most sublime spectacle in American nature, but it had noteworthy rivals. Thomas Jefferson, one of the first to be inspired by Edmund Burke's essay, *Treatise on the Sublime,* published in 1756, wrote in his *Notes on Virginia* that the Natural Bridge in Virginia was one of the most sublime of nature's works.[11] Johnson's painting (fig. 3) of this unique aspect of the landscape is one of his finest efforts. Completed in 1860, *The Natural Bridge of Virginia* clearly reveals the artist's interest and ability to detail finely the surface textures of the rock formation in a draftsmanly style of Ruskinian persuasion. The picture is, however, more than an accumulation of naturalistic detail; the size and majesty of the bridge is given perspective and scale by the inclusion of figures

Fig. 2   Jasper Francis Cropsey, *Niagara Falls*, 1860

along the river, and the whole coheres in a fusion of rich color and light that marks this as one of Johnson's best pictures.

The intensity of the realist vision inspired by Ruskin and nurtured by the Pre-Raphaelites had other interesting parallels in American art. Several paintings in the Ganz collection provide an opportunity to study the varied approaches to naturalism taken by American artists whose style was informed by Ruskinian principles but whose approach to naturalism was personalized by their own temperaments. Paintings and drawings in the Ganz collection by William Trost Richards and Aaron Draper Shattuck reveal uniquely different landscape expressions which depict the natural world viewed through the "Ruskinian telescope."

Interest in Ruskin on both sides of the Atlantic was high in the 1850s and sixties. The publication of *Modern Painters* in Great Britain in 1843 was followed by an American edition in 1848. Ruskin's ideas were further disseminated in the United States by *The Crayon,* an important periodical founded in 1855, whose coeditor, William J. Stillman, had visited Ruskin in England. In addition an English expatriate, Thomas Charles Farrer, a disciple of Ruskin, founded in 1863 a society called the "Association for the Advancement of Truth in Art," whose members were known as the American Pre-Raphaelites and whose work was predicated on the principles of adherence to nature formulated by Ruskin in *Modern Painters.* In the year of its forming, Farrer nominated William Trost Richards for membership in the association, and it was at this time that Richards's painstaking and meticulous draftsmanship most closely approximated Ruskin's formal ideals of naturalism.[12]

Richards was born and educated in Philadelphia where he received his early artistic training from Paul Weber, a German landscape painter who practiced a realistic style then favored in Europe. He also had commercial experience in art, as did many American landscape painters in their early years. In 1855–56 Richards traveled and studied in Europe, completing his stay in Düsseldorf, an academy well known for its dedication to realism and one which exerted a strong influence on artists in Europe and America. Richards returned to the United States in 1856 and continued to develop his landscape style with sketching trips in rural New York. In February 1858 he viewed the popular exhibition of the *British School of Art* held at the Pennsylvania Academy, and it was at this time, according to Linda Ferber, that his interest in the mode of landscape expression favored by the Pre-Raphaelites crystallized.[13] During this period in his development Richards drew and painted detailed studies of individual plants, or groupings of plants, in shaded forest interiors. These works were botanically accurate and precise in draftsmanship. Richards gradually increased the scale of his work, introducing more complicated problems of light, space, and atmospheric illusion. Between 1864 and 1866 Richards produced a group of large-scale charcoal and pencil drawings which are remarkable not only for their size but for their extraordinary precision of technique. The large Ganz charcoal, \Landscape with Brook (fig. 4), 1865 (37¼ x 50¾ in., sight) belongs to this group and is characteristic of Richards's attempt to transcend the compositional restrictions imposed by the closed space of a forest interior. The drawing clearly demonstrates Richards's talent at clinical delineation of form, but it moves beyond the Pre-Raphaelite concern for objective detail to encompass and develop more complex formal issues involving spatial recession and light reflecting from still water. In many ways this and other related drawings by Richards have formal commonalities with the work of the luminist painters Fitz Hugh Lane and Martin Johnson Heade; all share a particular concern for depicting nature stilled and frozen in time.

Richards and the Pre-Raphaelites were criticized as well as admired for their rigid adherence to Ruskinian principles. Tuckerman, in his famous *Book of the Artists*, published in 1867 at the high watermark of Pre-Raphaelitism, correctly identified Richards as a landscape painter who carried out in practice "the extreme theory of the Pre-Raphaelites."[14] He went on to note, however, his reservation concerning Richards's consummate realist techniques.

So carefully finished in some of them are the leaves, grasses, grain stalks, weeds, stones and flowers, that we seem not to be looking at a distant prospect, but lying on the ground with herbage and blossom directly under our eyes. Marvelous in accurate imitation are the separate objects in the foreground of these pictures . . . but the relative finish of the foreground, centre, and background is not always harmonious; there is little perspective illusion; what is gained in accuracy of details seems lost in aerial gradation and distances. Though for miracles of special study these works are interesting, even while enjoying the perfection of minutiae, we cannot but question the principle upon which they are executed, and doubt the ultimate triumph of a literalness so purely imitative.[15]

Richards had obviously realized the limitations of strict adherence to a graphic realist style, and in such works as *Landscape with Brook* he has clearly expanded the range of his interest in landscape beyond the focused and restrictive impression of such enclosed spaces as that depicted in *Woods*, also of 1865.[16]

In 1867 Richards traveled to Europe again, and following this trip he began to paint marine pictures of various American coastal scenes. In many of his landscapes a Pre-Raphaelite

Fig. 3   David Johnson, *The Natural Bridge of Virginia*, 1860

Fig. 4   William Trost Richards, *Landscape with Brook,* 1865

concern for the detail of rocky coasts is clearly evident. But in these works his style matured, and a feeling for atmosphere and light, particularly light reflected from wet surfaces, caused his style to become more generally expressive and less attentive to the minutiae of nature. This openness and lucidity can be observed in the 1877 seascape entitled *At Atlantic City* (fig. 5). The lowered horizon and the sun, filtered and suffused through the cloud cover, create a sense of open space and luminosity that characterizes many of Richards's later works. While this painting emphasizes the detail in the foreground grasses with Pre-Raphaelite precision, along with the gnarled stump and the trees, it does not focus with intensity on that aspect of realist depiction; instead, the style is much broader and more painterly than in his earlier Pre-Raphaelite works.

Aaron Draper Shattuck's *Leaf Study with Yellow Swallow Tail* (fig. 6), dating from about 1859, consummately articulates the Pre-Raphaelite concern for accuracy to nature. Tuckerman remarked that Shattuck, "was one of the first of our landscape painters to render foreground with care and fidelity."[17] The care and attention to foreground detail that characterized Pre-Raphaelite formal concerns are clearly apparent in this small, pristine canvas. In the magnified detail of this picture Shattuck intensified the reality of nature and encapsulated the experience within a bell jar. This type of study became popular in the late 1850s and was practiced by many artists who were influenced by Ruskin. Richards, who admired Shattuck's work greatly, also produced similar studies using the popular arched-top format employed by Shattuck in this magical work of art. Such works concentrate on groupings and organizations of living plants and grasses, which occupy the entire space of this picture and which press visually outward toward the viewer. In this and other related studies one is acutely conscious of the objective reality of nature in all its profuse details. However, while one is always aware in such landscapes of a contrived formal arrangement of elements organized in the shallow surface space of the picture, artists working in the Ruskinian tradition consistently drew from living nature, not studio arrangements. These pictures are fascinating to contemplate and offer a similar, indeed related experience, to the luminist canvases of Lane, Kensett, and Heade. In the stillness and intensity of their vision, the presence of the artist is diminished to such a degree that one is aware only of the reality of nature and of suspended time. If Lane's mature style has affinities with transcendental meditation, Shattuck's narrower, more acutely formed vision articulates with consummate clarity Ralph Waldo Emerson's interest in "the still, small voice" of nature.

Interest in the organization and depiction of foreground

Fig. 6   Aaron Draper Shattuck, *Leaf Study with Yellow Swallow Tail*, c.1859

detail had been a particular concern of English picturesque theorists. William Gilpin, as early as 1782, had directed British artists to study nature, "which, however slovenly in her composition, is the only school where he must study forms."[18] These attitudes and convictions about landscape composition in particular were passed on to Ruskin who, as the spokesman for his generation, continued to encourage artists to work toward accuracy of detail and fidelity to nature. His writings added a new chapter to the long tradition of the picturesque, providing a base of theoretical support for the compositional and formal principles of picturesque theory which had widespread and continuing importance for landscape art in the nineteenth century in America.

The pristine, highly refined realism that dominated the American art world in the late 1850s and sixties was an indigenous manifestation of an interest in not only naturalistic realism per se but a simultaneous concern in both Europe and America for the phenomenon of light in nature. In the United States this movement coalesced in the emergence of a mode

Fig. 5   William Trost Richards, *At Atlantic City*, 1877

of landscape expression now called luminist. The style of the artists who developed luminism in America reflected an intensity of concern for an empirical rendering of landscape that in its extreme realism and classically ordered composition reflected a mood of nature. In the best of the works of Fitz Hugh Lane, John Frederick Kensett, Martin Johnson Heade, and Sanford Robinson Gifford nature is painted directly as a clinical, geometrically ordered space, primarily horizontal in conception, in which radiant light glows. These paintings push the very definition of the term "realism" to an extremity opening into a new world of spiritual or transcendental experience of nature. These pictures, and the concept of naturalism which supports them, have nothing to do with the contemporary French realism of, for instance, Courbet or Millet, and the comparison is an interesting one. French realist art was charged with social significance which related to subject matter and issues of social concern. Pictures of humble workers, which outraged many Parisian critics, charged French realism with a political significance that did not exist in realist painting in America. Proudhon's defense of Courbet in which he celebrated "the right to work and the right of the worker"[19] specified a different purpose for realist painting than that which interested American artists. Theirs was a different form of propaganda.

Fitz Hugh Lane was the earliest of his generation to evolve a style that encompassed the formal characteristics we have defined as central to luminism. He was also one of the first landscape painters to utilize the higher intensity cadmium paints and orange colors which became available in the 1840s. Lane, who painted primarily in New England, began his career as an apprentice to Pendleton, a lithographer in Boston, and then studied with the marine painter Robert Salmon. During the 1840s he began painting coastal subjects in the quiet, understated luminist style that he would continue to refine. In the 1850s he produced many of his most beautiful canvases, including several of Boston Harbor. The Ganz picture, *Boston Harbor, Sunset* (fig. 7), painted probably between 1850 and 1855, is a classic example of the artist's mature style and one which displays Lane's interest in ordered compositional components seemingly frozen in an atmosphere irradiated with tinted light. This marine can be compared with a similar work of the same period in the Boston Museum of Fine Arts. Both paintings depict Boston Harbor with Charles Bulfinch's State House in the distance. They are both sunset pictures and together are interesting mirror images, in color as well as formal composition. The Ganz picture is blue in tonality, while the Boston picture is pink. In the Ganz painting the ships, on the right side, project bow forward toward the viewer; and the visual axis is established by the small rowboat moving diagonally back into space from the lower left center. The Boston picture is organized along an opposite compositional geometry. Both pictures are ordered, mathematically precise compositions. Stillness and silence are emphasized by the gravity of the slack sails of the ships, which seem resolutely anchored in time. This harbor scene is a classic example of mid-century luminism and has its stylistic counterpart in the works of Kensett and Heade.

Martin Johnson Heade developed a style of landscape painting closely associated with that of Fitz Hugh Lane, and there are remarkable stylistic affinities between Lane's painting of the early 1860s and Heade's achievement of the same years. He, like Lane, distilled the experience of light in nature into a unique space-time continuum that eternalizes a static perception and experience of silence and light in nature. Heade's

Fig. 7 Fitz Hugh Lane, *Boston Harbor, Sunset*, 1850–1855

paintings of the Newburyport marsh were, as Theodore Stebbins has noted, "his wilderness and his Niagara."[20] In many of these compositions Heade is particularly concerned with changing appearances of light and atmosphere, and the gray-green palette which he favored is enhanced by a splash of yellow sunlight offset by intense cadmium pinks in distant cloud banks. The marsh pictures of the 1860s and later form a unique chapter in Heade's development. Yet his concern for abstractions of space and time in his art is even further distilled in a remarkable series of charcoal drawings which, in the quality of the draftsmanship and in their conceptualization of nature, are unique in his work. Stebbins notes that the drawings, of

which at least eight are known, were completed in 1867 or 1868. They might have been based on a small watercolor study, *Sailboat Near Plum Island*, which Heade then translated into charcoal, a medium he had not previously used. Stebbins believes these charcoals were influenced by William Morris Hunt, who became acquainted with recent French efforts in this medium, such as those of Jean François Millet, during his visit to Paris.[21] The drawings depict a catboat moving slowly through the marsh, flanked by haystacks. In the distance are the towers of Newburyport. The drawings appear to represent different times of day, from noon to twilight. The Ganz drawing, which contains two boats, is entitled *Twilight on Newbury*

Marsh (fig. 8). It is the largest of the series (13½ x 29 in., sight) and particularly emphasizes the horizontality of the scene. This drawing, which accentuates the spatial dimensions both along the horizon and into space (note how the orthogonal lines formed by the haystacks cross at a point on the horizon that precisely touches the diagonal edge of the sail on the boat) might be the culmination of the series. Whether this is true or not, the fragile and delicate spatial geometry of the Ganz drawing appears to be the most sensitively balanced of the drawings in this series.

Luminist composition and color were highly refined by both Lane and Heade, and the quiet beauty of their paintings, emphasizing contemplative, transcendental qualities of light in a seaside atmosphere, clearly influenced the work of other artists, although no "school" of luminism emerged as a coherent entity on the American art scene. One artist whose work was clearly inspired by classic luminism was Francis A. Silva, a self-taught painter who began his professional career in 1868 in New York City. His 1874 painting entitled *Sunrise at Tappan Zee* (fig. 9) is as highly finished as Lane's work and even more emphatic in its cadmium-based, intense pinks and yellows. Silva's composition is emptier and more sparse than Lane's and confirms the continuing American interest in still landscape painted in a tight, realist style in the years following the Civil War.

Another work, virtually contemporary with Silva's in the Ganz collection, is Alfred Thompson Bricher's *On the Meadows of Old Newburyport* of 1873 (fig. 10). If Silva was inspired by Lane, then Bricher, who worked first in Newburyport and

Boston before moving to New York in 1868, must be identified with Heade. This strongly painted watercolor exhibits Bricher's ability to paint water as a reflecting surface as well as to imply depth in its moving shadows. One is not aware of the underlying geometry of the landscape composition which is so apparent in the work of Lane and Heade. Bricher's primary concern was for the changing effects of clouds and light.

Bricher painted seascapes almost exclusively after 1868, and his ability to paint water with waves breaking and reflecting on beaches was fascinating to the critics of his time; it is no less compelling now. His watercolor *Beach at Little Boar's Head, New Hampshire* (fig. 11) in the Ganz collection is a case in point. "Mr. Bricher has studied waves and can paint them," declared a writer in *The New York Times*. When asked how he painted waves, Bricher said: "I watch a wave as it comes in onto the shore, and then I turn my head away the second before it breaks."[22]

Bricher's masterpiece was *Indian Rock, Narragansett Bay*, 1871 (fig. 12), one of his largest canvases and somewhat uncharacteristic for him in a couple of respects. The warm colors and light of this major painting differentiate it from the clearer blues and bright atmosphere of his smaller marine compositions. The panoramic view of Indian Rock and Rhode Island Sound is composed in classic luminist style, emphasizing the long horizon and the stillness of the sea. But especially unusual for Bricher is his choice of the elevated vantage point, in contrast to his more familiar shoreside vistas. The misty atmosphere and yellow, tinted light unify the composition in a golden haze of summer afternoon, distilling a vision of natural perfection.

Fig. 10   Alfred Thompson Bricher,
On the Meadows of Old Newburyport, 1873

John Frederick Kensett painted a number of views of Lake George, and it is provocative to compare the Ganzes' *Lake George* (fig. 13), painted in 1858, with Lane's harbor scene. The two pictures, which at first might appear to have little in common, together reveal the magic of the luminist sensitivity to color and light and for balanced composition and refined, understated realist style. Kensett also began his career as an engraver and, unlike Lane, toured Europe on several occasions for extended periods: in the 1840s he visited England and France with Casilear and Durand, lived in Paris from 1841 to 1843, in London in 1843–44, and visited Germany, Switzerland, and Italy. He returned from Europe to his studio in New York where he established an important reputation as a landscape painter. The Ganz picture, *Lake George,* a subject he painted often, is resonant with low-keyed purple, aquamarine, and lavender tonalities and is a prime example of Kensett's interest in this scene and subject. Tuckerman notes that a picture entitled *Reminiscence of Lake George,* one similar in style and composition to the Ganz painting, "is wrought up to the highest degree of truth from the autumn mist to the lucent water and gracefully looming mountain."[23] The composition in the Ganz picture is ordered with a concern for balance and harmony. There are no unaccountable, disjunctive, or jarring imbalances. It is less complicated, less mathematically ordered in its components than Lane's harbor scene. But it is related in sensibility in that the final impression is one of absolute stasis. In the distance the framing mountains balance the view through to the far peak and the plane of the picture, an open expanse of water (a feature in many luminist canvases) appears to extend the pictorial space beyond the framed limits of the composition to encompass the viewer. Kensett's careful, tight realist style and his sense for an almost palpable atmospheric haze characterize his art and make it unique among the luminists. His style was clearly appealing to advocates of Ruskin; Tuckerman notes, for instance, that

In some of his pictures the dense growth of trees on a rocky ledge . . . are rendered with the literal minuteness of one of the old Flemish painters. It is on this account that Kensett enjoys an exceptional reputation among the extreme advocates of the Pre-Raphaelite school.[24]

Tuckerman goes on to praise Kensett, citing his "evenness of manner, the patience in detail, the harmonious tone"[25] of his paintings; but it is clear that the correspondence of style and composition that exists between Kensett and the other luminist artists relates all their work to a conceptual attitude toward nature, time, and space that is similar and related to Pre-Raphaelite formal concerns.

Sanford Robinson Gifford, of all the classic luminist painters, advanced the potential of color in landscape made possible by the new cadmium colors to a point of fascinating exaggeration. His particular interest in warm color intensities caused the writer James Jackson Jarves to complain that Gifford's color "is artificial and strained, often of a lively or deep brimstone tint as if he saw the landscape through stained glass."[26] In his art, however, Gifford was recognized in his own day as incorporating all of the stylistic aspects associated with luminist aesthetics. Tuckerman praised Gifford for his talent at

Fig. 9 Francis A. Silva,
Sunrise at Tappan Zee, 1874

. . . photographing in color a foggy day in early autumn on the Bronx river, with its pale sunlight, leafless trees, and still water—cathedral-like in its dim and pensive impressiveness.[27]

Tuckerman associated Gifford's work with what he discerned was a more general interest in the atmospheric effects we now identify with luminism:

Gifford has also been successful in the experiment which, of late, has been tried by several American landscape painters, to reproduce the effects of a misty atmosphere so often witnessed by summer travellers among the mountains; when the thick vapor which sometimes, at early morning, shrouds their lofty summits from view, is partially dissolved by the sun, the thinned fleecy moisture expands, and clings in half-dense, half-luminous wreaths. . . . Two remarkable instances of Gifford's skill and feeling in this special phase of mountain scenery, are his "Mansfield Mountain" and "Catskill Clove;" the latter is a deep gorge, tufted with trees and thickets; its proportions and profundity are made wonderfully sensitive to the eye, and over them broods a flood of that peculiar yellow light born of mist and sunshine.[28]

Gifford is the most comprehensively represented artist in the Ganz collection, and the eight paintings in the exhibition, consisting of finished paintings and studies and dating from 1856 to 1878, cover the mature range of his development and illustrate his continuing interest in "that peculiar yellow light born of mist and sunshine." The Ganzes intentionally collected small works by Gifford which they believe to be generally more successful than their larger counterparts.

Gifford was single-minded in his attempt to visualize the subtleties of atmosphere and light, and in virtually all of his art, whether foreign or American in subject matter, colored light is an overriding concern. He began the formal study of art in New York in 1845 and, following a tradition established by Thomas Cole and the early Hudson River School painters, began making sketching trips into the country soon thereafter. He began to exhibit in New York at the American Art Union and the National Academy in 1847 and was elected a full academician in 1854. During the following year Gifford made his first trip to Europe and visited picturesque cities in England. He made it a point to call on John Ruskin at his home. Shortly thereafter he visited Paris and then traveled through the North countries and the Alps before he settled in a studio in Rome for the winter. During his stay in Italy he visited many of its cities with Worthington Whittredge and Albert Bierstadt. Gifford returned to New York in 1857 and moved into the Studio Building on 10th Street.

In England Gifford had seen J.M.W. Turner's work, and while he did not particularly care for the world of dissolved light Turner had moved into in his later work, he admired Turner's earlier achievements, as had Thomas Cole before him.

Color and atmosphere were primary in Gifford's work but he did not dissolve the natural landscape as Turner did in his light-filled watercolors.

The earliest picture in the Ganz collection by Gifford is a small study of *Lake Nemi* (fig. 14), painted in Rome in 1856. This work is evidence of Gifford's sensitive fusion of color and light in the Italian landscape. William Gerdts believes that Gifford's earliest major luminist canvases, executed following his European sojourn and beginning with this picture, suggest the experience of Italy as seen through the eyes of Turner.[29] The rich, painterly effects and loose brushwork in this work are characteristic of a sketch and show the artist's indebtedness to both Thomas Cole and Turner. The completed painting in the Toledo Museum of Art (40 x 60 in.) is much larger than the small study exhibited. The finished picture was the largest Gifford had painted up to that time and was favorably reviewed in *The Crayon*.[30] The studies for the large picture were made in October, and Gifford worked on the picture that winter, completing it on April 4. He varnished it with several layers of boiled oil to increase the atmospheric density of the finished impression.[31] Except for the size, the final version of the picture is virtually identical to the sketch: both record the artist's dazzling impressions of sunlight filtering through atmospheric haze in the afternoon.

Back in New York Gifford painted some European subjects based on sketches and memories of his experiences and travels, but beginning in August 1858 American landscape subjects begin to enter the formal vocabulary of his art.[32] He made a sketching trip to northern New England at that time, and the small study *The Camp on Mansfield Mountain, Vermont* (fig. 15) was one of a group of pictures that resulted from that trip. Again in this picture Gifford's interest in rich impasto to define the textural surfaces of the rocks is apparent; but light is also important, the low, angled, slanting light which refracts from the rocks, accenting their massiveness and erecting a visual drama of cast shadows and reflections. It is interesting to compare this painting with the earlier sketch for *Lake Nemi*, which is similar in light rendition and color. However, the attention to detail and finish of the rocks is more thoroughly developed in the Mansfield picture, more "Ruskinian" in its concern for recording the details of the natural world, and the atmosphere far less smoky in appearance.

In 1862 Gifford painted several versions of his favorite subject, *Kauterskill Clove, in the Catskills* (fig. 16), a large version of which is in the collection of the Metropolitan Museum of Art (48 x 39⅞ in). Ila Weiss notes that three smaller oil versions of the same year were probably related to this large canvas, a

Fig. 14 Sanford Robinson Gifford, *Lake Nemi*, 1856

Fig. 15 Sanford Robinson Gifford, *The Camp on Mansfield Mountain, Vermont*, 1858

Fig. 16 Sanford Robinson Gifford,
Kauterskill Clove, in the Catskills, 1862

Fig. 17 Sanford Robinson Gifford,
Riva — Lago di Garda, 1863

favorite subject of the Hudson River School painters. The Ganz painting, signed and dated 1862, is one of the three smaller interpretations of the scene. It differs from the Metropolitan painting in that Gifford more clearly articulates the rock ledges at the right and incorporates different figures on the left. Their fragmented surfaces reflect the brilliant, enveloping light of the setting sun, accenting, along with the river and falls in the distance, the consuming brilliance and intensity of the light. Weiss observes of the scene:

It is not only a recasting of the same view of 1861, but a development, too, of the invention introduced in *Lake Nemi* of 1857. The clove, occupying more than half of the area of the format, is explored as a container for air—the palpable sky.[33]

The colored atmosphere conveys an almost tangible, sensual experience of American light that is perhaps the most intense such depiction in the luminist corpus. It is this scene and that "peculiar yellow light born of mist and sunshine" that Tuckerman was referring to in the passage cited earlier.[34]

The painting of *Riva-Lago di Garda* (fig. 17) was completed the following year in 1863 and illustrates classic luminist interest in horizontal composition. The town is depicted in the middle distance against a mountainous background. The water in the foreground occupies almost half the space of the picture and captures the stilled reflections of the topography as well as the pale, opalescent light. The Ganz picture is a study for a larger version of the scene painted in the same year. As in Gifford's earlier studies, this one shows more pronounced contrast of light and shade than the finished surfaces of the larger work.

The Artist Sketching at Mount Desert, Maine of 1864–65 (fig. 18) documents a sketching trip Gifford made to the Massachusetts and Maine coast. The type of composition, overlooking a vista of space from a high promontory, is one of Gifford's favorites. In this work the artist depicts himself sketching, and the painting contains a wonderful conceit—the scene on the open cover of the artist's paintbox is the same as the view shown in the painting. This work is a remarkable tour de force of color, emphasizing opalescent grays and delicate purples, set off by the rough textures of the foreground rocks. It is a visual paradigm of Asher Durand's enjoinder to artists in "Letters on Landscape Painting" in which he states:

When you shall have acquired some proficiency in foreground material, your next step should be the study of atmosphere—the power which defines and measures space.[35]

Another study, *A Home in the Wilderness* of 1865–67 (fig. 19), depicts a quiescent luminist scene of the type that occupied Gifford even during the war years. The large composition (30½

Fig. 13 John Frederick Kensett,
Lake George, 1858

x 54¼ in.) is in the Cleveland Museum of Art. Again Gifford's interest in what Weiss describes as "aerial luminism" is clearly visible in the study. It is interesting to note that many of the luminist pictures of 1860–65 by American artists reveal nothing of the turbulence and psychic dislocation caused by the Civil War and resonate of escapist nostalgia, a longing for the peace and eternal quiet of American nature. Weiss comments of this scene,

Perhaps the experience of the Civil War, which for Gifford was largely one of patriotism, and the sacrifice of one of his brothers lives to that cause, combined with a longing for the wilderness stimulated by the war situation, heightened his awareness of his personal connections with American history.[36]

Gifford made a second trip to Europe in 1868–69 and also ventured farther, visiting the Middle East, Constantinople, and Athens. Like Church, he was captivated by the ancient ruins but he was likewise transfixed by the brightness and clarity of the light. The painting of *The Desert at Assouan, Egypt* (fig. 20) dates from February of 1869 and is a continuing confirmation of Gifford's devotion to light and color in nature, revealing also his acute sense for the open space of the desert.

Sunset Over New York Bay (fig. 21) is a study for a large version of the scene in the collection of the Everson Museum of Art in Syracuse. Dating from around 1878, two years before the artist's death, the loosely brushed and scumbled paint reminds one of Turner's views of Venice. It is, indeed, fascinating to compare the two artists' styles. Gifford has, in this work, moved toward a more specifically European conception of light and atmosphere. The finish is not as highly refined or transparent as his earlier work, and the appearance of the picture relates closely to Turner's more tactile and facile style.

Throughout his development, Gifford's interest in colored atmosphere rarely wavered, and of the luminist painters, he, more than the others, showed a sustained interest in exploring the optical potentials of color and light as spatial phenomena.

The imperatives of Ruskin and classic luminism influenced other practitioners of American landscape outside of the core group of Lane, Heade, Kensett, and Gifford. The small *View on the Hudson River*, early 1850s (fig. 22) by Jervis McEntee is evidence of the pervasive interest in still, over-water views painted in a tight realist style.

William Stanley Haseltine, while not a luminist per se, was a marine painter who, like William Trost Richards, was a pupil

Fig. 18   Sanford Robinson Gifford, *The Artist Sketching at Mount Desert, Maine*, 1864–1865

Fig. 19   Sanford Robinson Gifford, *A Home in the Wilderness*, 1865–1867

of the German Paul Weber and chose the rocky shores of the East Coast as subject matter for his art. When Weber returned to Germany, Haseltine accompanied him and studied in Düsseldorf, along with Whittredge and Bierstadt. The Ganz painting, *Rocks at Narragansett* (fig. 23), is a superb example of the artist's work. Tuckerman commented that Haseltine gave

. . . ample evidence of his Düsseldorf studies, whereof the correct drawing and patient elaboration are more desirable than the color—although herein also he has often notably excelled. Few of our artists have been more conscientious in the delineation of rocks; their form, superficial traits, and precise tone are given with remarkable accuracy. His pencil identifies coast scenery with emphatic beauty; the shores of Naples and Ostia, and those of Narragansett Bay, are full of minute individuality.[37]

This is the language of Ruskin, and Haseltine's light-splashed "rock portraits," as Tuckerman called them, represent a style of realism that ran deeply throughout the American landscape school during the 1860s (see also, for example, Charles Temple Dix's *Marina Grande—Capri* of 1866, fig. 24). The overhead light, emphasizing horizontal surfaces, applied strongly and directly, can also be seen in Winslow Homer's pictures of the period. This small marine, like other coastal pictures by Haseltine, is anchored visually by a small area of intense blue water in the lower center of the composition. This kind of painting, with its clear, direct light and unaffected realism, was extremely popular in its time, identifying an experience of outdoor summer pleasure shared by the viewer. It was this aspect of experience which captured Tuckerman's imagination in his brief discussion of a Haseltine picture similar to the Ganz painting:

The waves that roll in upon his Rhode Island crags look like old and cheery friends to the fond haunters of those shores in summer. The very sky looks like the identical one beneath which we have watched and wandered; while there is a history to the imagination in every brown angle-projecting slab, worn, broken, ocean-mined and sun-painted ledge of the brown and picturesquely-heaped rocks, at whose feet the clear, green waters splash: they speak to the eye of science of a volcanic birth and the antiquity of man.[38]

The quiet reflections of still light in classic luminist canvases by Fitz Hugh Lane, Martin Johnson Heade, and others encapsulated a visual experience that corresponded with transcendental attitudes toward nature. The depiction of American light in the work of many mid-century painters was thus endowed with both meditative and theological significance. In the work of Frederic Edwin Church and Albert Bierstadt, however, light in nature, indeed nature itself, was visualized in modes of expression that emphasized the grandeur and spectacle of the landscape. Church had been the only pupil of Thomas Cole, and in the 1850s he emerged as the successor to Cole. Like his teacher, Church believed in the efficacy of landscape as history painting, and the emergence of his art coincided with developing American attitudes concerning manifest destiny. As David Huntington has noted,

Nature for Church was the theater of the world and man's mystic regeneration. This Puritan painter was imbued with his century's belief in the "Science of Design;" it was his second Bible . . . the work of no other American painter of his generation has proved so susceptible to the same methods of criticism and analysis that have been applied to a Thoreau, a Dana or a Whitman. Like Melville, Church

Fig. 20   Sanford Robinson Gifford,
The Desert at Assouan, Egypt, February 1869

Fig. 21   Sanford Robinson Gifford
Sunset Over New York Bay, c.1878

was a symbolic realist. Like Emerson, Church sought to reveal the hidden spirituality of nature.[39]

Church moved into a studio in New York in 1846 following his period of study with Cole and soon joined the Sketch Club and the Century Club; in 1849, when he was only twenty-three, he was elected to full membership in the National Academy of Design.[40] Like most American landscape painters he traveled and worked out of doors during the summer months, exploring and recording sites in the Catskills and other popular locations, and in 1850, 1851, and 1852 he visited Mount Desert

in Maine. In 1852 he traveled to Grand Manan Island in the Bay of Fundy, extending his interest in landscape into virtually unexplored areas. At this time Church was also reading Alexander von Humboldt's grand theories, which viewed geography as the determinant of civilization. Under von Humboldt's influence Church was inspired to record not only American nature but exotic landscapes in faraway lands. In 1853 he traveled to Colombia and Ecuador on a trip inspired by von Humboldt's writings. As Huntington has noted, South America had been the primary setting for the development of the the-

Fig. 23   William Stanley Haseltine, *Rocks at Narragansett,* 1860s

ories of natural history which von Humboldt formulated in *Cosmos, Personal Narratives* and *Aspects of Nature,* and Church's trip was to have been a grand tour of geographical determinism.[41] When Church crossed over into Ecuador he saw his first view of the Cordilleras, a range of mountains in the Andes, and sketched from a landscape which provided him with subjects he would translate into major works of art, such as *Heart of the Andes.*[42] This series also produced the Ganz painting, dated 1854 and entitled *The Cordilleras: Sunrise* (fig. 25). Church first saw that view on August 30, 1853, and described it in his diary as follows:

After a disagreeable journey across an elevated plain with a cold piercing wind and a sprinkling of rain we finally came to the edge of an eminence which overlooked the valley of Chota. And a view of such unparalleled magnificence presented itself that I must pronounce it one of the great wonders of Nature. I made a couple of feeble sketches this evening in recollection of the scene. My ideal of the Cordilleras is realized.[43]

Following this trip Church painted several South American landscapes in his New York studio, which he exhibited at the National Academy of Design in 1855 to great critical acclaim. A critic for *The Albion* remarked:

Mr. Church has adventured, and with brilliant success, into an entirely new range of subjects. He has recently made extensive travels through the finest regions of Central and South America, whose matchless colors and flowing atmosphere are precisely suited to his type. The result is seen in several landscapes of extreme beauty . . . of his several views, we do not know which to prefer. The Cordilleras: Sunrise No. 49 is an exquisite composition, treated with extremest delicacy, and most carefully finished. The distant air tints are admirably true.[44]

Church, consistent with the style of many of the American landscape painters of his time, adopted and practiced a painstaking realism, and his interest in the higher-keyed tonalities of light and atmosphere made possible by the new cadmium colors permitted him to explore and develop the light and drama of landscape with consummate success. *The Cordilleras: Sunrise* is particularly interesting to compare with his earlier

Fig. 27   T. Worthington Whittredge,
Indian Encampment on the Platte River, c.1870–1872

Fig. 22 Jervis McEntee, *View on the Hudson River*, early 1850s

composition *New England Scenery*[45] of 1851. Both pictures display the same compositional organization; a framing tree in the right front with a view over still water to a cascade in the middle distance and a wild landscape beyond. The two pictures relate closely in technique and composition, as Huntington notes,[46] but the South American picture displays a more direct concern for the subtleties of a softer, more generalized, and glowing atmosphere that Church would continue to develop in his art.

If South America provided Church with a vision of cosmic landscape, the American West compelled Albert Bierstadt to develop an equally grandiose imagery, also relating to popular notions of manifest destiny which were associated with the expanding western frontier. Indeed, Tuckerman credited the art of both Church and Bierstadt for extending the dimensions of landscape beyond a hitherto limited geographical region:

Precisely herein has been the signal triumph of such American artists as Church and Bierstadt; both have explored distant regions for characteristic and fresh themes; and both have succeeded in giving the true expression of local atmosphere, so that the sky that overhangs and the aerial environment that surrounds the Andes and the Rocky Mountains, truthfully fill the imagination through the vision.[47]

Albert Bierstadt was a German immigrant whose family brought him to America as an infant. He was raised in New Bedford, Massachusetts, and at twenty-three he decided to become a painter. In 1853 he returned to Europe to study at the academy in Düsseldorf. Worthington Whittredge joined him there, and the two later spent a winter in Rome and traveled in Europe with Sanford Robinson Gifford and William Haseltine. His early work was characteristic of the highly refined and technically accurate realism practiced by the

Düsseldorf artists. Tuckerman noted that one of the reasons for Bierstadt's phenomenal success was that the Düsseldorf style was a novelty in America at the time he returned to begin his career.[48]

Bierstadt traveled to the West for the first time in 1859 with Colonel F. W. Landers's survey party and photographed and sketched a wide variety of subjects which were translated into large canvases when he returned to New York. His first major successes were later in coming, however, following his second trip west in 1863, when he visited northern California and Oregon. It was on this trip that Bierstadt made the sketches of the Yosemite Valley which provided the compositional framework for the 1866 picture in the Ganz collection entitled *Yosemite Valley* (fig. 26). After 1863 Bierstadt's western scenes combined Düsseldorfian realism with the high drama of the traditional sublime inspired by the scale and majesty of the Rocky Mountains. He painted his highly acclaimed *The Rocky Mountains* in 1863 (Metropolitan Museum of Art, New York), which established his reputation at a level with Church, and in the landscapes of this period Bierstadt achieved his greatest triumphs. In *Yosemite Valley*,

the artist's view is from the north bank of the Merced River (in the foreground) somewhere in the west end of the valley. Seen are Sentinel Rock on the right, Royal Arches and Washington Column with a bit of North Dome slightly left of center, and probably Cloud's Rest in the center background, moved from its normal location. At the time Bierstadt visited Yosemite, broad, open meadows with very few conifers were the typical scene.[49]

The painting belongs to a group of pictures in which the artist combined a facility for depicting naturalistic detail, consistent with his Düsseldorf training, but sublimating it, like Church, to the larger vision and grandeur of the landscape. This results in a balance and harmony of color, atmosphere, and realistic articulation characteristic of Bierstadt at his best. This picture has more in common stylistically with the quietist and static views of nature associated with luminism than with the melodramatic images of the sublime that Bierstadt cultivated in many of his landscapes.

Bierstadt's friend and traveling companion in Europe, T. Worthington Whittredge, also visited and painted the American West. Whittredge left for Europe in 1849 where he traveled widely, studied for four years in Düsseldorf, and later lived in Rome. He returned to America in 1859 and established a studio in New York. In 1866 Whittredge accompanied Major General Page on a western expedition and first experienced the vastness of the high plains, which impressed him greatly, as did the mountains of the American West. He joined Sanford Gifford

Fig. 24   Charles Temple Dix,
Marina Grande — Capri, 1866

and John F. Kensett on another trip west in 1870 and returned once again in 1877. Whittredge painted several oils of scenes such as *Indian Encampment on the Platte River*, c. 1870–72 (fig. 27). This picture shows Whittredge's interest in the quiet waters of a still river, in the tradition of the classic luminism of Kensett, Lane, and Heade, and reveals his particular concern for the flatness and space of the plains rather than the scale and majesty of the mountains. It is possible that the small Ganz landscape was the original version from which a larger picture of the same scene entitled *On the Plains, Colorado* (30 x 50 in., 1872, in the St. Johnsbury Atheneum, St. Johnsbury, Vermont) was derived.[50]

After the Civil War landscape painting in America fragmented into pluralistic tendencies. Luminist quietism continued to interest certain artists, and more traditional concerns in which American painters interpreted landscape as history painting, were developed in the work of Church and Bierstadt. Simultaneously a new and emerging interest in French impressionist art began to attract the interest of younger painters. But the mood of the nation was different, and the art of the latter half of the century, the so-called Brown Decades, was itself a verification of a sense of uncertainty which came from a loss of confidence in traditional values. The nation had clearly embarked on a new historical era, but only reluctantly were its artists willing to visualize the new world that industrialization had wrought.

The landscapes in the Ganz collection do not offer a complete survey of the history of this genre in America in the nineteenth century. Rather, this part of the collection comprises a history of some of the variations of style which occurred as America changed abruptly from a pastoral to an urban society. Aside from the outstanding quality of the pictures, the collection offers a unique opportunity to examine some of the fascinating changes which American landscape underwent during and after the Civil War, reflecting changing attitudes toward nature and nation. Thomas Cole's *The Old Mill at Sunset* signaled the beginning of the end of the pastoral tradition. The luminist paintings of the 1860s, with their transcendental, quiet, and resonant light, are particularly poignant by contrast to the convulsions of a nation divided by war. American landscape had always reflected American history, and in the year following the war, as an industrialized and rapidly urbanizing country offered new values to a changing society, the arts reflected this remarkable diversity. These changes are apparent in the pluralization of styles which are shown in part in these selections from the Ganz collection.

Fig. 25   Frederic Edwin Church
The Cordilleras: Sunrise, 1854

Fig. 26   Albert Bierstadt
Yosemite Valley, 1866

Notes

1. Owned by the New-York Historical Society.

2. Asher B. Durand, "Letters on Landscape Painting," 1855, in *American Art 1700–1960*, ed. John W. McCoubrey (Englewood Cliffs, N.J., 1965), 113.

3. Howard Mumford Jones, *The Age of Energy: Varieties of American Experience, 1865–1915* (New York, 1971), ix–x.

4. Richard N. Murray, "Painting and Sculpture," in *The American Renaissance* [exh. cat., The Brooklyn Museum] (New York, 1979), 154.

5. Louis Legrand Noble, *The Life and Works of Thomas Cole*, ed. Elliot S. Vesell (Cambridge, Mass., 1964), 268–269.

6. Versions owned by Munson-Williams-Proctor Institute, Utica, New York, and the National Gallery of Art, Washington (1842).

7. "Sketches and Scenery of Niagara," *The North American Review* (March, 1861), 324–325.

8. Owned by Mrs. James H. Dempsey, Cleveland, Ohio.

9. Cited, William S. Talbot, *Jasper F. Cropsey 1823–1900* (Ph.D. diss., New York University, 1972; Garland series, 1977), 391.

10. Durand, "Letters on Landscape Painting," *American Art*, 111.

11. See Paul Shepard, *Man in the Landscape, A Historic View of the Esthetics of Nature* (New York, 1967), 176.

12. See Linda Ferber, *William Trost Richards* [exh. cat., The Brooklyn Museum] (New York, 1973), 26.

13. Ferber, *Richards*, 26.

14. Henry T. Tuckerman, *Book of the Artists* (New York, 1867), 524.

15. Tuckerman, *Book of the Artists*, 524.

16. Owned by the High Museum of Art, Atlanta.

17. Tuckerman, *Book of the Artists*, 560.

18. William Gilpin, *Two Essays: One on the Author's Mode of Executing Rough Sketches; The Other On the Principles on Which They are Composed*, ill. by Sawrey Gilpin, Esq., R. A. (London, 1804), II.

19. Pierre-Joseph Proudhon, "Concerning the Principles of Art and Its Social Destiny," in *Realism and Tradition in Art 1848–1900*, ed. Linda Nochlin (Englewood Cliffs, N.J., 1966), 49–53.

20. Theodore E. Stebbins, Jr., *The Life and Works of Martin Johnson Heade* (New Haven and London, 1975), 42.

21. Stebbins, *Heade*, 57–58.

22. Cited in *Nineteenth-Century Painting and Sculpture* [exh. cat., The Metropolitan Museum of Art] (New York, 1970), cat. no. 153.

23. Tuckerman, *Book of the Artists*, 511.

24. Tuckerman, *Book of the Artists*, 511.

25. Tuckerman, *Book of the Artists*, 514.

26. James Jackson Jarves, *The Art Idea*, ed. Benjamin Rowland, Jr. (Cambridge, Mass., 1960; first edition 1864), 193.

27. Tuckerman, *Book of the Artists*, 525.

28. Tuckerman, *Book of the Artists*, 526–527.

29. William Gerdts, *American Luminism* [exh. cat., Coe Kerr Gallery] (New York, 1978).

30. Ila Weiss, *Sanford Robinson Gifford 1823–1880* (Ph.D. diss., Columbia University, 1968; Garland series, 1977), 145, 147.

31. Weiss, *Gifford*, 148.

32. Weiss, *Gifford*, 176.

33. Weiss, *Gifford*, 227.

34. Tuckerman, *Book of the Artists*, 527.

35. Quoted in John I. H. Baur, "Early Studies in Light and Air by American Landscape Painters," *Brooklyn Museum Bulletin*, 9, no. 2 (Winter 1948):6.

36. Weiss, *Gifford*, 256.

37. Tuckerman, *Book of the Artists*, 556.

38. Tuckerman, *Book of the Artists*, 557.

39. David C. Huntington, *The Landscapes of Frederic Edwin Church* (New York, 1966), xi.

40. Huntington, *Church*, 29.

41. Huntington, *Church*, 41.

42. Owned by the Metropolitan Museum of Art, New York.

43. Huntington, *Church*, 43.

44. "Fine Arts/The National Academy of Design," *The Albion or British, Colonial and Foreign Weekly Gazette* (March 24, 1855): 141.

45. Owned by the George Walter Vincent Smith Art Museum, Springfield, Mass.

46. Huntington, *Church*, 43.

47. Tuckerman, *Book of the Artists*, 370–371.

48. Tuckerman, *Book of the Artists*, 392.

49. Letter from Jack Gyer, curator at Yosemite National Park, to Julian Ganz, Jr., October 1, 1980.

50. Anthony Janson to Linda Ayres, February 6, 1981.

Fig. 25 Church, *The Cordilleras: Sunrise* (detail)

Fig. 58   Winslow Homer,
Blackboard, 1877

The American Figure: Genre Paintings and Sculpture

Linda Ayres

How fitting that a country founded "of the people, by the people, and for the people" should give special attention to individuals in its art. American art concentrates not only on the concrete form of the human figure but also on the relationships of people to each other, to their surroundings, and to their country. The figure, more directly than still life or landscape, reflects the society that created it. The faces of America's people and the portrayal of their everyday activities tell us what happened to the country, what its interests and values were, where its strengths and weaknesses lay. By studying the Ganz figure group—which ranges in date from the Revolutionary War to the beginning of the twentieth century—one can learn a great deal about the United States in a period of radical change that saw the country transformed from an agrarian colony to an industrialized nation.

The predominance of the figure in this specific private collection echoes American art in general. Even though the popularity of figure painting began to wane with the rise of landscape painting in the 1840s, it remained important throughout the nineteenth century and reasserted its dominance at the end of the century.

A strong academic art tradition has been typical of this country, concentrating on the figure as the basis for study and as the ultimate artistic ideal. Young artists at the academies were asked to study plaster casts of antique sculpture, copy engravings after old masters, and draw from life models.[1] Thomas Eakins's basic concern with the figure led him to attend anatomy classes at Jefferson Medical College in Philadelphia and later caused his resignation as director of the Pennsylvania

Academy because he insisted on completely nude male models for his own life classes for women.

An additional reason for the figure's predominance is its ability to serve the cult of the individual, the cult of the hero, and the cult of the ordinary man. The figure also has been employed as palpable form, as still life, as an agent for narrative, sentiment, and subjectivity, and as decoration.

Since its beginning, the nation has celebrated self-reliance and individual worth. America was conceived as the home of freedom and democracy, a new country with endless resources and a promising future founded by noble, hard-working men and women. The likenesses of these individuals were recorded for posterity beginning with the colonial limners. Copley's strong, clearly defined portraits show their character. Stuart and Sully present their elegant, timeless images. Charles Loring Elliott's bravura portraits mirror the country's vigor and optimism. In a romantic era that thrived on stories of the individuals and personalities of the day, the cult of the individual achieved its fullest expression in the nineteenth century in works such as John Neagle's *Pat Lyon at the Forge* of 1826–27.[2]

Even after the daguerreotype had made it possible for nearly every citizen to be immortalized, the wealthy and famous still preferred to sit for oil portraits by the illustrious artists of the day. Some, like banker James Brown and Wall Street broker Alfrederick Smith Hatch, commissioned Eastman Johnson to paint group portraits which surrounded the proud individual with his relatives and material possessions.[3]

The monumental figures painted at close range by such contemporary photo-realist artists as Chuck Close, Alfred Leslie, and Alex Katz reflect the resurgence of concern for the individual in our own mechanized and dehumanizing times.

The cult of the hero is another aspect in American art in which the human figure has played a dominant role. It flourished following the War for Independence, one of the few times when the American public accepted the grand or epic style of history painting. Artists set out to commemorate not only the great events of the Revolutionary War but also its heroes, the founding fathers of our country who, as Thomas Paine said, deserved "the love and thanks of man and woman."[4]

The battles and leaders of the war were immortalized in John Trumbull's monumental and melodramatic series now owned by the Yale University Art Gallery.[5] Following the lead of his teacher Benjamin West, who in 1771 had broken with tradition in his own *Death of General Wolfe,* Trumbull portrayed the protagonists of the American Revolution in not classical but contemporary dress.

Charles Willson Peale, who had commanded troops as a militia captain during the war, painted a series of well over one hundred Revolutionary War heroes which provided the basis for his Philadelphia gallery, the first art museum in America. Portraits of John Adams, Thomas Jefferson, Lafayette, Benjamin Franklin, and other patriots were painted by many artists, but the figure who best captured the spirit of the era was George Washington. "Nothing can more powerfully carry back the mind to the glorious period which gave birth to this nation—nothing can be found more capable of exciting the noblest feelings of emulation and patriotism"[6] than a portrait of George Washington, according to Rembrandt Peale, who created over eighty replicas of his famous "porthole" portrait of our first president. The Washington, or "pater patriae," cult produced other secular icons for the public by Edward Savage, Emanuel Leutze, Charles Willson Peale,[7] and Gilbert Stuart, best known for his Athenaeum, Vaughan, and Lansdowne portraits. A portrait of Washington the man became an important symbol for the young nation.

The cult of the hero also followed the Civil War when enormous statues were erected in honor of the heroes of that conflict. Augustus Saint Gaudens's *Sherman Monument* (1903) and *Admiral David Glasgow Farragut Memorial* (1877–1881)[8] are heroic in scale as well as in content.

At the other end of the spectrum from the cult of the hero lies the cult of the ordinary man. For every American hero, there were countless nameless people who were also important to the country. Jacksonian democracy brought about a general interest in the common man and the commonplace; Americans were curious about each other, about the lives, dress, and characters of their fellow citizens. Genre painting, which arose from the cult of the ordinary man, concerned itself with the figure, at work or at play. Thus in the works of Eastman Johnson, George Caleb Bingham, and William Sidney Mount we see American "types" in American settings pursuing American activities in uncomplicated, familiar, and often humorous scenes.[9] Walt Whitman, speaking for the "divine average" and the "en-masse," wrote in the 1850s:

I celebrate myself, and sing myself,
And what I assume you shall assume,
For every atom belonging to me as good
    belongs to you.[10]

Like Whitman's verse, American figure painting celebrated the common man. In both word and picture, there is a sense of optimism, security, and well-being.

In mid-century landscape painting, however, the figure shrinks dramatically in size and importance. The interest in the life of the ordinary man was replaced by interest in the land. Artists painted America's wilderness (already beginning to be destroyed), which expressed both the country's nationalism and its relationship with God, its "manifest destiny." The small, relatively inactive figures in these works help to create a feeling of awe and grandeur upon viewing America's scenery and a sense of harmony between man and nature, or between man and God as seen through nature. These early romantic landscapes picture man at one with the world, but in many luminist canvases, the figure disappears altogether. Beginning in the 1870s, however, in works by Eastman Johnson, Winslow Homer, and Thomas Eakins especially, the figure regained a prominent and active demeanor in outdoor scenes. Then, at the turn of the century, many artists depicted the figure outdoors as quiescent. Aristocratic, elegant women are shown in repose: picking flowers, dreaming, holding musical instruments.

Three-dimensional solid forms, the naturalistic rendering of objects, and sound structure have been important to American artists from the beginning. An indication of the deep roots of palpable form in the art of this country is the fact that the American impressionists (whose works are not collected by the Ganzes), unlike their French counterparts, never lost sight of solid form in their paintings. In American art the artist has used the human figure to express his concern with concrete form, direct realism, and visual fact. This can be seen in Copley's colonial portraits. It is also reflected in Charles Willson Peale's trompe l'oeil portrait of his sons Titian and Rembrandt entitled *The Staircase Group,* in John Vanderlyn's controversial painting of the beautiful, sculptural nude figure, *Ariadne Asleep on the Island of Naxos,* and in Thomas Eakins's *William Rush Carving the Allegorical Figure of the Schuylkill River*[11] for which the artist made three-dimensional studies. In addition, the neoclassic marble sculpture created by other artists was truly three-dimensional and solid, one of the reasons for the tremendous success of this form of art.

Ingvar Bergstrom has defined still life as objects grouped together for artistic purposes, for the study of texture, light, color, and structure.[12] Figures can serve this purpose just as well as apples, pipes, books, teapots, or other material objects. This is evidenced by what might be described as figural still lifes in the Ganz collection: Thomas Sully's *Portrait of the Misses Mary & Emily McEuen* (fig. 29), Winslow Homer's *Blackboard* (fig. 58), and Elihu Vedder's *Girl with a Lute* (fig. 54). In these canvases, the formal arrangement of the solid, volumetric figures constitutes as much a still life as the bouquet of flowers in the Sully, the geometric configurations on the blackboard in the Homer, or the group of objects on the table in the Vedder. The Vedder is as exotic as a Heade orchid and hummingbird painting, while the Homer invokes a mood of brooding introspection like Peto's arrangement of old books.

Most nineteenth-century art is not obscure in its meaning. Indeed, Americans were very fond of stories, especially sentimental stories, from which a moral lesson could be derived. This strong narrative strain in American art has been well served by the human figure. The figure, as we have seen, was instrumental in presenting the stories of the Revolutionary War. Later the figure, in such allegorical paintings as Thomas Cole's *The Course of Empire* and *Voyage of Life,*[13] helped to bring forth a moralizing narrative. Some mid-nineteenth-century paintings were strictly literary, depicting the tales of Washington Irving, James Fenimore Cooper, and Henry Wadsworth Longfellow. And in the neoclassic sculpture of Hiram Powers, Randolph Rogers, and William Henry Rinehart, the figure became the primary agent of narration. Moralizing themes were taken from the Bible, mythology, classics, and contemporary literature to educate and elevate the minds of the public. Many nineteenth-century Americans knew the myths and stories behind these works and would have understood the moral lessons involved, but for those who needed some edification, exhibition catalogues usually printed a synopsis of the narrative.

In addition to specifically literary works, genre paintings brought a more general and anecdotal aspect to nineteenth-century American paintings. J. G. Brown, Seymour Guy, and Lilly Martin Spencer told easily comprehended stories about family life, love, and customs of their times. In these works, the figure becomes not only an agent of narration but of sentiment as well.

Because of the influence of European schools—especially those of Paris and Munich—American artists began to use the human figure for emotional expression and aesthetic communication, not for portraiture or narrative but as a vehicle for mood.[14] Artists discovered the expressive possibilities of the human figure. Whereas in earlier nineteenth-century American art the artist had concentrated on closely observed details and attempted to imitate nature, the turn-of-the-century artists considered this approach to be theatrical and mechanical, preferring instead a poetically evocative style. Objective reproductions of nature were no longer the primary goal of the artist. Emphasis was given instead to the expression or suggestion of feeling, emotion, and mood. In works such as Thomas Wilmer Dewing's *Woman with Violin* (fig. 65), everything is simplified so that the viewer can concentrate on the figure's mood and bearing. Thomas Eakins's later portraits strike a similar subjective chord of melancholy preoccupation. Again, it is the human figure that can best convey the emotions that the artist is trying to express. No story is needed or even desired; mood and atmosphere are what the artist is trying to capture. Like the human still lifes discussed earlier, these figures are in repose. As is evident in the woman depicted in Francis Coates Jones's *Lady and Lyre* (fig. 66), many are drained of all energy and vitality, conjuring up an image of fin-de-siècle ennui.

In an age that believed you "proved the existence of an abstract truth if you capitalized the noun,"[15] idealized images of Truth, Justice, and Beauty appeared in the arts, and the human figure was used to convey specific universal ideals to the public. Though taken from Renaissance and Greek art, the female figures embodying these concepts were metamorphosed during the American Renaissance (see fig. 71) into genteel American virgins to act as improving adornments. Representing science and the arts, among other disciplines, these Beaux-Arts figures by muralists like Frederick Dielman, George Willoughby Maynard, Kenyon Cox, and Edwin Blashfield served as decorations for libraries, courthouses, and government buildings erected in the latter part of the nineteenth century. The artists created female figures with fluid, graceful lines that followed the architectural design of the buildings. Again, the human figure proved to be a very adaptable form.

With these thoughts on the figure generally, let us now turn to the individual figural works in the Ganz collection.

Painters in the colonial era were greatly influenced by English art and artists, and this influence can be seen in the earliest work in the Ganz collection, *Sketch for "The Copley Family"* (fig. 28), painted by John Singleton Copley just after he settled in London at the beginning of the Revolutionary War. Copley, stepson of printmaker and teacher Peter Pelham, was America's leading eighteenth-century portraitist. After Pelham's death in 1751, the young Copley comfortably supported the family by engraving and painting realistic, sophisticated portraits of Boston's elite. But a combination of factors led Copley in 1774 to go abroad. One consideration was Benjamin West's strong advice that Copley study the old masters in Europe. Perhaps a more pressing concern was the safety of his family since Copley's father-in-law, Richard Clarke, was a prominent Tory and one of the consignees of the infamous tea which the patriots had dumped in Boston Harbor in 1773.

The Ganz painting is a preparatory oil sketch for the National Gallery's *Copley Family* (1776–1777) which documents the warmth of the family's reunion in 1775 in its new Leicester Square home. Since this is a portrait of the artist's family, it is a much less formal work than most of Copley's paintings. The *Sketch for "The Copley Family"* (1776) focuses on the triangular group on the right side of the canvas. At the center is Copley's wife, Susanna Farnum Clarke, flanked on the left by her son John, Jr. (who later became Lord Lyndhurst, Lord Chancellor of England) and on the right by her daughter Mary. The presence of another daughter, Elizabeth, is faintly discernible in the outline at the far left of the picture.

Because of the absence of the other family members and many of the details (costumes, toys, furniture), the isolated trio of figures offers moving insights into the psychological characters of the sitters. Copley has captured an intimate, unguarded moment between a mother and her children. Although it is a portrait, it also contains genrelike elements which relate it to nineteenth-century works in the Ganz collection by such artists as Lilly Martin Spencer, Eastman Johnson, and Edward Lamson Henry, who also depicted loving, mother-child relationships.

The Ganz sketch comes from a transitional period in Copley's career, displaying not only his freer brushwork, a skill acquired after he moved to England, but also the fine draftsmanship he learned in America from Peter Pelham. Jules Prown has described the painting as "spirited and strong, demonstrating for the first time what remains true throughout Copley's English career, that he is at his virtuoso best in his oil sketches."[16] The

Fig. 28   John Singleton Copley, *Sketch for "The Copley Family,"* 1776

solid figures are very clearly outlined, with bits of landscape and costume suggested. They form a stable, tightly knit group. Copley placed special emphasis on the faces and hands, following Benjamin West's counsel that they were the "Parts of Most Consequence."[17] And it is these that tell the story.

From what is essentially a colonial American work—though painted in England—we move to the federal period, where the main artistic theme was still relatively formal portraiture in the British style. An exemplary work is Thomas Sully's double *Portrait of the Misses Mary & Emily McEuen* (fig. 29), fully documented in 1823 in the artist's Register of Paintings.

Born to English actors, Sully began his artistic career painting miniatures in Charleston, South Carolina. He later received advice from such established artists as Henry Benbridge, John Trumbull, and Gilbert Stuart before returning to England for a year's study with Sir Thomas Lawrence. Settling in Philadelphia, Sully soon became that city's foremost portraitist, immortalizing the faces of its wealthy families.

The fashionable McEuen sisters sit on a rose velvet settee in an informal pose, as if the artist had interrupted their intimate conversation. Silhouetted against a neutral background, they

Fig. 29   Thomas Sully, *Portrait of the Misses Mary & Emily McEuen,* 1823

form a tightly coherent unit of sisterly affection. The painting's fluid, elegant lines serve to reinforce the bond between the two women. The young woman in the light dress rests her right hand on her sister's shoulder. The viewer's eye moves easily from the hand down the twisted shawl that crosses the second sister's dark dress and from there to the first woman's curving arm and then back to her face. It is one of the most touching and affectionate, though unsentimental, of Sully's early portraits.

One sister holds a portfolio labeled "Sketches from nature/ TS 1823." It is believed that the sketchbook is Sully's own and that the artist allowed the McEuen sisters to look through it because of his friendship with their family. An unusual and charming note is the addition of a sumptuous still life to the right.[18] Wolfgang Born, in his *Still Life Painting in America,* has

pointed out that the bouquet, with its rose at the center and tulip at the top, is typical of the compositions seen in young ladies' decorative watercolors and velvet paintings of this period.[19]

Sully's indebtedness to eighteenth-century English portraiture in general and Sir Thomas Lawrence in particular is evident in both the bravura brushwork (noted especially in the pale blue gown, shawl, still life, and sky) and the rich coloration. The entire canvas breathes an air of delicate refinement, order, and stability typical of the idealistic era of Thomas Jefferson.

Sully believed that his sitters did not object to flattery and advised young painters that, while resemblance was essential, "no fault will be found with the artist, (at least by the sitter,) if he improves the appearance."[20] Prosperous families evidently agreed, for Sully's portraits, at the time of his death at the age of eighty-nine, numbered over two thousand.

In the early nineteenth century, American art was romantic and moralistic; the public believed that works of art should uplift the viewer to thoughts of the good and pure. Americans not only wanted a story, but one with a moral. The landscapes of Thomas Cole, the essays of Ralph Waldo Emerson, and the neoclassic sculpture of Hiram Powers shared this lofty purpose.

Idealism in the form of white marble neoclassic sculpture, as in Sully's painting, was refined in both surface and sentiment. Almost all American neoclassic sculpture was produced by expatriates living in Italy (first in Florence, then in Rome), a country that provided a good climate, modest expenses, nude models, the pure white marbles of Carrara and Seravezza, examples of Greek and Roman sculpture (unearthed in the mid-eighteenth century and on view at the Vatican galleries), and, perhaps most important, skilled workmen to carve the marble statues.

Although American sculpture came into its own as an art form at this time, it was still very much dependent on European examples. Nineteenth-century sculptors such as Antonio Canova, Albert Bertel Thorwaldsen, and Lorenzo Bartolini served as sources along with the antique Greek statues that Emerson thought breathed "a confession of moral nature, of purity, love, and hope."[21]

By the 1840s, Greek revival was in its heyday in America. The young republic looked to the ancient Greek democracy for inspiration and supported Greece's recent War for Independence that echoed our own battle for freedom. Classicism was to serve a symbolic role in American art through much of the nineteenth century. American towns were named Utica, Syracuse, Troy, and Athens, and their libraries, colleges, churches, and mansions were built to look like Greek temples.

Fig. 30   Hiram Powers, *Proserpine*, 1844

sculpture acceptable to most of the public, but an outraged Nathaniel Hawthorne, in his novel, *The Marble Faun,* expressed the opinion that naming a "specimen of womanhood" Eve or Venus did not "apologize for lack of decent clothing."[24] He was in the minority, though, as many Americans on the Grand Tour made obligatory visits to the artists' studios and brought home both portrait and idealized busts for their parlors or libraries as a symbol of wealth and culture. Others who wanted to have the same sculpture could order replicas from the artist, who would have his carvers again transfer his plaster model into marble.

A few years after settling in Florence, where Hiram Powers was to remain for the rest of his life, he created an idealized bust of *Proserpine* (1844, fig. 30). The daughter of Jupiter and Ceres and the wife of Pluto, she is depicted emerging from a base of acanthus leaves, symbol of immortality. The Ganz work is one of two known busts dated 1844, indicating that it is one of the first of over 100 replicas made by Powers. According to Richard Wunder, the bust became the "most favored single piece among Powers's work and it was copied more times than any other work ever produced by an American sculptor."[25]

Proserpine, goddess of agriculture (she wears a wheat wreath in her hair), was well received not only because of the beauty of the naturalistically rendered female form but because she was a truly fitting symbol for the young republic. Austere and pure, Proserpine had been abducted by Pluto. She was forced to spend one-third of each year in Hades but returned every spring with the flowers. This story of the seasons must have held special significance for the agrarian American nation. In addition, the story's strong symbolic Christian overtones, with thoughts of life, death, and resurrection, would have satisfied the age's requirements for spiritual and moral content.

The bust-length replica (after 1845, fig. 31) of Powers's *The Greek Slave* may be considered a companion piece to *Proserpine. The Greek Slave* was the epitome of the nineteenth-century neoclassic aesthetic and, in its full-length form, the most famous American sculpture of its day. The form is borrowed from antiquity[26] and is classical in its perfect proportions and quiet simplicity.

The exotic tale behind the statue involves a young Christian woman taken captive by the Turks to be sold in Constantinople. Initially, the full-length nude version created an outcry, but after lengthy explanations by the artist and supportive statements by the clergy, the nude became acceptable both in Europe and in the United States. Indeed, she became a Christian heroine and a lesson in faith and morality. Hiram Powers described *The Greek Slave* as possessing "what trust there could

The neoclassic sculptors strove not only for the perfection of human form, but also to endow that form with spiritual and moral content to elevate the soul. For art was considered the "sister of religion . . . the interpreter of the high and pure."[22] Those spiritual and moral ideals were represented more often than not by a female figure who was totally naked or naked to the waist, and this at a time of extreme prudery in America. The leading American sculptor, Hiram Powers, believed that a marble statue of a nude was an "unveiled soul" imbued with spiritual meaning.[23] This moralistic point of view made the

Fig. 31 Hiram Powers, *Bust of the Greek Slave*, after 1845

Appeal, fair stone
From God's pure heights of beauty against man's wrong!
Catch up in thy divine face, not alone
East griefs but west, and strike and shame the strong,
By thunders of white silence, overthrown.[29]

The Reverend Orville Dewey also sanctioned the work, to nearly universal satisfaction, by proclaiming that the nude was "clothed all over with sentiment, sheltered, protected by it from every profane eye."[30]

The Greek Slave's symbolism appealed to Americans on the basis of Christian ethics and also on a political level in terms of sympathy for Greece's war against the Muslim Turks and for the growing antislavery movement in America.

Another work by Hiram Powers in the Ganz collection is the tender sculpture of his baby daughter's hand emerging from the center of a daisy. *Loulie's Hand* (fig. 32) was cast by the artist in 1839 and transferred into marble by the artisan carvers in his studio as a surprise. Powers gave the work to his wife at Christmas that year, and it remained in the family until it was acquired by the Ganzes. Delicately carved, the pure white marble form of *Loulie's Hand* summons forth the idea of childhood innocence.

One sculptor who did not join the others in Italy was John Crookshanks King, a Scot who eventually settled in Boston,

still be in a Divine Providence . . . with utter despair for the present mingled with somewhat of scorn for all around her. She is too deeply concerned to be aware of her nakedness. It is not her person but her spirit that stands exposed, and she bears it all as Christians only can."[27] Thus, the slave, turning her face away from her contemptible captors, is elevated above them by her Christian faith. Its white marble, Powers believed, "removed the object . . . into a sort of spiritual region,"[28] and Elizabeth Barrett Browning's sonnet praised its purity and power:

Fig. 32 Hiram Powers, *Loulie's Hand*, c.1839

Fig. 33   John Crookshanks King, *Cat on a Cushion*, mid-19th century

specializing in realistic portrait busts rather than ideal sculpture. King's *Cat on a Cushion* (fig. 33), with its matted fur and languid feline pose, reflects the artist's realistic strain. Although William Gerdts has pointed out that animals were used as accessories for sculptural monuments, it would have been rare to see an independent statue of a cat such as this one.[31] This fact, along with the sensitive treatment of the animal, leads one to suspect that this is a loving portrait of the artist's pet.

By the 1840s, genre painting was at its most popular. The realistic depiction of everyday activities had emerged at this time with the rustic, anecdotal, and humorous paintings of George Caleb Bingham and William Sidney Mount. Genre scenes captured the nationalistic days when Jacksonian democracy prevailed; self-confidence was in the air, and native subject matter was the vogue. The realistic mode paralleled the development and growing importance of the camera and the distribution and sale of popular genre scenes by the art unions.[32]

The more flamboyant school of portraiture, typified by Thomas Sully's works, declined, while straightforward realism, epitomized by Charles Loring Elliott's *Self-Portrait*, increased in popularity. Contrast Elliott's *Self-Portrait* (c. 1850, fig. 34) with the Sully painting of the McEuen sisters (fig. 29). Although one is a large, formal portrait and the other a more private, intimate work, they serve as examples of the difference in style and taste between federal and Jacksonian America.

Elliott, a leading New York portraitist who had studied with John Trumbull and John Quidor, was noted for his skill in painting remarkable likenesses. His *Self-Portrait* brings us into direct confrontation with the subject. There are no flowers, elaborate costumes, furniture, or landscape elements as accessories. The man himself is important, not his possessions or surroundings. Indeed, there are no surroundings at all, only a neutral background from which the Rembrandtesque figure emerges. It is a democratic, solid American portrait. A nationalistic individual, Elliott believed that no artist he knew had ever benefitted from a trip to Europe.[33]

The portrait, in which the artist appears to be between thirty-five and forty years of age, is one of a series of at least seven self-portraits that Elliott painted during various stages of his

Fig. 34   Charles Loring Elliott, *Self-Portrait*, c.1850

life. The image exudes optimism, confidence, and independence. With auburn goatee and moustache, black hat and jacket, and intense eyes, Elliott presents us with a dramatic and vigorous sense of himself. Using a bravura "Salvatoresque touch of brush,"[34] as James Jackson Jarves termed it, and placing the figure close to the picture plane, Elliott brings to the portrait a new sense of immediacy.

Sculpture at mid-century also began to move toward realism, and this evolution can be seen in several works by the second generation of American sculptors in Italy. One of those artists, a pupil of Lorenzo Bartolini named Randolph Rogers, settled in Rome, which had replaced Florence as the expatriate artistic colony. Although most of his commissions were for portrait busts, Rogers in 1853 modeled his first important ideal sculpture, *Ruth Gleaning*, a charming mixture of neoclassicism and realism. The Ganzes have one of a group of reduced figures executed after 1867 (fig. 35). It is clear at first glance that a change in style and taste has begun. Unlike the classic, cool, and serene sculptures of Hiram Powers, Rogers here has captured both motion and emotion.

Rogers has chosen for his subject the narrative about one of the most popular heroines of the Old Testament.[35] The story of Ruth is one of bravery, loyalty, love, and virtue's rewards; it depicts a harmonious and peaceful society characterized by God-fearing and loving people. In addition, it illustrates how a foreigner can become identified with an adopted country: in Ruth's case, Israel; in the case of the neoclassic sculptors, Italy.

It is important to note that Rogers chose to depict the most dramatic moment in the story—when Ruth meets her future husband Boaz and kneels before him to thank him for allowing her to glean in his fields. Not only is her humble expression realistic, but the representation of her hair and drapery, the intricate carving of the hem of her dress, and the rendering of the wheat she holds are all very naturalistic. In Rogers's later works, such as *Nydia, Blind Girl of Pompeii* (1855–56), he intensifies both expression and movement to become the most baroque of the neoclassic sculptors.[36]

Another expatriate in Rome was Harriet Hosmer, who found it a "moral, physical, and intellectual impossibility to live elsewhere"[37] and who studied there with English neoclassic sculptor John Gibson. A native of Massachusetts, she had been raised by her father to be an independent spirit. Thus, at the age of twenty-four, when she found herself alone in Rome, with her father no longer able to support her, she sold her horse, canceled a vacation, and created a work that would

Fig. 35   Randolph Rogers, *Ruth Gleaning*, after 1867

eventually bring her more than its "weight in silver."[38] This was *Puck* (fig. 36), whom she often referred to as her son. The Ganz collection includes a replica of *Puck*.

Considered a "conceit" or "fancy" piece, *Puck* is the antithesis to the serious and dramatic story of Ruth. This little figure—the source of which may have been Shakespeare's *A Midsummer Night's Dream*—sits on a toadstool, playing with a lizard with one hand while holding a beetle with the other. Full of "mischievous self-will," the statue was thought by contemporaries to be "a laugh in marble" and "the very embodiment of diablerie."[39]

Puck could well have been a personification of the artist herself who was recognized as the leader of the group of female sculptors that Henry James dubbed "The White Marmorean Flock." Described as perky, spritely, and "carefree as a child," Hosmer was one of the most colorful, unconventional personalities of her day.

Two of Harriet Hosmer's friends in Italy were Elizabeth and Robert Browning, of whose hands she made casts during the winter of 1853. Hosmer's *Clasped Hands of Robert and Elizabeth Barrett Browning* (fig. 37) unites the couple for eternity and is a lasting symbol of their love and devotion for each other as well as their close personal relationship with their "great pet," Hattie Hosmer. Robert Browning's sturdy yet tender hand holds the slender fingers of his wife, whom Hosmer described as being "so fragile that the gentlest zephyr might have borne her away." Van Wyck Brooks has written about the Brownings' constant devotion (Robert Browning dined away from home only once in fifteen years and could not bear to leave his "Ba"

Fig. 37 Harriet Hosmer, *Clasped Hands of Robert and Elizabeth Barrett Browning*, 1853

Fig. 36 Harriet Hosmer, *Puck*, after 1854

alone), and Hosmer wrote that the Brownings "lived in a world of their own, happiest when alone therein."[40]

The style of sentimental realism, as seen in the works of Lilly Martin Spencer, began in the 1850s with the emergence of middle-class art patronage and remained popular in American painting through the sixties and seventies. The contemporary values of a warm home life and a good education were favorite themes and can be seen not only in paintings by Spencer (fig. 38) but also by Seymour Joseph Guy (figs. 49–52) and Eastman Johnson (fig. 39). Although there had been British and French precedents for this type of art—in the works of Sir David Wilkie and Jean-Baptiste Greuze, respectively—the new influence came from Germany and the School of Fine Arts in Düsseldorf.

Even though patron Nicholas Longworth offered to send her overseas to study, Lilly Martin Spencer did not go abroad as did Harriet Hosmer or Mary Cassatt. While Hosmer had proclaimed that it was impossible to be artist, wife, and mother, Spencer combined all three careers. Her husband prepared her frames and canvases, varnished the paintings, and acted as her business agent. During the day, she painted and took care of her large family, and, at night, attended drawing classes at the National Academy of Design.

Spencer excelled in painting scenes of domestic tranquillity, depicting primarily kitchen activities or nursery themes like *Mother and Child* (1858, fig. 38) which may well be a self-portrait of the artist and her young son, Charles.[41] The rich colors of the palette, crisp outlines, concern with detail and texture (the still life in the background, the decoration on the gown and petticoat) reflect the contemporary influence of the Düsseldorf School. It is highly likely that Spencer would have seen examples of this popular European style at New York's Düsseldorf Gallery, open from 1849 until 1861. *Mother and Child* is an informal, intimate painting, like so many in the Ganz collection, and one filled with warmth and family love, an example of the emphasis that Victorians placed on home life.

The mother and child theme was a very popular one in this era. In 1872 Eastman Johnson painted an interior genre scene of middle-class Victorian family life entitled *Bo Peep* (fig. 39). Apprenticed first in Bufford's lithography shop in Boston—where Winslow Homer also worked—Johnson went abroad in 1849 to study art. Two years in Düsseldorf and three and a half years at The Hague (as well as a short stay in Paris studying with Couture) influenced the artist greatly.

Bo Peep, exhibited at the National Academy of Design in 1874, drew generous praise from *Appleton's Journal:*

"Bo-Peep" is a most graceful and spirited painting of a child, who has bound a handkerchief round her mother's eyes, the child full of life

Fig. 38 Lilly Martin Spencer,
Mother and Child, 1858

Fig. 39   Eastman Johnson,
Bo Peep, 1872

and laughter, and the mother so sweet and tender as to recall one's pleasantest impressions of such situations and such a relation. Eastman Johnson, more than any artist in New York, has the happy talent to render familiar scenes with elegance of style. His beautiful color and pleasant tone, added to spirit and completeness of conception, make his pictures popular with everybody, while to amateurs they have the solid advantage of being really wrought from a high artistic standard.[42]

Bo Peep reflects Johnson's Dutch training, especially, in its focus on a simple event from everyday life, muted palette, and dramatic lighting. Here the light not only serves to model form but also symbolically beams down on the head of the playful little child who was close in age to Johnson's own daughter, Ethel. The triangular composition of the two figures leads the viewer's eye to the outline of a cross—highlighted in the wooden shutters—behind their heads which makes the figures symbolic of the Madonna and Child and reinforces the Victorian idea of the sanctity of children. The Bible prominently placed on the prie-dieu to the right further imparts a religious feeling to the work.

Johnson sets a mood of maternal tenderness and love, an affirmation of life. The dark interior and the attention to details of the family's comfortable Victorian existence signal that the painting comes from the so-called Brown Decades after the Civil War, but the positive emotion shown here does not reflect the cynicism, disillusionment, or withdrawal—both physical and emotional—that characterized these years.[43]

The mother and child theme is further explored in three charming works by Edward Lamson Henry, a genre painter who studied at the Pennsylvania Academy of Fine Arts before spending two years in Paris with Gleyre and Courbet. Henry was principally known for scenes of the colonial and federal eras—particularly popular after the centennial celebrations of 1876 had revived interest in American history—that were archaeologically correct in costumes, furniture, and architecture and topographically correct in their scenery. But the Ganz paintings, *Watching Mother Embroider* (1878, fig. 40), *Can They Go Too?* (1877, fig. 41), and *Mother and Child Under a Rose Trellis* (1877, fig. 42) faithfully document his own times and show another side of Henry's work. One delves into the world

Fig. 40 Edward Lamson Henry, *Watching Mother Embroider*, 1878

Fig. 41 Edward Lamson Henry, *Can They Go Too?*, 1877

portrayed within the frames and finds tiny jewellike paintings that chronicle in microscopic detail Victorian life—its dress, its architecture, its eclectic possessions, its ever-present sentiment. Even in *Mother and Child Under a Rose Trellis*, an outdoor scene filled with bright light and color (perhaps relating to his studies in Paris and the influence of the impressionist school), Henry adheres to a style of precise detail and form.

A very successful painter, Henry could count the Astors and Vanderbilts among his patrons. It is said that his paintings were in such demand that they were sold as soon as they were varnished, even before their exhibition at the National Academy.

The president of the academy, reading a memorial to Henry, stated: "In depicting on canvas the manners and customs, the inventions and habitations, the politics and pioneering of his native country . . . Mr. Henry stands unrivalled. Surely he

may be called the Meissonier of America."[44]

John George Brown, an Englishman who came to America in 1853, was one of the most popular figure painters of his time. The Ganzes have brought together an outstanding group of five paintings by Brown from the 1860s and seventies when the artist created his finest works. The first is an informal oval portrait of *John Jacob Astor III* (c. 1860, fig. 43),[45] one of Brown's wealthiest patrons. Drawn on canvas with a free brush, this engaging portrait displays the spontaneity and freshness, resulting from that approach, that relates it to Elliott's *Self-Portrait* (fig. 34).

Resting in the Woods (1866, fig. 44) depicts a pensive young girl in repose outdoors. The way in which the artist has rendered the various textures—of her straw hat, shoes, and luscious pink dress and of the mossy rock and the bark and leaves—is one indication of his skill. But the real artistic achieve-

Fig. 42   Edward Lamson Henry,
Mother and Child Under a Rose Trellis, 1877

Fig. 43   John George Brown,
John Jacob Astor III, c.1860

ment is revealed in Brown's early use of sunlight as it filters through the leaves. It is a hard, white light that objectively describes the figure and its surroundings. Predating by ten years similar works of solitary, introspective women outdoors by Winslow Homer, it is a work of enormous beauty and force. Brown's *Among the Trees* (mid-1870s, fig. 45) depicts another wistful young woman, but in a more painterly manner. Holding a nosegay of freshly picked wildflowers, she pauses among the tree boughs in a moment of reflection.

Different in setting, *Children at the Gate* (1872, fig. 46) is an example of Brown's paintings of rural children. These works came from the summers the artist spent in the countryside in the Adirondacks, Catskills, New England, and Canada. They bring to mind the paintings of country children by Winslow Homer executed during this period, although Brown's color and Ruskinian attention to surface and textures are very close to the British tradition. Brown, in fact, saw his painting as a

continuation of the English genre tradition of William Hogarth and Sir David Wilkie.[46] The two figures, poised at the gate, are precisely and clearly rendered, and the clear, bright light which falls on the straw hat of the young boy spotlights the charming Huckleberry Finn-like character.

Picnic Party in the Woods of 1872 (fig. 47), one of Brown's most delightful and complex works, also utilizes sunlight to spotlight a single figure. The brightly colored canvas shows a group of people—children and adults—at various stages of life: a man and woman courting, a young couple with their new baby, a group of children playing, and an old man observing and reflecting on the activities capture our attention. However, through the use of light and composition, it is the young girl dressed in white, bathed in light, and standing at the center of the canvas who dominates this allegory of life. She is thought to be Brown's own daughter.[47]

Samuel S. Carr's *The Beach at Coney Island* (c. 1879, fig. 48),

Fig. 99 John George Brown,
The Fur Muff, 1864

Fig. 45 John George Brown,
Among the Trees, mid-1870s

Fig. 44   John George Brown,
Resting in the Woods, 1866

like Brown's *Picnic Party in the Woods,* reveals the middle class enjoying their new-found leisure time out of doors. With straightforward color and light, Carr has painted an appealing picture of a Victorian day at the seashore, similar in spirit to works by Winslow Homer in America and Eugène Boudin in France. Carr used the same figures over and over again in many of his canvases, as can be seen by comparing the Ganz painting with one in the Smith College Museum of Art entitled *Beach Scene* (c. 1879). Some of the figures in *The Beach at Coney Island* seem to have been taken from photographs, especially the family group in the center that is posing for the beach photographer.

The paintings of another English-born artist, Seymour Joseph

Guy—strongly represented by four paintings in the Ganz collection—are very similar in subject and technique to those of J. G. Brown. After arriving in the United States in 1854, Guy began his career as a portraitist but soon became a specialist in genre scenes depicting children and adolescent girls. An *Art Journal* writer observed that "Mr. Guy's subjects mostly relate to scenes and incidents drawn from child-life, and in their composition and treatment he has no superior in American Art."[48]

In *The Pick of the Orchard* (c. 1870, fig. 49), *Unconscious of Danger* (1865, fig. 50), *Story of Golden Locks* (c. 1870, fig. 51), or *Making Believe* (1870, fig. 52), the viewer is confronted with the Victorian glorification of childhood. Artists and poets, Henry

Fig. 47   John George Brown, *Picnic Party in the Woods*, 1872

Tuckerman wrote in 1867, believe that the image of childhood is "a redeeming presence, a harmonizing and hopeful element, the token of what we were, and prophecy of what we may be."[49] As may be expected, these scenes of the hope, promise, and innocence of America's youth were especially prevalent following the devastation of the Civil War.

Guy's style evolved from his early training as a sign painter and is notable for its accomplished draftsmanship, meticulous rendering of each object, rich coloration, and smooth, enamellike finish. *The Pick of the Orchard* shows a young girl alone outdoors in a contemplative pose and recalls J. G. Brown's *Resting in the Woods* in both style and spirit. Both paintings, showing solitary figures in reverie, derive from the English Pre-Raphaelite tradition.

Unconscious of Danger tells a simple and straightforward story with solid forms and bright, pure coloring. It is best described by a contemporary critic as

one of the best pictures yet painted by this rapidly-improving artist. It represents a young lad, unconscious of danger, while dreaming of the future, walking to the edge of a high ledge of rocks, while his sister is in the act of striving to bring him back. It is excellent in drawing, exquisitely finished, and tender in expression.[50]

The two interior scenes provide us with the special opportunity to witness the artist's deft handling of light and shadow. Both *Story of Golden Locks* and *Making Believe* have hidden light sources that cast dark shadows and bring a mysterious air to the seemingly peaceful compositions. In *Story of Golden Locks*, similar to Guy's *A Bed Time Story*, the sister's large shadow appears on the wall above her frightened, wide-eyed little

Fig. 46   John George Brown, *Children at the Gate*, 1872

Fig 50   Seymour J. Guy, *Unconscious of Danger*, 1865

brothers. In *Making Believe*, which relates closely to *Making a Train* (1867),[51] the curvaceous shadow to the left of the semi-erotic depiction of the young girl playing "grownup" anticipates the woman she is about to become, while the large nebulous shadow looming behind her perhaps symbolizes the imminent loss of childhood innocence. Both interior scenes contain depictions of very specific American types of furniture (the Chippendale chair and the Victorian spool bed in *Story of Golden Locks*, for instance) which appear in many other works by Guy.

Straightforward realism is seen in the early work of John Ferguson Weir. Known for his paintings capturing the tenor of the growing industrial society such as *The Gun Foundry* (1866)

and *Forging the Shaft* (1877),[52] Weir in 1864 painted a loving and elaborate tribute to his father entitled *An Artist's Studio* (fig. 53). Robert W. Weir, also the father of Julian Alden Weir, was a painter of landscapes, portraits, and genre scenes and served as drawing instructor at the U. S. Military Academy. He is depicted at his desk in his studio at West Point which was built two stories high to accommodate his large painting of *The Embarkation of the Pilgrims* for the Capitol Rotunda. *An Artist's Studio* is crowded with furniture, easels, sculpture, musical instruments, frames, books, and a multitude of studio props. Scholars have begun to identify many of the works in the painting, such as two studies for *The Embarkation of the Pilgrims*, *Taking the Veil* of 1863, which was enthusiastically received in

Fig. 48   Samuel S. Carr,
The Beach at Coney Island, c.1879

New York (on the easel), *St. Nicholas* (1837), and the large portrait bust of the painter Washington Allston by Shobal Vail Clevenger on the cupboard.[53]

A critic described the elder Weir's studio in 1865:

One steps from brilliant sunshine into the quiet light and tranquil atmosphere of the artist's studio. . . .

At a table on one side or before an easel, sits the artist. His white hair shades a face full of intelligence. . . . It is a mind rich in knowledge of his art and keen in intellectual curiosity. Books are his tools; brushes and paints his familiar comrades. . . .

A studio like this, therefore, low in tone, rich in detail is "like an old chapel" which the prayers of saints and the petitions of longing hearts have vitalized to an almost living quality. . . . It has repose, culture, breadth of vision.[54]

An Artist's Studio, one of the two paintings with which John Ferguson Weir made his debut at the National Academy of Design, was a huge success and of crucial importance to the "aims and hopes" of the young artist: "the picture had sold itself . . . and my election [as an Associate] at the Academy was a verdict by the artists; it gave me confidence."[55]

Girl with a Lute (fig. 54), painted by Elihu Vedder in Paris in 1866, also depicts a solitary figure, yet leaves us with a different sort of feeling than the Weir painting. James Jackson Jarves considered Vedder to be "an artist of wider scope, greater vigor, more varied, intense, and original conceptions and thor-

ough executive skill, than has hitherto appeared.[56] Although the painting was executed in nineteenth-century France, it also speaks of fifteenth-century Florence—not only in the Renaissance costume but also in the stately Ghirlandaioesque figure and the sinuous lines reminiscent of Michelangelo. Vedder had lived in Florence in the 1850s, seen the recently restored frescoes of Ghirlandaio and Giotto, and made studies after them, drawing fifteenth-century costumes and scenes of Renaissance life.[57] But as Joshua Taylor has written, "the pensive young woman lives not in Florence but in a world of art, a world of artistic perception. There is no story to tell, and yet the senses and the imagination are transported to an arrested eddy of time in which their exercise had full rein." Taylor further noted that it was to this "vaguely designated time and place—historical without specific epoch—that Vedder habitually returned when he wanted to concentrate on physical beauty."[58]

The whole is rich in color and texture. The figure has a solid feeling of weight and form but also conveys grace, elegance, and sensuality. The interest in sculptural volumes is contrasted to the highly decorative background tapestry. These swirling lines of animals and foliage predate by almost twenty years the art nouveau style of Vedder's illustrations for the *Rubyáiyát of Omar Khayyam* (1885).

Girl with a Lute is the first in Vedder's series depicting women with musical instruments and tapestry backgrounds.[59] It also serves as predecessor and inspiration for many younger artists, such as Thomas Wilmer Dewing and Francis Coates Jones, who depicted beautiful, inward-looking women at the end of the nineteenth century.

Many of the female figures found in American sculpture in the last half of the nineteenth century were derived from literature. Joseph Mozier, who left a lucrative business in New York to become a sculptor in Rome, created one such figure entitled *Undine* (c. 1867, fig. 55). The literary source for the sculpture is Baron de la Motte-Fouqué's story of a water nymph, Undine, who being given a soul was rejected by her lover (a mortal) and ultimately caused his death. A popular figure for nineteenth-century artists, Undine was the subject of an opera and was carved by several other sculptors.[60] Mozier's version is very rare, there being only one other known example besides the Ganz piece. It illustrates the later neoclassic sculptor's fascination with and virtuoso treatment of surface textures. While Undine's gown is smooth, her drapery is distinguished by striations. The artist's skill, however, is particularly evident in the execution of the veil which has been called "one of the most notable American examples of the see-through illusionism popular in Italy at mid-century."[61] This technical virtuosity, also popular in Italy in the eighteenth century, was revived around 1850 in Europe and can be seen in works such as *The Veiled Nun* by Giuseppe Croff.[62] The complex handling of the carving and the beauty and grace of the female figure won *Undine* the grand prize at the Rome exhibition of 1867.

Another popular classical theme in the nineteenth century associated with a tragic love affair was *Hero* (1868, fig. 56), represented in the Ganz collection in a work by William Henry Rinehart, a Maryland man who settled in Rome in 1858. Hero, a priestess of Aphrodite, was visited each night by her lover, Leander, who lived on the opposite side of the Hellespont. One stormy winter night, the lamp that Hero had lit to guide Leander to her was blown out by the wind. He later was found dead, and Hero threw herself into the water and drowned.

Hero captured the romantic imagination of the nineteenth century. Not only did Turner paint the story (*The Parting of Hero and Leander*, 1837),[63] but Lord Byron wrote a poem about it and even successfully reenacted Leander's swim across the Hellespont. Although Rinehart also created a handsome statue of Leander, it is indicative of American preference for examples of the female figure rather than the male that he was commissioned to do only two Leanders, compared to eight Heros.

Rinehart's work is poignant, although not as dramatic as Rogers's *Ruth*. It shares with *Ruth* an emphasis on creating a sense of movement. *Hero* is a diagonal composition, with the

Fig. 49   Seymour J. Guy, *The Pick of the Orchard*, c.1870

Fig. 52   Seymour J. Guy,
Making Believe, 1870

Fig. 51   Seymour J. Guy, *Story of Golden Locks*, c.1870

figure leaning forward, eyes out to sea, her right hand to her breast in a pose of anticipation and anxiety. The presence of wind is indicated by the blowing drapery, the flickering flame in Hero's lamp, and the waves lapping onto the rock where she waits for Leander. Wayne Craven has noted that Hero's head bears a strong resemblance to that of the *Venus de Milo*.[64]

The post-Civil War period that Howard Mumford Jones has called ''The Age of Energy'' was characterized by movement. Jones cites as examples of this restless age the hundreds of thousands of soldiers being dispersed following the Civil War, settlers' wagons going west, immigrants from Europe coming to America, railroads stretching across the country, and ferries and steamboats plying its waters. People were fascinated by machines such as the gigantic Corliss steam engine, ''the beneficent Titan'' which was ''one of the greatest wonders of the [Centennial] Exhibition.''[65] There was an emphasis on speed and mobility.

In 1872, Eadweard Muybridge had captured on film the image of a running horse, and in 1874 Thomas Ridgeway Gould captured, in stone, movement in the guise of *The West Wind* (fig. 57). Gould, a merchant whose business failed during the Civil War, executed portrait busts of Bostonians before moving to Florence and concentrating on ideal sculpture. *The West Wind* was one of Gould's finest and most popular conceptions; at least seven replicas were eventually made. And, like the Corliss engine, the original sculpture (the Ganzes own a reduction)

Fig. 55   Joseph Mozier,
Undine, c.1867

Fig. 57   Thomas Ridgeway Gould,
The West Wind, 1874 (at right)

Fig. 101   William Henry Rinehart,
Harriet Newcomer, 1868 (at far right)

Fig. 56   William Henry Rinehart,
Hero, 1868

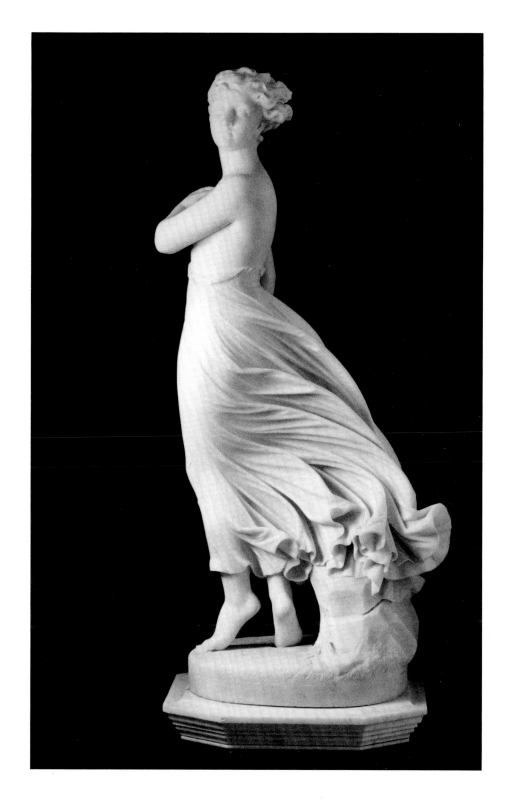

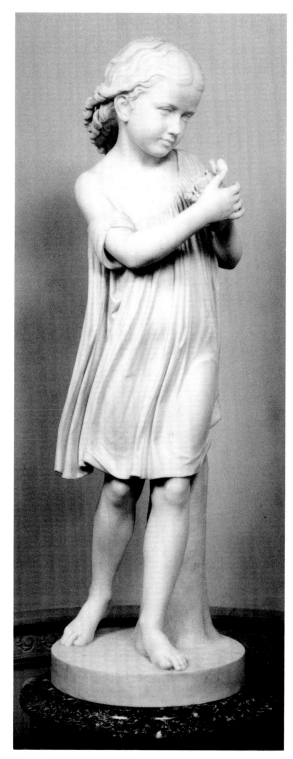

Fig. 53 John Ferguson Weir,
An Artist's Studio, January 1864

was on display at the Centennial Exhibition of 1876. The personification of the West Wind, a young ethereal girl, is shown running on tiptoe, the drapery pressed tightly against her body by the force of motion and billowing out behind her. She turns to look over her shoulder with a movement of remarkable grace and lightness.[66]

Certainly one of the strongest works of art in the Ganz collection is a watercolor painted in 1877 by Winslow Homer. One usually associates Homer with the outdoors, especially with the sea, yet this quiet interior entitled *Blackboard* (1877, fig. 58) is one of the most compelling images in his oeuvre. It is bold and powerful in its economy and realism and an exceptional example of Homer's mastery of the technique of watercolor which he had begun to use only four years earlier.

It is far removed from many other genre scenes of the Victorian era, far from the Gilded Age, the moralizing, the anecdotal, the idealized, and the sentimental, and it proves Homer to be one of the finest artists of the nineteenth century.

A reviewer writing about the Homers in the Tenth Annual Water-Color Exhibition (held in New York in 1877) criticized several of the artist's works but added that the *Book* and *Blackboard* showed that "Homer is himself again—one of the few American painters of originality and force."[67]

Blackboard was one of a series of works using the country school theme that Homer executed during the seventies, including *Snap the Whip, School Time,* and *New England Country School.*[68] And although the education of children was another moral virtue considered important by the Victorians, Homer

Not until the mid-1890s would Homer again work confidently in such a monochromatic manner.[69] Bands of thinly applied, muted color—also modern like those flat, abstract rectangles painted by Adolph Gottlieb and Mark Rothko in the twentieth century—form an ambiguous space in which the floor joins the walls: everything is parallel to the picture plane. But unlike Rothko, Homer has not abandoned form, has not abandoned the human figure, in this case an introspective woman with downcast eyes.[70] She is lost in thought, in her private world. The work is subtle in feeling as well as in color. There is a sense of isolation and delicate stillness in the air, just as there is in George W. Maynard's *A Geographer* (1880, fig. 59), in which a child is lost in contemplation of maps.

Fig. 54 Elihu Vedder,
Girl with a Lute, 1866

is not necessarily as concerned with the implications and symbolism of the subject as with formal considerations. In *Blackboard* he has taken the composition down to its essentials—the school mistress, the wall and floor, and the blackboard itself.

The Ganz painting is unusual among the country school series in that it employs a geometric motif on the blackboard. This modernistic configuration of angles and circles has been likened to the work of Sol LeWitt and Cy Twombly. Helen Cooper suggests that the simplified color scheme echoes the pure, minimal shapes of the white notations on the black slate.

Fig. 58 Winslow Homer,
Blackboard, 1877

Painting 1880–1900

Most of the figural works in the Ganz collection were created in the period during or following the Civil War when Americans were looking for order, searching for a style. The result of this search was an eclecticism seldom seen before or since. In architecture alone, we find the disparate styles of the French châteaux, Rhine castles, Venetian palazzos such as the one built by the National Academy of Design, Richardsonian Romanesque libraries, Second Empire government buildings, and Queen Anne dwellings. Rooms were furnished with Chippendale and Jacobean chairs, Oriental lamps, Moorish tapestries, Japanese prints, and bearskin rugs. The generation's artistic styles were as diverse as those of George de Forest Brush, John Singer Sargent, Winslow Homer, Edward L. Henry, and Thomas Dewing. These styles included realism, sentimentality, idealism, and the linear with the painterly. Literature of this period embraced the frontier spirit of Mark Twain and the gentility of Henry James.

America in the late nineteenth century was preoccupied not only with the art of Europe but with the art of the past. Many artists, both American and European, went back to one or more historical styles. In the late 1850s through the 1860s and seventies, the influence of the Düsseldorf and Munich schools created a sense of reverence for the old masters of the seventeenth century: Hals, Rembrandt, Vermeer, and Velázquez. And some of the turn of the century artists went back to the art of the Italian Renaissance.

The post-Civil War generation saw tremendous advancements in science and industry. Endless opportunities for success and wealth encouraged a wave of confidence and a new sense of nationhood. But these same opportunities also fostered widespread corruption (the Grant administration scandals and the tyranny of Boss Tweed), the "incredible rottenness" that Mark Twain and Charles Dudley Warner chronicled in the satirical novel, *The Gilded Age* (1873).

It was a dynamic but troubled era, a period of conflicting ideas and attitudes and of rapid change. Many Americans felt they were "wandering between two worlds, one dead, the other powerless to be born."[71] The country grew rapidly, expanding to its frontiers and taking in thousands of immigrants. Americans saw their old world transformed. Previous measurements no longer applied, standards changed drastically, and traditional values fell prey to uncertainty. Charles Darwin's theory of evolution, outlined in his *Origin of the Species* (1859) and *Descent of Man* (1871), challenged the uniqueness of man and profoundly influenced American thinking.

The uneasiness of the late nineteenth century was articulated by Henry Adams in his *Education*. Like so many others, Adams felt dislocated after the Civil War: "he could only wait for he knew not what, to send him he knew not where." After the horror of Lincoln's assassination, Adams described his world as "so changed as to be beyond connection with the past."[72]

These Brown Decades, as Lewis Mumford has termed them, reflected the somber feeling and loss of innocence following the Civil War. Disillusionment, skepticism, and frustration caused many to withdraw into private worlds, and in the art (save for the American impressionists) and literature of the period, one finds introspective themes, personal visions filled with poetic melancholy and mystery. Emily Dickinson captured the mood:

The Bustle in a House
The Morning after Death
Is solemnest of industries
Enacted upon Earth—

The Sweeping up the Heart
And putting Love away
We shall not want to use again
Until Eternity.[73]

Her poetry considered "too delicate" to publish, Emily Dickinson went into seclusion and wrote for herself and her friends. Winslow Homer, Thomas Eakins, John F. Peto, Albert Pinkham Ryder, and Henry Adams also retreated into private worlds. Art of this era suggests, rather than explicitly defines, feelings; it is full of shade and nuance. Feeling or mood becomes the subject matter. As one critic noted in 1880, "whereas it used to be the main effort of American painters to imitate nature, it is the main effort of the new men to express feeling."[74]

The other term used to describe these years, "The Gilded Age," brings to mind another side of Victorian life: the ostentatious display of wealth and material possessions seen in many of the images of the sophisticated urban class. The philanthropy of this group of Americans brought about a great expansion in the arts. Major museums (The Metropolitan Museum of Art in New York and the Museum of Fine Arts in Boston) and art schools were founded, and the new aristocracy—with an overwhelming desire to acquire gentility—spent more money on art during the thirty years after 1880 than had ever been spent by any similar group in history.[75] They wanted beauty and culture for America, but many felt it needed to be imported from abroad. While most Americans tended to collect mainly European art, there was one notable exception in Thomas B. Clarke (1848–1931), the New York connoisseur who was the foremost patron of American art from the 1870s until the end of the century.

The first big international exposition in the late nineteenth century, the Centennial, was held in Philadelphia in 1876. This exposition and the one that followed it, the World's Columbian Exposition in Chicago in 1893, provided the impetus for the rediscovery of European art by an American public that strove to be genteel and cosmopolitan. Indigenous American art lost favor, and American painters and writers like the sculptors before them felt the need to study and live abroad. Nathaniel Hawthorne had explained one reason in his preface to *The Marble Faun* (1860):

No author, without a trial, can conceive of the difficulty of writing a romance about a country where there is no shadow, no antiquity, no mystery, no picturesque and gloomy wrong, nor anything but a commonplace posterity, in broad and simple daylight, as is happily the case with my dear native land. . . . Romance and poetry, ivy, lichens, and wall-flowers need ruin to make them grow.[76]

Henry James and Mary Cassatt led expatriate lives. Henry Adams and his friend John La Farge went to the Orient and South Seas. While London in the eighteenth century had been the center for artistic study, the nineteenth century saw Americans going to Florence and Rome, to Düsseldorf and Munich, and, in the latter part of the century, to Paris. Except for Charles Loring Elliott, the artists examined throughout this essay were either Americans trained abroad or who had spent time in Europe or European-born artists who emigrated to the United States. The influence of Europe can be seen in almost every work discussed. Yet the artists, borrowing freely from other styles and civilizations, nonetheless felt they were transcending the European schools and creating a new art for America. The Society of American Artists boasted that most of its members had studied in France or Germany, but insisted that they were "thoroughly American in Spirit."[77] Similarly, it is interesting to note that despite his immersion in European life and art, John Singer Sargent turned down an English knighthood because he was an American citizen and refused the presidency of the Royal Academy in London.[78]

Sargent came from a family that seemed to be on a perpetual Grand Tour. Born in Florence, he studied in Italy, France, Spain, and Holland, countries where he found European models for his art. His teacher Carolus-Duran's rapid execution directly on canvas, Velázquez's light-filled interiors, and Frans Hals's brilliant brushwork are echoed in Sargent's spirited painting, *The Sulphur Match* (1882, fig. 60).

The Sulphur Match is one of several informal works which Sargent painted in Venice in the early 1880s.[79] A Sargent in the National Gallery of Art, *Street in Venice*, executed the same year as *The Sulphur Match*, is not only close in size but also shows the same man and probably the same woman in the scene. The Ganz painting is also similar in spirit to Sargent's famous large Spanish painting of 1882, *El Jaleo*.[80] Both are interior scenes that capture the romanticism that Europe held for Americans.

While most paintings from the 1860s, seventies, and eighties in the Ganz collection are essentially linear, *The Sulphur Match* is extremely painterly, executed with a sensuous delight in virtuoso technique. Like the impressionists, Sargent has captured a moment in time, a moment of leisure. A dashing man (possibly the artist J. Frank Currier) dressed in black lights a cigarette while the young flirtatious woman (a favorite model, Gigia Viani) in white dress and vivid red scarf tips back in her chair. A feeling of incipient seduction surrounds the couple, and an overturned wine jug on the floor adds to the romantic air.

In the 1870s and 1880s, Munich became an important center for artists, and two works from the Ganz collection—Charles Frederick Ulrich's *An Etcher in His Studio* (c. 1882, fig. 61), and

Fig. 61   Charles Frederick Ulrich,
An Etcher in His Studio, c.1882

Fig. 59 George W. Maynard,
A Geographer, 1880

Louis C. Moeller's *The Evening News* (1880s, fig. 62)—are indicative of the influence of the Munich Royal Academy.

Ulrich, the son of a photographer, had studied for eight years under Wilhelm Lindenschmidt and Ludwig Löfftz. When he returned to the United States in 1882 and began his series of pictures (1882–1885) depicting glassblowers, printers, and other craftsmen, his style was that of the Munich school: realistic genre scenes with precisely rendered details and dark colors. *An Etcher in His Studio*, a fine example of Ulrich's photographic realism, reflects the Munich school's emphasis on the old masters of the seventeenth century. The Dutch influence is especially present here in the brown and golden tonalities and in the Rembrandtesque prints that the etcher keeps before him.

It further reflects the artists' and country's growing interest in etching, a seventeenth-century medium that enjoyed a revival in the nineteenth century. French artists took up the process in the 1850s, followed by the English (1860s) and Americans (1870s). By the 1880s, etching was flourishing in the United States. Etching clubs were formed in all the major cities, the distinguished nineteenth-century etching collection at the Metropolitan Museum of Art was begun, and French treatises on the medium were translated into English. Exhibitions on etchings were popular, and the *American Art Review* published many etchings by such artists as James McNeill Whistler, William Merritt Chase, Ignatz Gaugengigl, Seymour Joseph Guy, and the Moran family.[81]

Louis Moeller's six-year stay in Munich overlapped with Ulrich's. Moeller's freer brushwork, however, is the result of the influence of an American, Frank Duveneck, Moeller's teacher in Munich. Although Moeller's typical painting consisted of figures in a dark interior, the subject of *The Evening News* is posed in afternoon sunlight. Again one can see the influence of photography in the harsh light and the desire to capture this informal moment. Straightforward, unsentimental realism and solid forms relate this painting to the earlier Elliott *Self-Portrait* and J. G. Brown's *John Jacob Astor III*.

Both Ulrich and Moeller, before leaving for Munich, had studied at the National Academy of Design in New York. In the late 1870s, in reaction to the conservatism of the academy and its refusal to exhibit the works of younger artists who had brought back other styles from Europe, the Society of American Artists was founded. These artists were influenced not by the dark Munich style but by the lighter palettes of the French Barbizon and impressionist schools which were coming into prominence. But while using European techniques, Americans

Fig. 60   John Singer Sargent, *The Sulphur Match*, 1882

never lost their feeling for material form, for substance, as did many of the French artists.

One of the members of the society—which included William Merritt Chase, John La Farge, John Singer Sargent, and George de Forest Brush—was Henry Siddons Mowbray, who had trained at the Atelier Bonnat in Paris. Mowbray was a friend of painters such as Chase, Willard Metcalf, and John Twachtman who were associated with American impressionism, and in his painting, *Studio Lunch* (c. 1880–1883, fig. 63), Mowbray's light and color, though not his structure, share an affinity with the impressionists. Known for his highly realistic harem and allegorical scenes, this painting is atypical of Mowbray's work.

Fig. 62   Louis C. Moeller,
The Evening News, 1880s

Fig. 64 Rhoda Holmes Nicholls, *After the Ball*, c.1885

Studio Lunch shows the artist and his model engaged in conversation in a studio decorated with various kinds of props (tapestries, paintings, drawings, pottery, Japanese fans), recalling the earlier painting, *An Artist's Studio*, by J. F. Weir.

In the last two decades of the nineteenth century, when the interest in landscape had subsided, the figure again became the main theme in American art. The female figure was particularly popular, but it was a different kind of American woman that the artists chose to paint or draw. There are many depictions of the female as a passive being, lost in her own thoughts, such as in the touching watercolor by Rhoda Holmes

Nicholls, *After the Ball* (c. 1885, fig. 64).

The Gilded Age had spawned a class of women with nothing to do. As Thorstein Veblen observed in his *Theory of the Leisure Class* (1889), the American woman of leisure was

petted, and is permitted, or even required, to consume largely and conspicuously—vicariously for her husband or other natural guardian. She is exempted, or debarred, from vulgarly useful employment—in order to perform leisure vicariously for the good repute of her natural (pecuniary) guardian.[82]

The antithesis of the loud, vulgar, and chaotic male world, the American woman was seen as contemplative, quiet, re-

Fig. 66   Francis Coates Jones,
Lady and Lyre, c.1900–1910

Fig. 65   Thomas Wilmer Dewing, *Woman with Violin*, 1891

Fig. 67   Francis Coates Jones,
Woman in Classic Dress, 1890s

fined, and gentle. She was a decoration, an ornament to the household of the Gilded Age.

Historian Samuel Isham explained in 1905 that Americans, having no saints or goddesses of their own, found in the "idealization of their womanhood" what goddesses, saints, and heroines represented to other cultures. Isham noted that this idealization was completely decorous, that there was no room for passion or sensuality. "The American girl is placed upon a pedestal and each offers worship according to his abilities, the artist among the rest."[83]

One of the artists who idealized the American woman as a delicate, graceful, aristocratic creature was Thomas Wilmer Dewing, who felt that his works belonged "to the poetic and imaginative world where a few choice spirits live."[84] As a

Fig. 63 Henry Siddons Mowbray,
Studio Lunch, c.1880–1883

student in Europe (in Paris at the Académie Julian and in Munich with Frank Duveneck), Dewing came under the influence of the tranquil domestic scenes of Vermeer and the dreamlike reveries of Utamaro prints.[85] Dewing's own later dreamlike works are in the style of American tonalism, a term coined by Wanda Corn to describe the use of a few muted colors, diffused light, and blurred atmosphere to evoke feelings of reverie, nostalgia, and longing.[86] One contemporary critic described Dewing's withdrawn women as living apart," in a medium of their own; they are no longer personal, individual; they are not figures and objects, they are Presences."[87]

The figure in *Woman with Violin* (1891, fig. 65) is not the typical Dewing female, however, in that she is more solidly modeled than his later, more ethereal, figures. She is aware of the viewer yet turns her head aside and ignores him, thus isolating herself. She is aloof, haughty, standing with her hand on her hip and her chin slightly tilted up in an attitude that

approaches defiance and determination. Not a part of the corruption and vulgarity of the outside world, she belongs to a nobler class; she is unapproachable. Placed in a dark, ambiguous space, there is only the small violin to tie her to this world.

The techniques of pastels, watercolors, and prints—the "genteel media" as Patricia Hills has termed them—increased in popularity at the end of the nineteenth century.[88] Francis Coates Jones's intimate pastels, *Lady and Lyre* and *Woman in Classic Dress* (figs. 66 and 67), are poetic evocations related to the tradition of the Paris salons and the École des Beaux-Arts where Jones had studied. These two works, less precisely rendered and therefore somewhat atypical of the collection, appealed to the Ganzes because of their beautiful classical subjects and rich use of pastel. *Woman in Classic Dress*, dating from the 1890s, depicts a figure who sits in contemplation in a light-filled room. The figure's dress is classical as is the figure itself, in her

Fig. 68   George de Forest Brush,
Orpheus, 1890

bearing, dignity, and poise. Jones's later work, *Lady and Lyre*, also depicts a haunting female figure gazing into space, but instead of turning her head away, she looks directly at the viewer.

An equally poetic composition of a man with a lyre was painted by George de Forest Brush, Jones's fellow student at the École des Beaux-Arts. Known for his idealized, noble figures in paintings of the American Indian and of mother and child themes (inspired by Renaissance madonnas), Brush painted few mythological subjects. The Ganz painting, created in 1890, depicts *Orpheus* (fig. 68), son of Apollo and Calliope and considered the most famous musician from classical mythology, charming a group of rabbits with his musicmaking.[89] The sentimental love story of Orpheus and Eurydice would have appealed to the Victorian public as would the myth's theme of the power of music and poetry to civilize and pacify both man and nature. The Brush shows the strong influence of the French

academician Gérôme in its hard surface and in its pose[90] and highly saturated colors. The solid, muscular nude figure is drawn and modeled in the academic manner with great precision.

Brush's *The Indian Hunter* (1890, fig. 69), like *Orpheus*, is a sensuous, richly colored image. Silhouetted against a dark background stands a statuesque, bronze Indian brave—as dignified and muscular as a statue of a Greek athlete—carrying a bright pink flamingo that hangs limply down his back. Brush, who had traveled among the North American Indians, felt sympathetic to their culture, and this painting particularly conveys the artist's romantic vision of the Indian and the solitude and silence of his serene existence before the white man's arrival.

Julian Scott also studied the Indians, especially during the early 1890s as he executed paintings and drawings to be used as illustrations in a report ("Indians Taxed and Indians Not

Fig. 69   George de Forest Brush,
The Indian Hunter, 1890

Fig. 70   Julian Scott, *Horseman, Anadarco, Oklahoma*, 1890

Taxed") for the Eleventh Census. *Horseman, Anadarco, Oklahoma* (1890, fig 70) is his realistic depiction of a chief on horseback holding an umbrella as an indication of his rank.

In turn-of-the-century American art, however, it is the female figure, not sensuous male nudes such as *Orpheus*, which is given foremost attention. Like Francis Coates Jones, artists such as Charles Caryl Coleman (fig. 74), Francis Davis Millet (figs. 75 and 76), and Frederick Dielman (fig. 71) portrayed contemplative women in classical garb for both exotic and symbolic purposes. These painters were part of the American Renaissance, a renaissance that Auguste Rodin said Americans did not realize had come, but one that has now begun to receive considerable attention from historians.[91] The renaissance spirit inspired collaborations between painters, sculptors, and architects (the handsome frame on Dewing's *Woman with Violin* was designed by architect Stanford White), and every art form, whether it be wallpaper, murals, or stained glass, was considered worthy of attention. The artists borrowed from antiquity, from the Greeks and Romans as well as the Renaissance.

The style they brought back from studies in Europe is a decorative one, stressing frontality, simplified forms, the play of lines, and flattened backgrounds,[92] all of which can be seen in Frederick Dielman's *Personification of Peace* of 1902 (fig. 71). The serene, idealized figure, set against a glowing golden background, is an image related to the classical figures symbolizing various nationalistic virtues that adorned courthouses and libraries at the turn of the century. The Dielman, a classical Greek figure, is the personification of the chaste, noble, and genteel woman: The American Virgin. While the figure is known to be a variation on *Peace* in the mosaic mural *Law* at the Library of Congress, the woman could also represent Columbia or a variation on the Statue of Liberty (which had been erected in New York Harbor in 1886). Although the American Virgin is presented close to the picture plane, there is a coolness, an emotional reserve, that prohibits us from getting too near. She is Goodness, Truth, Beauty, crowned with an olive wreath of peace, rising above the gritty industries and corrupt administrations of the Gilded Age.

At the turn of the century, everything—including the human figure—became a source for design, and the distinctions that had previously been drawn between artists and decorators began to blur. Albert Herter, a muralist, furniture and tapestry designer, and portraitist, was part of this design explosion. His marvelous watercolor, *Two Women on Stairs* (fig. 72), chosen for the cover of the October 1901 issue of *The Ladies' Home Journal*, is beautifully rendered in both drawing and coloration and is similar in style to the Dielman. Flat, decorative, and

Fig. 72   Albert Herter, *Two Women on Stairs*, 1901

Fig. 76 Francis Davis Millet,
After the Festival, 1888

idealized, the female figures are arranged as an ornamental still life. They live in a vacuum. Carefully carrying pottery and glass jars, the ethereal figures are expressionless and motionless. Appearing to be frozen in the midst of some sort of ritualistic procession, they are more of an illusion than reality, too perfect to exist in the mundane world. The other Herter watercolor in the collection, entitled *Pastoral* (1892, fig. 73), is a tranquil scene depicting a meadow where a Pan-like figure serenades a beautiful woman who reclines at his feet. Its beauty stems not only from its delicate colors but its lyrical mood.

Also sharing the style of aesthetic classicism with the Jones pastels and the Herter and Dielman watercolors are paintings by Coleman and Millet. Charles Caryl Coleman, a student of Thomas Couture and a close friend of Elihu Vedder, spent most of his life in Italy. There, in the 1880s, he bought a villa on Capri which he filled with Roman antiquities. His painting, *Vintage Time in a Capri Garden* (fig. 74), depicts a woman in classical gown relaxing on an exedra on a terrace planted with vines. Though painted in 1889 in Rome, the scene may well be the artist's villa which was set picturesquely against the steep hills overlooking the Bay of Naples.

The talented artist and writer Francis Davis Millet had a

passionate interest in classical costume and lectured on the subject at the Museum of Fine Arts in Boston and the National Academy of Design in New York. Posing and draping a live model in a variety of Greek, Roman, and Etruscan costumes, he stressed the need to study antique statues, the function and relation of classical clothing and its relationship to manners of antique culture.[93] Millet suggested the establishment of a costume library at the American Academy in Rome and traveled widely to study dress as well as landscape and architecture.

Millet began painting figures in archaeologically correct classical costumes in 1883 and continued his deep interest in the subject throughout the eighties. (Although he continued to paint classical subjects until 1897, most of these scenes date from the 1880s.) Two of his finest paintings in this genre are in the Ganz collection.

The Poppy Field (1884, fig. 75) shows Millet's keen eye for detail in painting classical dress. The painting features a precisely rendered female picking bright red flowers which dot the field near a Greek temple. The figure is statuesque in its dignity, grace, and beauty. *After the Festival* (1888, fig. 76) also depicts an elegant woman dressed in Greek costume. She is pensive, lost in reverie, her head resting on her right hand as she sits by a fluted column on an open porch. This painting shows Millet's talent as a colorist. The combination of her pale lavender sash, salmon-pink drapery, and red roses is a gift for

Fig. 71   Frederick Dielman,
Personification of Peace, 1902

Fig. 73   Albert Herter,
Pastoral, 1892

Fig. 74   Charles Caryl Coleman, *Vintage Time in a Capri Garden*, 1889

the senses. The painting also illustrates the artist's strong technical power in rendering the metal of the tambourine and bracelet and the veined marble of the bench on which the charming figure sits.

Millet's fondness for the work of English artists such as Albert Moore and Sir Lawrence Alma-Tadema can be seen here, though like those of Francis Coates Jones, these paintings of nineteenth-century figures in classical dress do not necessarily tell a story.

Having journeyed through more than a century of American art and traced the treatment of the American figure, we have seen it evolve from realism to sentimentality and idealism.

Reflecting American society, the scenes have changed from vigorous, self-confident, indigenous images, through various types of revivals, to works that are inward-looking, aesthetic, and cosmopolitan in spirit. They vividly bring to life the gentle, and genteel, Victorian age in America. This group of figural works, however, intentionally does not form a complete survey of American painting and sculpture. Rather, it is an enlightening and selective representation of American academic art. Works in other styles have been consciously omitted. A powerful group that is unsurpassed by any other private collection, it reflects the Ganzes' personal taste for precisely rendered objects of high quality from the academic tradition in America.

Fig. 75   Francis Davis Millet, *The Poppy Field*, 1884

1.   William H. Gerdts, Jr., "Figure Painting in the United States," in *From All Walks of Life* [exh. cat., National Academy of Design] (New York, 1979), 7.

2.   *Pat Lyon at the Forge* is in the collection of the Museum of Fine Arts, Boston. An 1829 replica is owned by the Pennsylvania Academy of the Fine Arts, Philadelphia.

3.   *The Brown Family* (1869, versions at the National Gallery of Art and The Fine Arts Museums of San Francisco); *The Hatch Family* (1871, The Metropolitan Museum of Art, New York).

4.   Thomas Paine, "The American Crisis," in *The Writings of Thomas Paine*, ed. Moncure Daniel Conway, 2 vols. (New York, 1969), 1:170.

5.   The series includes *Death of General Warren at the Battle of Bunker's Hill* (1786), *Death of General Mercer at the Battle of Princeton* (1787), and the *Declaration of Independence* (1786–97).

6.   Rembrandt Peale, *Porthole Portrait of George Washington* (Philadelphia, 1857), 5.

7.   Savage's *Washington Family* (1796, National Gallery of Art), Leutze's *Washington Crossing the Delaware* (1851, The Metropolitan Museum of Art, New York), and Peale's *George Washington at Princeton* (1779, Pennsylvania Academy of the Fine Arts).

8.   Both statues by Saint Gaudens are located in New York City.

9.   Eastman Johnson's *Corn Husking* (1860, Everson Museum of Art), Bingham's *Fur Traders Descending the Missouri* (1845, The Metropolitan Museum of Art, New York), and Mount's *Rustic Dance After a Sleigh Ride* (1830, Museum of Fine Arts, Boston).

10.   Walt Whitman, "Song of Myself," published in *Leaves of Grass* (1855), reprinted in *Walt Whitman,* Viking Portable Library Edition (New York, 1973), 32.

11.   Peale's *Staircase Group* (1795, Philadelphia Museum of Art), Vanderlyn's *Ariadne Asleep on the Island of Naxos* (1814, Pennsylvania Academy of the Fine Arts), and Eakins's *William Rush Carving the Allegorical Figure of the Schuylkill River* (1877, Philadelphia Museum of Art).

12.   Ingvar Bergstrom, *Dutch Still-Life Painting in the Seventeenth Century* (London, 1956), 3.

13.   Cole's *Course of Empire* (1836, New-York Historical Society) and *Voyage of Life* (1840, Munson-Williams-Proctor Institute, and 1842, National Gallery of Art).

14.   William H. Gerdts, Jr., *Revealed Masters: 19th Century American Art* [exh. cat., American Federation of Art] (New York, 1974), 31–32.

15.   Howard Mumford Jones, *The Age of Energy: Varieties of American Experience, 1865–1915* (New York, 1971), 23.

16.   Jules David Prown, *John Singleton Copley,* 2 vols. (Cambridge, Mass., 1966), 2:263.

17.   "John Singleton Copley: Correspondence, 1766–1767," in *American Art, 1700–1960: Sources and Documents* ed. John W. McCoubrey (Englewood Cliffs, N. J., 1965), 16.

18.   The National Gallery's *Coleman Sisters* of 1844 by Sully also has a still life, but it is not nearly so prominent a device.

19. Wolfgang Born, *Still-Life Painting in America* (New York, 1947), 20.

20. Thomas Sully, *Hints to Young Painters* (New York, 1965; first published 1873), 31.

21. Ralph Waldo Emerson, "Art," in *The Complete Essays and Other Writings of Ralph Waldo Emerson,* ed. with a biographical introduction by Brooks Atkinson, Modern Library Edition (New York, 1950), 309.

22. William Wetmore Story, quoted in Russell Lynes, *The Art-Makers of Nineteenth-Century America* (New York, 1970), 111.

23. Letter, Hiram Powers to Elizabeth Barrett Browning, August 7, 1853, quoted in Donald Martin Reynolds, "Hiram Powers and His Ideal Sculpture" (Ph.D. diss., Columbia University, 1975; Garland series, 1977), 211.

24. Nathaniel Hawthorne, *The Marble Faun* (1860; reprint ed. Indianapolis and New York, 1971), 119.

25. Powers began to make replicas of *Proserpine* in 1844. The other bust from that year is in the Honolulu Academy of the Arts. See letter, Richard Wunder to Malcolm Stearns, Jr., July 12, 1973. That Powers considered this a special replica is indicated by the fact that he dated the work, something he rarely did, especially on replicas. See also Richard P. Wunder, *Hiram Powers: Vermont Sculptor* (Taftsville, Vermont), 18.

Gerdts describes the process by which the artist would "form a conception in plaster or clay, and this would then be enlarged to the full scale intended for the finished work. The artist would also acquire a block of marble . . . and this, together with the large plaster, would be turned over to the workmen. These men, with the aid of a pointing machine which acted as a three-dimensional guide in transferring proportions from plaster to marble, would do the actual carving." Gerdts further explains that upon receiving an order for a replica, the artist again turned over the large plaster and block of marble to the artisans to carve another sculpture. See William H. Gerdts, Jr., *American Neo-Classic Sculpture: The Marble Resurrection* (New York, 1973), 17–18.

26. Both William Gerdts and Wayne Craven have cited Powers's indebtedness to the classical Venus. See Craven, *200 Years of American Sculpture* [exh. cat., Whitney Museum of American Art] (New York, 1976), 41. See also Gerdts, *American Neo-Classic Sculpture,* 32.

27. Letter, Hiram Powers to Edwin M. Stoughton, November 29, 1869, quoted in Reynolds, "Hiram Powers," 141.

28. "Nathaniel Hawthorne: A Visit to the Studio of Hiram Powers, 1858," in *American Art,* ed. McCoubrey, 89.

29. "Hiram Powers' 'Greek Slave' " in Margaret Farrand Thorp, *The Literary Sculptors* (Durham, North Carolina, 1965), 118.

30. Gerdts, *American Neo-Classic Sculpture,* 53.

31. Gerdts, *American Neo-Classic Sculpture,* 142.

32. The art unions, formed during the 1840s and fifties, provided a market for American art and reinforced the public's taste for American genre and landscapes. Artists exhibited and sold their work at the art unions. Members (numbering in the tens of thousands) annually received a steel engraving of a painting and were eligible to win an original painting or sculpture at lottery. The most prominent organization of this kind was the American Art-Union in New York, but cities such as Boston, Philadelphia, and Cincinnati also had art unions.

33. Colonel Thomas B. Thorpe, *Reminiscences of Charles L. Elliott* (New York, 1868), 9.

34. James Jackson Jarves, *The Art-Idea* (1864; reprint ed. Cambridge, Massachusetts, 1960), 189.

35. Ruth, after her husband's death, left her people to follow her mother-in-law, Naomi, to Bethlehem. She went to glean in the fields of Boaz who was a wealthy kinsman of Naomi and had heard of Ruth's sacrifice. Soon thereafter Ruth became Boaz's wife and bore him a son who later became the grandfather of King David.

36. Gerdts, *American Neo-Classic Sculpture,* 34. One version of *Nydia* is in the Los Angeles County Museum of Art.

37. Letter, Harriet Hosmer to Mrs. Carr, October 30, 1854, in Cornelia Carr, ed., *Harriet Hosmer: Letters and Memories* (New York, 1912), 42.

38. Carr, *Hosmer,* 123. At least thirty marble replicas were sold at about $1,000 each. In catalogue entry no. 5 of *The White Marmorean Flock: Nineteenth Century American Women Neoclassical Sculptors* [exh. cat., Vassar College Art Gallery] (Poughkeepsie, New York, 1972), the authors observe that the source for *Puck* is not necessarily Shakespearean. However, William Gerdts, in *American Neo-Classic Sculpture,* p. 116, states that "*Midsummer Night's Dream* provided not only the popular *Puck* by Harriet Hosmer, but a *Titania and Nick Bottom* by John Adams Jackson."

39. Carr, *Hosmer,* 79 and 278.

40. Carr, *Hosmer,* 33, 49, and 50. Also see Van Wyck Brooks, *The Dream of Arcadia: American Writers and Artists in Italy 1760–1915* (New York, 1958), 78.

41. It is very similar in its arched format, woman's gown, and other details to *This Little Pig Went to Market* (1857, Campus Martius Museum, Marietta, Ohio), thought to be Spencer and her son. See Donelson F. Hoopes, *American Narrative Painting* [exh. cat., Los Angeles County Museum of Art] (Los Angeles, 1974), 116.

42. Anonymous, "Art: Composition Pictures at the Academy," *Appleton's Journal* 11 (May 16, 1874): 636.

43. The Amon Carter Museum, Fort Worth, Texas, recently acquired another version of *Bo Peep*. *Bo Peep* is related in date, style, and spirit to several works by Johnson that portray women engaged in private activities: *The Earring* (1873, Corcoran Gallery of Art); *Not At Home* (c. 1872–1880, Brooklyn Museum); and *Day Dreams* (1877, private collection). See Patricia Hills, "The Genre Painting of Eastman Johnson: The Sources and Development of His Style and Themes" (Ph.D. diss., New York University, 1973; Garland series, 1977), 141–142.

44. Elizabeth McCausland, *The Life and Work of Edward Lamson Henry N.A.,* (*New York State Museum Bulletin 339*) (Albany, 1945), 30 and 66.

45. Until recently, the subject of this portrait was identified as John Jacob Astor II.

46. Walter Montgan, ed., *American Art and American Art Collections,* 2 vols. (Boston, 1889), 2:941–943. I would like to thank Earl A. Powell for sharing his observations on the outdoor genre scenes in the Ganz collection.

47. Hoopes, *American Narrative Painting*, 140.

48. Anonymous, "American Painters: Seymour Joseph Guy, N.A.—Lemuel E. Wilmarth, N.A.," *The Art Journal*, 1 (1875): 277.

49. Henry T. Tuckerman, "Children," *The Galaxy*, 4 (1867): 318, quoted in Patricia Hills, *The Painter's America: Rural and Urban Life, 1810–1910* (New York, 1974), 74.

50. Letter, William H. Gerdts, Jr., to Jo Ann and Julian Ganz, Jr., September 9, 1978, quoting from microfilm of *New Pictures At Goupil's Gallery*, 772 Broadway, N.Y. (probably late 1860s) in the Archives of American Art.

51. *A Bed Time Story* is unlocated. *Making a Train* is in the collection of the Philadelphia Museum of Art.

52. *The Gun Foundry* is owned by the Putnam County Historical Society, Cold Spring, New York, and *Forging the Shaft* is in the collection of The Metropolitan Museum of Art, New York.

53. *Taking the Veil* is in the collection of the Yale University Art Gallery. Versions of *St. Nicholas* are owned by the New-York Historical Society, New York, the Butler Institute of Art, Youngstown, Ohio, and the National Museum of American Art, Washington. The National Academy of Design, New York, owns a plaster bust of Allston by Clevenger of c. 1839–40.

54. Irene Weir, *Robert W. Weir, Artist* (New York, 1947), 58–59.

55. Theodore Sizer, ed., *The Recollections of John Ferguson Weir* (New York, 1957), 47.

56. Jarves, *The Art-Idea*, 202.

57. Joshua C. Taylor, "Perceptions and Digressions," in *Perceptions and Evocations: The Art of Elihu Vedder* [exh. cat., National Collection of Fine Arts] (Washington, D. C., 1979), 45–47.

58. Taylor, "Perceptions and Digressions," 77.

59. For instance, *Musical Inspiration* (1875, The Parthenon, Nashville, Tennessee) and *Dancing Girl* (1871, Barbara B. Millhouse).

60. Thomas Ridgeway Gould, Chauncey B. Ives, and Paul Akers, among others, created sculptures of *Undine*. See Gerdts, *American Neo-Classic Sculpture*, 88–89.

61. Gerdts, *American Neo-Classic Sculpture*, 89.

62. *The Veiled Nun* is owned by The Corcoran Gallery of Art, Washington, D. C.

63. *The Parting of Hero and Leander* is in the collection of The National Gallery, London.

64. Wayne Craven, "Images of a Nation in Wood, Marble and Bronze: American Sculpture from 1776 to 1900," in *200 Years of American Sculpture*, 44.

65. Jones, *The Age of Energy*, 138–139 and 142.

66. Several other pieces with an aerial theme (*The Lost Pleiad* by Randolph Rogers and *Pleiades* by Henry Kirke Brown) appeared in the last half of the nineteenth century, simultaneously with the paintings of the Barbizon and impressionist schools which similarly sought to capture on canvas the effects of light, clouds, and atmosphere. See Gerdts, *American Neo-Classic Sculpture*, 84–85.

67. *Scribner's Monthly*, 13 (April 1, 1877): 866–867. *The Book* is now called *The New Novel* and is in the collection of the Museum of Fine Arts, Springfield, Massachusetts.

68. *Snap the Whip* (1872, versions at The Metropolitan Museum of Art and The Butler Institute of Art), *School Time* (1874, Collection of Paul Mellon), and *New England Country School* (1873, Addison Gallery of American Art).

69. Letter, Helen Cooper to Linda Ayres, September 15, 1980. An example of a later watercolor using a monochromatic scheme—though in a much freer style—is *Trout Fishing, Lake St. John, Quebec* (1895, Museum of Fine Arts, Boston). Helen Cooper is curator of American Paintings and Sculpture at the Yale University Art Gallery and is currently at work on a dissertation on Homer's watercolors.

70. Gordon Hendricks has pointed out that the same model was used in several other canvases painted in Homer's New York studio in 1876–77. See Gordon Hendricks, *The Life and Work of Winslow Homer* (New York, 1979), 129.

71. Matthew Arnold, paraphrased by Henry Adams, *The Education of Henry Adams* (1918; Sentry ed., Boston, 1961), 108.

72. Adams, *Education*, 109 and 209.

73. Emily Dickinson, "The Morning After Death," in *The Complete Poems of Emily Dickinson*, ed. Thomas H. Johnson (Boston and Toronto, 1960), 489.

74. William C. Brownell, *Scribner's Monthly*, 20 (1880): 1–2.

75. Wendell Garrett, "A Century of Inspiration," in *The Arts in America: The Nineteenth Century* (New York, 1969), 33.

76. Hawthorne, *The Marble Faun*, 5.

77. Lois Marie Fink and Joshua C. Taylor, *Academy: The Academic Tradition in American Art* [exh. cat., National Collection of Fine Arts] (Washington, D. C., 1975), 81.

78. *A Catalogue of the Collection of the Corcoran Gallery of Art*, 2 vols. (Washington, D. C., 1973), 2:24.

79. Others include *Venetian Glass Workers* (Art Institute of Chicago), *Venetian Bead Stringers* (Albright-Knox Gallery, Buffalo), and *Street in Venice* (National Gallery of Art). All date from the year 1882.

80. *El Jaleo* is owned by the Isabella Stewart Gardner Museum, Boston.

81. See James Laver, *A History of British and American Etching* (London, 1929), 124–151. Also see facsimile copies of S. R. Koehler's *American Etchings* (Boston, 1886) and *American Art* (New York, c. 1886), reprinted in 1978 as part of the Garland series, *The Art Experience in Late Nineteenth-Century America*, ed. H. Barbara Weinberg.

82. Thorstein Veblen, quoted in Hills, *Painter's America*, 97–106.

83. Samuel Isham, quoted in Patricia Hills, *Turn-of-the-Century America* [exh. cat., Whitney Museum of American Art] (New York, 1977), 74.

84. Wanda M. Corn, *The Color of Mood: American Tonalism 1880–1910* [exh. cat., The Fine Arts Museums of San Francisco] (San Francisco, 1972), 20.

85. See Judith Elizabeth Lyczko, "Thomas Wilmer Dewing's Sources: Women in Interiors," *Arts*, 54, no. 3 (November 1979): 152–157; Nelson C. White, "The Art of Thomas Wilmer Dewing," *Art and Archaeology*, 27, no. 6 (June 1929): 253–261; and Richard Boyle, *American Impres-*

sionism (Boston, 1974), 174.

86.   See Corn, *The Color of Mood.*

87.   Charles H. Caffin, "The Art of Thomas W. Dewing," *Harper's Monthly Magazine,* 116 (April 1908): 724.

88.   Hills, *Turn-of-the-Century America,* 74.

89.   His musical talents not only soothed wild beasts, according to the myth, but persuaded Pluto and Proserpine to free Orpheus's wife, Eurydice, from Hades. Orpheus subsequently lost her again, however, and this fact most likely accounts for his mournful expression.

90.   Gérôme's *Diogenes* of 1860 (Walters Art Gallery, Baltimore) has been suggested as the source for the pose. See Carol L. Troyen, *A Private Eye* [exh. cat., The Heckscher Museum] (Huntington, New York, 1977), 26.

91.   Lewis Mumford, *The Brown Decades: A Study of the Arts of America 1865–1895* (1931; reprint ed., New York, 1955), 190. *The American Renaissance 1876–1917,* exhibition held at The Brooklyn Museum of Art, New York, and other museums, 1979–80.

92.   Hills, *Turn-of-the-Century America,* 16.

93.   H. Barbara Weinberg, "The Career of Francis Davis Millet," *Archives of American Art Journal,* 17, no. 1 (1977): 7.

Fig. 39   Johnson, *Bo Peep* (detail)

Fig. 83   Severin Roesen, *Flower Still-Life with Bird's Nest*, 1853

The American Object: Still-Life Paintings

John Wilmerding

THE GANZ COLLECTION affords a distinctive opportunity to appraise the character of American still-life painting on several related levels. Foremost, it provides a broad, selective survey of still-life subjects painted throughout the nineteenth century. It also offers us the special pleasures of examining, within the context of an overall presence of high quality, a few works that stand as the masterpieces of the artists in question. Furthermore, we have eloquent material for ruminating on the possible national characteristics of the American still life. The still lifes, though not quite so numerous as the figure paintings in the Ganz collection, nonetheless reveal the continual interplay of American styles with European art. Of equal interest are the suggestive stylistic parallels and connections between American still-life paintings in various periods and other subjects artists were painting at the same time.

Some of these issues have received only cursory treatment in the studies of American art, largely because we tend to isolate the subject in a near-hermetic tradition of its own. The primary literature on the field has come in three successive periods of concentration. The first was the pioneering general survey *Still-Life Painting in America* by Wolfgang Born, published in 1947. Alfred Frankenstein's investigative thoroughness next marked his research on William M. Harnett and the trompe l'oeil painters in particular at the end of the nineteenth century. His findings appeared in 1953 in *After the Hunt, William Harnett and Other American Still Life Painters, 1870–1900,* with an updated edition published in 1969. Most recently, William H. Gerdts and Russell Burke collaborated to produce their comprehensive and informative volume, *American Still-Life*

Painting, in 1971.[1] This last not only brought to light numerous interesting figures heretofore almost unknown, but also made available for the first time in published form extensive illustrations in both black and white and color.

The result of these admirable efforts has been the imprinting on the field of certain assumptions, perceived to be so definitive as to be almost inhibiting. For example, the very title of Frankenstein's book implies John F. Peto to be a follower of Harnett, an anonymous "other." Yet a glance at the Ganz pictures by these painters makes clear that the questions of relative originality and connoisseurship within their oeuvres remains provocatively open for discussion. Indeed, Frankenstein's apparent comprehensiveness in outlining the careers of Harnett and Peto was sufficiently persuasive to Gerdts and Burke that they virtually repeated the former's argument intact. Their chapter 10 is titled "Trompe l'oeil: William Michael Harnett and His Followers," and in it they admit: "Frankenstein really covers Harnett well and completely. For that reason the authors would here like to acknowledge their debt to Frankenstein's essay."[2]

Similarly, the basically self-contained overviews by Born and by Gerdts and Burke of American still life have given us thorough artists' biographies and distinguishable individual styles. At the same time, they have tended to make us see the material as separate from mainstream traditions which were pervasive and dominating in landscape or figure painting. While there is an iconography obviously special to still-life painting, there are equally treatments of form, composition, and ideas which directly link still life to a larger cultural context. Not only do styles in still-life painting relate to a broader evolution of taste, evident more familiarly perhaps in architecture, sculpture, or landscape painting, but in so doing, these styles can reveal identifiable cultural visions and attitudes.

Partially because historians have tended to see still life more than any other subject as an idiosyncratic development in American art, stylistic issues surrounding the work of major artists have been blurred. For example, consider the following statement:

Place a Harnett still life of the middle 1870's next to a Raphaelle Peale of 1815 and it is impossible to believe that they are separated by two generations, that one belongs to the era of James Madison and the other to that of U. S. Grant.[3]

Again, a look at the Ganzes' Peale (fig. 77) alongside their Harnett (fig. 96) demonstrates that, for all their shared precision of rendering, the still lifes by these two painters are as different as Jeffersonian federal and Richardsonian Romanesque architecture, to which they may be respectively compared. The significance is that beyond surfaces Peale's elegant and balanced image tells us as much about the ideas of order in early republican America as Harnett's somber arrangement reveals about the dark years following the Civil War. In other words, we ought not to confuse tabletop still lifes any more than we should the different appearances of classical forms in building styles. Even in periods so close as federal and Greek revival, the styles reflect aspirations as different as those embodied in Peale's work compared to that of John F. Francis (fig. 78) only one generation later.

What are some of the recurring characteristics of American still-life paintings? Historians regularly note our concern for the palpable and real world, for solid things naturalistically rendered and fixed in measured spaces.[4] Such observance of physical realism is apparent in the Ganz still lifes from Peale to Severin Roesen to Martin Johnson Heade (figs. 77, 83, and 91). Americans have also traditionally valued the practical and the functional, and art has often served the needs of documentary recording and scientific illustration. This element dominated the first drawings of the New World made by European explorers in the sixteenth century. We may regard John White's watercolors of fish and flowers as the earliest body of still-life images painted in America. While remarkably artistic in their sensitivity to detail, coloring, and expressive pattern, their foremost role was fulfilling the impulses of science. Such record-taking continues in the early nineteenth century with the comprehensive and meticulous achievements of George Catlin and John James Audubon. The latter's several hundred watercolors for *The Birds of America*, 1827–1838, are unusual still-life compositions fusing the aesthetic and the scientific.

To a large degree American still-life painting, like genre and landscape, owes a certain inheritance to Dutch seventeenth-century precedents. These were variously known to Americans through occasional originals and more pervasively through imported copies, prints, or eighteenth-century English derivations. Dutch art had a natural appeal because it reflected a shared culture in part grounded on Protestantism, commerce, material well-being, and scientific exploration. In writing about Dutch still-life painting, Ingvar Bergstrom has stressed the interest in the things and activities of daily life, a fascination just as common in nineteenth-century America. Such an impulse, he points out, derived from the emergence of naturalism at the beginning of the Renaissance (around 1400) and manifested itself in the subsequent flourishing of the natural and biological sciences.[5] Concurrent with the inclination to categorize stimulated by scientific disciplines, Dutch artists were similarly turning to increased specialization in their devotion to subjects. Further, within the area of still life there emerged by the seventeenth century specific subdivisions according to typologies of flowers, foods, and so forth.

Much of this spirit carried over into American painting as artists became freer to explore a varying range of subject matter during the first half of the nineteenth century. Obsession with the specific characteristics and details of the national landscape also encouraged interest in recording its individual botanical and faunal components. At the same time American painting is still generally distinguishable from Dutch prototypes. More secular, technologically minded, and pragmatic, our younger culture seldom embraced the particularized mythological, religious, or allegorical content of European painting. While we shall see later that Dutch still-life painting made elaborate and exact associations between flower types and certain Christian virtues, American artists were usually far less dogmatic and intellectually calculating in making symbolic references. Rather, they preferred more unpretentious celebrations of daily realities and familiar things.

We may also see separable differences between American and French painting. For instance, there are refinements of touch, as well as a strongly moral current, in the eighteenth-century still-life works of Jean Simeon Chardin, which are essentially alien to the businesslike realism in the American tradition. Neither are we likely to see here the concerns with pure paint and color of a Manet or Renoir, nor the probing into issues of perceiving form to be found in Cézanne. Interesting comparisons have been drawn between the flower pictures of Fantin-Latour and Heade[6] and could be made between Peto and Chardin, but in general the French artist more consciously engaged in questions of art for its own sake. By contrast, his American counterpart preferred to hold to image-making as illustration, decoration, or storytelling.

Before further pursuing matters of a native style in American still-life painting, we might well ask why any artist chooses this subject for his creative expression. Just what is still life, and what distinguishes it, beyond superficial iconography, from other general types of imagery? Bergstrom provides a very useable definition to focus our initial consideration: "A still-life painting is a representation of objects which lack the ability to move . . . and which are for artistic purposes grouped into a composition."[7] Possibly the most interesting phrase here is "for artistic purposes grouped," as this signals the fundamentally centripetal nature of the art of still life. That is to say, foremost the artist must select and arrange objects for a still life before painting them. This means his initial conceptual acts have to do with assembling forms for their inherent properties of shape, texture, color, or sensuous association.

Still lifes simply do not preexist in front of us the way a landscape or active figure or human face does. Thus, one of the primary levels of meaning in a still-life painting is its attention to pure artistic form. It is no accident, for example, that the momentous breakthrough in cubism from the analytic to the synthetic phase in the winter of 1912–13 took place not through the subject matter of portraiture or landscape, but crucially by means of such still-life components as bottles, playing cards, mandolins, pipes, newspapers, and other tabletop objects. This was because cubist investigations were addressing issues of pure form: how three-dimensional entities could be reconciled with a two-dimensional surface, the relationship between the surface and the interior of something, the connection among simultaneous views of an object from different vantage points—in short, questions less of meaning than of perception. The still life has a neutrality about it which allows the examination of strictly formal elements. In this sense, then, still life is probably the most artificial of all art subjects, but wherein artifice has literally to do with calling attention to the making of the art.

If still-life painting has this essentially self-referential aspect, on another level it also refers to its arranger. We are not always attentive to the artist's hand, but it has been present successively in the choosing, composing, and painting of objects. To this extent his imprint gives us clues to his life, whether the circumstances of his artistic career or his personal biography. On yet a broader level a still life will tell us something about its period and place, how it issued from a particular time embodying certain values and attitudes and from a recognizable

culture carrying the genes of a nation's identity. Mindful of style as individual, period, and national, let us now return to the still-life works in the Ganz collection.

Raphaelle Peale's *A Dessert*, 1814 (fig. 77), is the earliest of this category in the collection. The artist's very name informs us he was already immersed in a world of art. His father was Charles Willson Peale (1741–1827), the celebrated inventor, scientist, patriot, museum founder, and head of a large family of artists working over several generations. The spirit of the eighteenth-century encyclopedists motivated him to name his children by his first wife after famous artists, and by his second after renowned scientists. As a painter, the elder Peale established himself as a master of an equally comprehensive variety of subjects from portrait and landscape to history and still-life painting. With great ingenuity he could adapt the traditional subject areas of painting to fresh combinations and variations best suited to contemporary American needs. In his own paintings are to be found most of the subjects later taken up as specialties by his children and grandchildren.

Appropriately, the senior Peale chose his own family as the subject for one of his first major works. Painted in 1773, *The Peale Family* (New-York Historical Society) included members of three generations grouped around a table, one with palette and brushes in hand, and in the background a canvas showing the muses as well as pieces of sculpture, intimating a larger world of art. Placed at the center of the table is a modest still-life arrangement, not unlike that which Raphaelle would isolate for attention a few decades later. Thus, in one composition are brought together portraiture, family history, interior genre, and still-life elements. Whether subsequently depicting the *Exhumation of the Mastodon*, 1806 (Peale Museum, Baltimore), or *The Artist in his Museum*, 1822 (Pennsylvania Academy of the Fine Arts), Charles Willson Peale made his own life and profession the subject of his art.

It was a natural consequence that his son, Raphaelle, should devote himself so constantly to finely arranged and lovingly crafted still-life designs. Like his father's work, these are indirectly about the actions of art. We are to savor *A Dessert* above all for its aspiration to perfect balances, unmarred surfaces, and pure geometries. Peale had exhibited his first still-life painting only two years before, and this one is typical of the austere and quiet beauty which mark his best work from here on. In placing his remarkable technical dexterity in the direct service of an almost glassy illusionism, he draws attention to our very processes of seeing the reality of things. Peale here incorporated his own metaphoric presence by his full signature. As if a natural scientist taking a precise temporal and spatial

reading, he put on record: "Raphaelle Peale, Augt. 5th 1814, Philad."

Although dating from the early years of the nineteenth century, this picture owes its animating feeling and raison d'être to the philosophical inheritance of the eighteenth. That earlier century had placed its broad stamp across American taste and thought during the country's formative years surrounding and following the Revolution. Scottish and French philosophers in particular had nurtured systematic methods of inquiry, and the desire to order and categorize affected scientific and political thinking alike.[8] The image that Peale provides us here bears something of this period's attitudes in its stress on clear relationships, hierarchical order, and equilibrium among disparate parts. These same values were those shaping the discourse of America's founding political documents, from the Declaration of Independence through the Constitution to the Federalist Papers. Review Jefferson's calculated list of grievances in the Declaration and its total structure of reasoned logic, or the give-and-take leading to a tripartite government of checks and balances framed by the Constitution, or the dialogue on social order artfully composed and exchanged in the Federalist Papers. In painted form Peale's still life evokes a private parallel vision.

We might say that in his way Peale was declaring for American art the still life as a new and independent form. Through the seventeenth and eighteenth centuries aspiring artists in America had the primary obligation of answering functional needs: to provide shelter or protection in architecture, or likenesses for posterity in painting, or serviceable furniture and silverware in the decorative arts. Within the conventions of portraiture, painters occasionally introduced still-life elements as accessory details, the most noteworthy being the skull as a *vanitas* symbol in Captain Thomas Smith's *Self-Portrait*, c. 1690 (Worcester Art Museum), and the various tabletop objects appearing next to sittters painted by John Singleton Copley. Copley painted one true still life, *Corkscrew Hanging on a Nail*, c. 1766–74 (Museum of Fine Arts, Boston), one of the earliest illusionistic renderings in American art. But it is not really until the career of Raphaelle Peale that we find the still life liberated as a complete and separate entity for sustained artistic attention.

As suggested already, his still-life designs observe a notably discrete sense of order and harmony. In the Ganz painting *A Dessert*, the three perfectly spherical oranges gently sitting in the bowl in a very slightly curved grouping anchor the center of the composition. This gentle arc in turn complements the smooth bulge of the dish below and finds a further minor echo

Fig. 78 John F. Francis,
*Still Life: Yellow Apples and
Chestnuts Spilling from a
Basket,* 1856

in the four walnuts at the lower right. To either side rest the highlighted shapes of a glass decanter and goblet, one narrowing as it rises upward, the other splaying outward in a reverse conical form. Overall, the colors here are clear and restrained, the materials delicate and elegant, the arrangement crisp and ductile. There is an almost aristocratic refinement of taste here; at the same time we feel an assertion of individual parts even as they convene in the unity of the whole.

These same values inform the style of federalist architecture, as typified in the contemporary buildings of Charles Bulfinch, Samuel McIntire, and Thomas Jefferson. Drawing on the graceful and delicate style of English Adamesque architecture, the federal style expressed those virtues of chaste serenity and controlled reserve which perfectly suited the elevated aspira-

tions of eastern seaboard Americans. William Pierson has persuasively demonstrated in his analysis of early American architecture how building forms and styles evocatively articulated the new nation's emerging cultural identity.[9] Consider his description of McIntire's Pingree House of 1805 in Salem, Massachusetts, as a "system of sharply defined self-contained and independent parts, rhythmically joined in a coherent decisive whole. . . ."[10] or Bulfinch's second house for Harrison Gray Otis in 1806 in Boston as "an experience of proportions,"[11] or Jefferson's Monticello at Charlottesville, Virginia, built between 1793 and 1809, as "disarmingly simple at the same time that it is intricate; it is practical at the same time that it is easy, flowing, and gracious; it is dignified and yet is filled with charming informality."[12] We may transfer such phrases almost intact to Raphaelle Peale's painting.

But it is not only the operating principles and overriding feeling of federal architecture which painting shares. Pierson also points out the specific introduction of circular and elliptical shapes in repeated curving arrangements.[13] Again with Peale's still life before us, we can recognize a stylistic language from the cognate forms of McIntire's carved fireplace mantles, Bulfinch's oval drawing rooms, and Jefferson's central rotundas. For that matter we may discover something of the same informal elegance and harmonious design in the portrait paintings by John Singleton Copley and Thomas Sully in the Ganz collection. The former's Sketch for "The Copley Family," 1776 (fig. 28), and the latter's Portrait of the Misses Mary & Emily McEuen, 1823 (fig. 29), present us in effect with beautifully modulated figural still lifes. Private in mood and intimate in scale, the work of Raphaelle Peale glows as an eloquent microcosm of this idealistic yet sensible age.

If we compare this Peale still life with Still Life: Yellow Apples and Chestnuts Spilling from a Basket by John F. Francis (fig. 78), painted in 1856, we can see changes in style as subtle yet definitive as those from federal to pure Greek revival architecture, or from the figure paintings of Sully to those of Seymour Guy and J. G. Brown (figs. 29, 50, and 46). Francis began his career as a portrait painter in the 1830s and forties, and something of his sense for the individuality of things, along with the rather stiff formality of posed objects, seems to have carried over into his still-life compositions. Born in Philadelphia, he certainly knew the solid traditions for this subject matter established in preceding decades by various members of the Peale family.

Ostensibly, we have in these two works by Peale and Francis very similar images: close-up views of a tabletop, with fruits and nuts piled high in a dish in the earlier, and in a basket in the later. But readily the differences become more significant. Where Peale has patiently rendered his surfaces with creamy smoothness, Francis works with painterly vigor. In the former the table surface is clean and flat; in the latter the tablecloth is heavy and creased. Peale's spare forms rest serenely and comfortably in their positions, while the densely packed apples and nuts of Francis tumble out onto the table surface toward the viewer. Instead of the fragile thinness of good glass and porcelain, we now have a sturdy basket and ordinary kitchen dishcloth. Peale's oranges appear ideal in their refined circumferences; Francis's apples bulge with equal roundness, but bear variously irregular silhouettes and mottled surfaces, suggesting a down-to-earth ripeness. Finally, Francis's colors and textures are stronger and more aggressive. Even the scale of his painting is larger and bolder, as if evoking a more expansive world. We have moved from the soft shadows and polished surfaces of a federal dining room to an ordinary kitchen table in Jacksonian America.

Here again Pierson's examination of mature Greek revival architecture in America provides us with applicable insights. He cites the crucial shift from the federal tastes for refined elegance toward a new "bold system of simple massing,"[13] as reflective of emerging vitality and pragmatism of the young, self-confident country. Examples of the style appeared early in the century and flourished through the 1850s and sixties. Compare Francis's still life with the description of Benjamin Latrobe's Center Square Pump House, 1801, in Philadelphia as a "bold piling of geometric shapes, from a cube to a cylinder to a hemisphere"; or Robert Mills's Monumental Church, 1812, in Richmond, Virginia: "The effect is solid and muscular, with all the essentials stripped away, only the bare bones of the geometry to define the spaces."[14] Pierson goes on to argue that "nothing could have been more expressive of the broad common strength of the new nation than the primitivism of Neoclassical forms and the stark sometimes awkward way with which Mills used them."[15]

It is just this same awkwardness, solid massiveness, and simple strength which characterize mid-century still-life painting. The apples in a basket of Francis belong to an ordinary workaday world, and pure neoclassic architecture articulated the same values across the country throughout the second quarter of the nineteenth century. In formal terms the fundamental change was from compositions conceived in plane to solid geometry. This was also the period when the intellectual politics of Jefferson gave way to the physical energies of the age of Andrew Jackson. The latter inaugurated the day of the common man, and the down-to-earth realism of subject matter at this time may also be readily seen in such contemporary genre works in the Ganz collection as J. G. Brown's Children at the Gate (fig. 46) and Seymour Guy's Unconscious of Danger (fig. 50). But it is clear in these figure paintings that we have also moved from the sinuous lines and enamel-smooth surfaces of Sully or Copley to more simplified and compact volumes.

This Francis still life is typical of his first mature works in the 1850s. Gerdts and Burke have shown how his early style tended toward relatively tight delineation of forms and rendering of textures, whereas by the 1870s his handling of paint had gradually become more fluid and sensuous. Once turned full-time to still-life subjects, Francis concentrated on three principal types: the dessert grouping with dishes of berries and cakes, cream pitcher, and sugar bowl; the luncheon setting of

Fig. 81   Edwin Whitefield, *Formal Still Life*, 1840s

compotes surrounded by varied wine bottles and glasses; and the open basket of fruits such as the Ganzes'.[16] Occasionally, he opened up his compositions, especially in the dessert type, with a bright airy view to some landscape in the upper right corner. This device has the effect of suggesting a bigger environment for these food pieces and links them to the larger growing world of nature. In this regard we are reminded of the still life being both an actual and symbolic piece of American bounty at mid-century.

By and large, however, these window vignettes in Francis's work have a touch of contrivance and superfluity about them. *Yellow Apples and Chestnuts* gains its particular effectiveness, rather, through the power of simplicity. In keeping with its unpretentious directness is the overall warmth of its coloring. Between the extremes of the warm dark background and the pasty white tablecloth are the ruddy brown nuts, the one red apple to the left, and the some dozen yellow ones across the center. The total effect is one of earthy mellowness, appropriate to a golden hour of national well-being and self-assurance. The solid, weighty masses we see here, the aura of abundance, and the celebration of humble foods are shared by numerous painters at work through the middle decades of the century.

For example, both the imagery and very title of William Mason Brown's work, *The Bounties of Nature* (fig. 79), indicate the pervasiveness of these stylistic elements. Where Francis had come to still-life painting from portraiture, Brown, a native of Troy, New York, began first as a landscapist. Consequently, when he turned to still-life subjects in the late 1850s, it may have been more natural for him to choose ones which were arranged on the ground itself. But the same ripened volumes of fruit preoccupied him, as they did in more intimate works by Helen Searle Pattison and Edwin Whitefield. The former's surprisingly small but strong oil sketch *Still Life: Plums, Peach and Grapes* (fig. 80) and the latter's delicate watercolor *Formal Still Life* (fig. 81) convey both strength and charm, even in this very reduced scale. Pattison's sketch is additionally compelling for its near-abstract design. Intentionally unfinished, it nonetheless convincingly presents these rounded bodies at once resting on a flat surface and rhythmically floating in empty space. Variances and continuances of this originally mid-century mode of painting can be found well after other styles came to dominate American painting, as in Joseph Decker's *Their Winter Hoard* (fig. 82).

The analogies to neoclassicism are apparent both in architectural references and in contemporaneous Greek revival marble figures, such as Hiram Powers's *Proserpine* (fig. 30), with its leafy bodice. In fact, his carving of *Loulie's Hand* (fig. 32), along with the bronze by Harriet Hosmer, *Clasped Hands of Robert and Elizabeth Barrett Browning* (fig. 37), constitute counterpart still lifes in sculpture. Powers was one of the leading American sculptors who had joined the expatriate community in Florence in the middle of the century; Hosmer preferred Rome as her base. Their names, and these two works in particular, are coincidentally linked at this time by Nathaniel Hawthorne in his novel *The Marble Faun*, 1860. In a chapter titled "A Sculptor's Studio" the character Miriam, a painter, makes a visit to her friend Kenyon.

Hawthorne uses the image of the hand to draw several metaphors. First, it signifies the connections and distances between people. Miriam broods about her colleagues as "she approache[s] the edge of the voiceless gulf between herself and them. Standing on the utmost verge of that dark chasm, she might stretch out her hand, and never clasp a hand of theirs."[17] White marble further summoned contrasts of the heart's human warmth and the cool permanence of timelessness: "an infinite, shivering solitude, amid which . . . human beings . . . turn to cold, chilly shapes of mist."[18] The hand is also that of the sculptor himself at work on his actual carving and chiseling. It is, as Kenyon says, "grimy with Cleopatra's clay,"[19] engaged

Fig. 79 William Mason Brown,
The Bounties of Nature, c.1867

in the creative act itself. Lastly, in more general terms the neoclassic form embodied idealized beauty and pure innocence, what Hawthorne calls "remote and shy divinity."[20]

When Kenyon shows Miriam a modeled hand of a woman he has done, the associations with Powers and Hosmer immediately come to mind:

it is as good in its way as Loulie's hand with its baby-dimples, which Powers showed me in Florence, evidently valuing it as much as if he had wrought it out of a piece of his great heart. As good as Harriet Hosmer's clasped hands of Browning and his wife, symbolizing the individuality and heroic union of two high, poetic lives![21]

Thus, these hands in hard stone and metal respectively acquire both the formal and metaphoric purity of still life. As isolated portions of the body, they additionally stand for the larger organic unity of the human figure. Horatio Greenough foremost articulated the connecting principles between Greek architecture and the human body by perceiving both as integrated, functional systems. Like a temple, the structure of man was "the most beautiful organization of earth, the exponent and minister of the highest being."[22] Man, too, as much as fruits and flowers, was a part of nature's higher order and totality.

Emerging concurrently with mature neoclassicism and succeeding it as an architectural style in the third quarter of the nineteenth century was the Gothic revival. There are revealing parallels to be drawn with the related emergence in these years of flower still lifes. Just as the classicism we have noted in different forms in the work of Peale and Francis relied on the clear, self-contained integrity of component parts, so now a much more varied and intricate set of relationships begins to appear in both Gothic revival architecture and in the floral still-life subjects painted after mid-century. To make this point directly we need only compare Severin Roesen's quintessential *Flower Still-Life with Bird's Nest* of 1853 (fig. 83) with Pierson's partial description of the Gothic: "Its fragmented irregular shapes, its lofty tapered profiles, its constantly shifting surfaces, its interlacing proliferous forms, all so reminiscent of the world of natural growth. . . ."[23]

We might also note the repeated preference by Roesen and many of his contemporaries represented in the Ganz collection for the vertical format; see, for example the still lifes by George Henry Hall, George Cochran Lambdin, Aaron Draper Shattuck, Henry Roderick Newman, and Martin Johnson Heade (figs. 84, 89, 6, 90, and 91). On the one hand, some of these (even when in vases) continue the expression of abundant plenitude present in Francis's apple group; at the same time, they also allude to certain chapellike enclosures of nature's wilderness. In contrast to the imagery of Francis, many of these floral and leafy subjects seem to have shifted subtly from an emphasis

Fig. 80 Helen Searle Pattison, *Still Life: Plums, Peach and Grapes,*
August-September 1868

Fig. 82 Joseph Decker,
Their Winter Hoard, c.1889

Fig. 83   Severin Roesen,
Flower Still-Life with Bird's Nest, 1853

dering nature's growing things accurately as living organisms. To this end they often sought to suggest or depict a precise natural environment.

Severin Roesen was surely one of the American masters of this mode. Born in Germany, he is thought to have had some early training as a painter of porcelains before coming to New York in 1848. Bringing with him an awareness of German still-life painting and the traditions of the subject grounded in Dutch and northern European art of the seventeenth century, Roesen soon established himself as a specialist in fruit and flower compositions. His *Flower Still-Life with Bird's Nest* is one of his finest achievements in the latter category. The polished refinement of touch, precision of detail, and gleaming textures recall the character of porcelain painting, at the same time that the lush assemblage of these myriad flowers constitutes almost an almanac of America's living promise. Frequently Roesen dots his bulbs or leaves with glistening droplets of water or an occasional fly, as he does here, to amplify our sense of the uttter ripeness and perfection of these bright, buoyant bouquets.

In George Henry Hall's *Still Life: Pink Rose in Green Vase* (fig. 84) and in George Cochran Lambdin's paintings of lilies and roses (figs. 85 and 86), we have more concentrated and specialized variations of this theme. It is as if Roesen had itemized a garden's produce, leaving for painters of a subsequent generation to isolate a single species or flower for examination. Something of Hall's clarity of form must have derived from his earlier study with the Düsseldorf school. Here his accuracy in rendering the individuality of form is delicately tempered by the muted color complementaries of pink and green and by the emotional associations of the rose with personal affection. Whether Lambdin intended a similar allusion to purity with his *Lilies* (fig. 85) is uncertain. The brilliant illumination and intense coloring of his flowers against the warm, somber background have the effect of creating a brooding, even threatening, air of eroticism.

In painting a similar vase of lush roses (fig. 86) Lambdin created a work which makes a striking pair with the *Lilies,* yet ultimately possesses a different expressive power. Where the intensity of form and exoticism of feeling seem to dominate his bunch of lilies, this arrangement captures our attention by its consciously asymmetrical design. The full vase sits clearly to the right of center, balanced on the left by the low but bright blue dish. Lambdin makes playful echoes on the living and artificial nature of his floral imagery, as we take note first of the central flowers themselves and then the floral patterns on the vase and tablecloth in darker tones below. Likewise the

on rational order to a new infusion of imagination, emotion, and expressive feeling. To this end the colors and textures of Roesen and Lambdin especially appear more intense, varied, and complex.

There were at least three major forces coming to bear on the flourishing of this type of still life at this time: a sense of nature's moral and spiritual content (which had the associations noted with the Gothic revival), John Ruskin's philosophical examination of nature's details, and the evolutionary theories of Charles Darwin. The more traditional composition gathered and placed cut flowers in a vase on a table, much in the manner of earlier fruit assemblages. Flowers tended to retain closer ties than foods with their original growing contexts, but also freely allowed the creative act of purely formal and abstract arrangements. The heightened concern at this time with individual species owed much to Ruskin's influential books on drawing and painting, which went through numerous popular editions from the 1850s on. Likewise, Darwin's ideas occasioned intense interest among both landscape and still-life painters for ren-

Fig. 84 George Henry Hall, *Still Life: Pink Rose in Green Vase*, 1880s

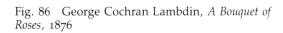

Fig. 86 George Cochran Lambdin, *A Bouquet of Roses*, 1876

Fig. 85   George Cochran Lambdin,
Lilies, 1872

Fig. 89   George Cochran Lambdin,
Roses on a Wall, 1877

vital buds above have as footnotes at their base the fallen petals and snapped stem, hints of mortality in this world of nature's evolution.

To some extent the symbolic meanings given to particular flowers goes back to conventions of Renaissance and baroque painting, though American artists seldom followed the precedents of explicit allegorical content. Ingvar Bergstrom has itemized many of these associations, such as those suggesting transience, like the hourglass, candlestick, and soap bubbles; or vanity of human existence, alluded to by the presence of a skull, musical and scientific instruments, and jewelry; or Christian resurrection, indicated by the beaker of wine, the walnut, and butterflies.[24] Within this tradition formulated during the sixteenth and seventeenth centuries there were further references to be drawn from the iconography of various flowers. For example, ivy signified eternal life, the lily virginal purity, the iris royalty, the columbine the Holy Ghost, violets Christian faith and humility, the peony transience, the carnation hope for redemption, and laurel the Resurrection.[25]

While these exact correlations may not have been precisely employed by mid-nineteenth-century American painters, it is

Fig. 87 Edwin Whitefield, *Blue and Yellow Violets in a Landscape*, 1855

Fig. 88 John William Hill, *Pineapples*, after 1855 (at right)

clear that there were elaborate allusions kept in mind for many native flowers. In conjunction with his research on Heade, Theodore Stebbins has shown that floral dictionaries and lexicons were published extensively during the middle decades of the century, and American painters were certainly aware of their contents. Among blooms often appearing in their work, a number carried particular significance, such as the heliotrope devotion, the orange blossom purity, the hibiscus delicate beauty, heather solitude, the carnation refusal or disdain, exotic flowers sexual bliss, trailing arbutus inseparable love, daisies innocence, and the magnolia nature's magnificence. Roses were further subdivided: generally considered the flower of lovers, the red rose specifically recalled bashful love, the pink rose devotion, the white rosebud a "heart that knows not love" or silence, and the fallen pink rose a lost maiden.[26] While we do not know to what degree painters like Roesen, Hall, and Lambdin intended their still-life subjects to carry such associational conventions, these cultural tables of organization provide an indispensable context for appreciating their work.

The English critic John Ruskin widely influenced many aspects of American painting in these years, and not least affected by his ideas was still life. In his essays on the principles and practice of drawing he encouraged the recording of those details which expressly differentiated one species from another and which conveyed the organic growth of a subject. Pronounced Ruskin: "The flower exists for its own sake—not for the fruit's sake."[27] To him and to his generation of followers in America, flowers and trees possessed a divine as well as scientific beauty, both of which required understanding. But equally important to Ruskin was the notion that "a flower is to be watched as it grows."[28] In this regard his stress on knowing the appropriate natural environment for any plant gained even greater acceptance from the concurrent popularization of Charles Darwin's theories.

On the Origin of Species was published in 1859 and had an immediate impact on both sides of the Atlantic. Notions such as evolutionary selectivity and survival of the fittest gave new consciousness to the processes of organic life and growth.[29] As Darwin's ideas filtered down to specific perceptions of plants and flowers, and to their interpretation in turn by artists, two definitive effects occurred. First, growing things were no longer artificial or isolated abstractions, but active living forms. Second, from the 1860s on artists were moved to depict flowers no longer cut in vases but alive in their natural outdoor habitat.[30]

The Ruskinian way of thinking is readily evident in what has come to be called American Pre-Raphaelitism, a style of meticulous rendering and close scientific observation. By the mid-

1850s the manner was followed in such diverse examples as Edwin Whitefield's *Blue and Yellow Violets in a Landscape* (fig. 87), Aaron Draper Shattuck's *Leaf Study with Yellow Swallow Tail* (fig. 6), and John William Hill's *Pineapples* (fig. 88). In following decades the Darwinian sensibility caused flower subjects to be integrated into outdoor settings to a point where still-life and landscape painting became virtually fused. This development is apparent in such Ganz pictures as Lambdin's *Roses on a Wall* of 1877 (fig. 89), Henry Roderick Newman's *Italy*, 1883 (fig. 90), and Heade's *An Amethyst Hummingbird with a White Orchid* from the 1870s (fig. 91).

There are several literary parallels we could cite to these mid-century attitudes in painting, but none perhaps is as apt or eloquent as the nature writing of Henry David Thoreau. His sense of place is of course well known in a masterwork such as *Walden*, but throughout the journals from these years are innumerable passages which will serve to remind us what joy

Fig. 100   Martin Johnson Heade,
Victorian Vase with Flowers of Devotion, c.1870–1875

Fig. 91 Martin Johnson Heade,
An Amethyst Hummingbird with a White Orchid, 1870s

and edification the American imagination found in scrutinizing nature's smallest corners. Let us savor a paragraph on hazel blossoms, taken almost at random from an entry of March 28, 1858:

I go down to the railroad, turning off in the cut. I notice the hazel stigmas in the warm hollow on the right there, just beginning to peep forth. This is an unobserved but very pretty and interesting evidence of the progress of the season. I should not have noticed it if I had not carefully examined the fertile buds. It is like a crimson star first dimly detected in the twilight. The warmth of the day, in this sunny hollow above the withered sedge, has caused the stigmas to show their lips through their scaly shield. They do not project more than the thirtieth of an inch, some not the sixtieth. The staminate catkins are also considerably loosened. Just as the turtles put forth their heads, so these put forth their stigmas in the spring. How many accurate thermometers there are on every hill and in every valley! Measure the length of the hazel stigmas, and you can tell how much warmth there has been this spring. How fitly and exactly any season of the year may be described by indicating the condition of some flower![31]

Here are familiar efforts to locate and measure, technically precise names, and the growth of plants equated with a season's progress as well as with the greater laws of nature. To carry these latter truths worthily, leaf and petal had now to be seen spread upon the tabletop of nature.

Such elements return us to the contemporary flourishing of the Gothic revival in American architecture. Aside from its spiritual frame of reference and its structure of systemically related parts, the Gothic encouraged the integration of a building with its surrounding natural setting. As Andrew Jackson Downing, one of the great architectural critics and designers of the day, put it: "architectural beauty must be considered conjointly with the beauty of the landscape or situation."[32] Downing further eschewed the abstract white of Greek revival and recommended colors and textures that would harmonize a structure with nature. It is significant that Downing, along with his equally influential colleague, the architect Alexander Jackson Davis, devoted special attention to the design and placement of country villas and cottages. In them the intricacies, irregularities, and proliferations of form might perfectly match the picturesque aspects of adjacent scenery.[33]

We are in the same stylistic world as we glance at the wall-climbing roses of George Lambdin, A. D. Shattuck's leafy ground cover, or Roderick Newman's garden grapevine view, and listen to William Pierson's characterization of Lyndhurst in 1865:

each arch, each molding, each tracery bar conveys the impression of being there as a result of natural growth . . . the later windows of

Lyndhurst seem to emerge from the substance of older parts as living organisms, capable of perpetual renewal, and appear more as blossoms on a flowering tree than as cut flowers arranged for a special occasion.[34]

The emergence of landscape gardening as a profession and of the parks movement in America in the decades following the Civil War only confirmed a larger context for these concerns of painters and architects alike with the powerfully vivifying role of nature.

But there was an exotic element entering American still-life and landscape painting during the 1860s and seventies. One of the exemplars of this was Martin Johnson Heade, represented at his strongest in the Ganz collection by *An Amethyst Hummingbird with a White Orchid* (fig. 91). Heade had grown up in Pennsylvania and after an early trip to Europe concentrated on painting landscapes along the New England coast. He also began producing conventional tabletop still-life paintings of roses and apple blossoms in vases, some of exquisite delicacy and suggestive feeling. During the 1860s he made the first of several voyages to Central and South America in search of new subjects. A number of his contemporaries, like Sanford Gifford and Frederic Edwin Church, also undertook extensive travels to distant landscapes with exotic climates or geography. Partially, this impulse seems to have been an American pursuit of an endless wilderness frontier and, coming in the apocalyptic twilight of the Civil War, also an escape from the disruptions of the national Eden at home.

This may help to explain Heade's fascination, as much emotional as scientific, in his later still-life work for the passion flower and the orchid. Stebbins has explained how the former, in shape, number of petals, and color, came to be associated with Christ's final Passion, while the orchid, whose name is derived from the Greek word meaning testicle, carried a "dangerous aura of sexuality and was thought to be an aphrodisiac."[35] By the same token, the hummingbird was perceived to occupy a grove in Eden, and in his South American visions Heade closely juxtaposed that bird with various orchids in compositions that were powerful still lifes grafted on to steamy jungle landscapes. Sometimes he contrasted the male and female bird, in other cases two fighting males. These sexual observations had provocative echoes in the visibly erotic shapes of the orchid's vaginal flower and phallic pistils. Heade's seductive imagery reflects the drives of species postulated by Darwin paradoxically fused with the hidden sexuality of the Victorian age.

Albert Bierstadt's small oil of 1890, *Butterfly* (fig. 92), brings many of these foregoing themes to conclusion at the close of

Fig. 94   S.S. David (pseudonym of De Scott Evans), *A New Variety,* after 1887

the nineteenth century. In earlier centuries butterflies were symbols of the soul, obviously deriving from their processes of metamorphosis into evanescent creatures of beautiful coloring.[36] Thus they assumed roles related to certain flowers in referring to the transience of life, the fragility of human existence, and the hopes for resurrection. Presumably, the butterfly which darts about Lambdin's roses is one of mere factual observation appearing in the artist's garden. But Bierstadt's intentional isolation and abstraction of the form suggests further psychological and aesthetic impulses at work. Technically intricate, these intimate oils were the result of pigments carefully laid at the center of the page, which Bierstadt then folded in half, spreading and blotting colors out to a butterfly shape. Each side is nearly symmetrical, as if in an artistic Rorschach

Fig. 90   Henry Roderick Newman,
Italy, 1883

test. Surpassing scientific accuracy, then, this image is more private. In effect, the emerging butterfly is both the metaphor and actuality of the artistic act. Its bright, pure colors come from a world as exotic as Heade's, as immediate as Lambdin's, as creatively artificial as Peale's.

The tradition of Edenic still lifes represented an effusive age of self-confidence and national promise. Even though exuberant blossoms continued to grow luxuriantly from artist's palettes through the later nineteenth century, another type of realism and subject matter emerged at the end of the century, representing a graver and more worldly outlook. This changed view is apparent in the work of elusive or little-known figures like De Scott Evans (S. S. David) and Claude Raguet Hirst, and in the three foremost exponents of this fin-de-siècle style, John Haberle, William Michael Harnett, and John Frederick Peto, all shown at the top of their form in the Ganz collection. Together, the decorative, manufactured, and commercial objects of their compositions return American still life to a darkened world indoors. These three artists belonged to a generation born just at mid-century and who came to artistic maturity during the 1870s. Their outlook was therefore tempered by a post-Civil War world of unsettled turbulence and retrenchment, new industrialism and encroaching technology, further territorial expansionism and regionalism. Corruption and deceit marked national politics; great accumulations and expenditures of wealth directed the attention of entrepreneurial America to property and possessions of substance.

All of this meant that the youthful optimism and naive innocence of the country during the ante-bellum decades now constituted an inadequate vision for a changed national spirit. No wonder that Haberle would paint tricky illusions of paper currency, Harnett the pipes, mugs, books, and tangible acquisitions of personal value, or Peto the sober artifacts of his desk and bookshelves. Haberle was the most consciously whimsical and technically clever of the group. A native of New Haven, Connecticut, he had an early job assisting with exhibits at the Yale paleontology museum. This helps to explain his long artistic fascination with painting labels and notes on drawers, itemizing individual coins and dollar bills, and packaging lots of small objects for display. His life-size rendering of a one dollar bill lying across a ten is typical (fig. 93). Entitled *U.S.A.*, it bears Haberle's printed signature and place of work on the illusionistic boards at the upper right, along with a childlike drawing of a smiling face. These witty marks of the artist's presence in his own work have a further counterpart in the painted clipping of newspaper below, which in part reads: " 'Imitation' by John Haberle, is one of those clever pieces of

Fig. 93   John Haberle,
U.S.A., 1889

artistic mechanics showing an old greenback. . . ." In terms of
subject Haberle is calling our attention to the reality and illusion
of money in an acquisitive age, while in terms of art he is
equally challenging our perceptions about the reality and illusion of painting.

One of the most idiosyncratic and wittiest illusionists of this
period was De Scott Evans, who began by playing with the
reality of his own name. He was actually born David Scott
Evans but later changed it to acquire a more French character.
Known at present by only a couple of dozen paintings, he
further confounded his artistic identity by signing his works
with a variety of initials and name combinations derived from
his own, including Stanley David and S. S. David. The Ganz
picture *A New Variety* (fig 94) bears the latter name and in
format is close to one so signed in the Yale University Art
Gallery. Yale's and several other versions depict roasted peanuts in this shallow box, a popular subject taken up by other
colleagues at the time, most notably Joseph Decker, John Haberle, and John F. Peto. The Ganzes' *Their Winter Hoard* (fig.
82) by Decker belongs in this company, though its animated

squirrels introduce elements of both the natural world and
anecdotal genre.

Yale's painting illustrates peanuts also massed behind broken
panes of glass, while the Ganzes' *A New Variety* is special in
its more rarified depiction of almonds. Typical of Evans is his
fascination with objects in a narrow space at once extending
back into depth and forward toward the viewer. Here only one
almond at the lower center achieves the second illusion of
projecting beyond the planes of the glass and the canvas surface. The smooth, tight handling of paint lends an air of true
visual foolery, while the sense for abstract design in this spare
delineation of shapes and muted colors creates an overall air
of aesthetic artifice quite beyond Decker's more illustrational
approach. One has to wonder if Evans did not intend a final
conceit in his title, suggesting for himself a fresh subject,
treatment, and even artistic personality.

Harnett, for his part, was a Philadelphian by upbringing and
training, and his early tabletop compositions belong to that
city's still-life tradition going back through Francis and Lambdin
to the Peales. Trained at the Pennsylvania Academy in the

Fig. 95   William Michael Harnett,
La Flûte Enchantée, 1887

early 1870s, he established himself locally as an accomplished still-life painter but went to Munich for the first half of the next decade. There the grittier textures and humble library objects of his first period yielded to tighter arrangements of more refined antiques, treated with a new jewellike precision and polish. This stylistic change was a response to the more exacting manner of delineation, paint handling, and coloring prevalent in much mid-nineteenth-century German painting, although the art of the French painter Jean Meissonier has also been

proposed as a possible influence.[37]

After six years in Munich, Harnett returned in 1886 to settle for the last part of his career in New York. It is at this juncture that he painted the Ganzes' *La Flûte Enchantée* (fig. 95). The preference for the vertical format, relatively compact design of refined objects, and purity of these highlighted surfaces all reflect his recent European work. This was one of a series of very similar versions he painted in this period, including a nearly identical version from the next year now in the National

Fig. 96   Claude Raguet Hirst,
Still Life with Clippings, 1891

Gallery. The objects in both these paintings come from a cosmopolitan world of eclectic tastes. As evidence of his worldly travels Harnett brings together recognizable emblems of diverse arts, such as a vellum-bound volume of Shakespeare's comedies and a music cover inscribed "Rigoletto." In *La Flûte Enchantée* we can specifically identify Dante's *Divine Comedy*, the music sheets of a popular romantic melody, along with a Roman lamp and Dutch jar, as well as the flute itself and Harnett's familiar meerschaum pipe. The artist rearranged a number of these elements yet again in a much larger canvas of 1888, *The Cincinnati Enquirer*, now in The White House collection. This last replaced the lamp with a common candlestick and the French music with the American newspaper.

Occupying a position stylistically between the precise brushwork of Harnett and the rougher textured paintings of John F. Peto is the neglected work of Claude Raguet Hirst. Probably unchallenged as the most able woman painter working in this illusionist still-life tradition in the later nineteenth century, she came from Cincinnati in the mid-1880s. She had begun painting more traditional flower and fruit still lifes, but upon Harnett's return from Europe to New York in 1886, she readily adapted his familiar motifs. Unquestionably one of her finest performances is the example of her work in the Ganz collection entitled *Still Life with Clippings* (fig. 96). The inkwell, pipe, tobacco pouch, and newspaper are all personae from Harnett's tabletop stages, though the gleaming pair of scissors and the bright reds of the ink label, pen, and pouch string are distinctively her details. Given the technical level of accomplishment here, it is not surprising that both drawings and paintings by Hirst have periodically ended up on the market as works attributed to Harnett or Peto. A work of this quality at once brings to light a fascinating artist heretofore overlooked and illustrates the nuances of connoisseurship called for in this complex area of American painting.

The imagery in the Ganz Harnett, Hirst, and their companions belongs to a Victorian world of substantial material possessions, of men's comfortable and crowded libraries, much in tune with those social aspirations which raised the great marble palaces and shingle-style mansions in Newport and the massive Beaux-Arts brownstones in New York. In Harnett we observe an environment of casual but clear order, cultivated tastes based not on the spiritual values of nature but on the solid physical world of stuffs and things. Henry Hobson Richardson's dark, heavy architecture in wood and stone perhaps epitomized this cultural style dominating the last third of the nineteenth century, in what Lewis Mumford has set aside for us as the Brown Decades.

Mumford's term alludes to several interrelated aspects of culture in this period: the dark colors of painting, the monumental forms and earthy textures of buildings, the somber brooding images of many painters and sculptors, the uninspired dreariness of national politics. A worldly air characterizes the stark realism of Winslow Homer's mature landscapes and the contemplative tone of Thomas Eakins's saddened faces. Browns, with associations both physical and psychological, pervade the mood of John F. Peto's still-life paintings especially. A Philadelphia native, Peto was a fellow student with Harnett at the Pennsylvania Academy and for his first years as an artist much under his friend's influence. This has been one of the primary reasons, along with the fact that Peto was often uneven in quality and capable of repetitiveness, that he has been so consistently described as a follower of Harnett. But this view does not fairly take into account such remarkably personal and original achievements by Peto as the Ganzes' *Office Board for Christian Faser* and *Old Companions* (figs. 97 and 98).

Indeed, following Harnett's lead, in the late seventies he had begun painting small compositions of pipes, books, beer mugs, and newspapers spread across simple wooden tables. Yet early on, even in this most derivative youthful period, there were hints of Peto's independence in choice and handling of subject. In 1878, for example, he painted a bunch of candy canes tumbling from a paper bag, the first of several unusual food subjects undertaken in subsequent years, which have been virtually overlooked by his critics. Later Peto was able to imbue the common raspberry or cucumber, a simple teacup or dented brass pot, with a remarkable aura of mystery and sensuous feeling. Although never the dazzling illusionist that Harnett was, Peto was equally concerned with purely formal issues. In fact, while he was perfectly capable of creating witty visual deceits in his own more painterly style, he always insisted on reminding his viewer of being in the presence of art. Whether by playing with wonderful patterns of lines, planes, and volumes or romantic melodies of evocative colors and textures, or using an always evident brushwork and sometimes intentionally not finishing details, Peto tells us that these marks are the very elements and actuality of painting *as painting*.

His office boards initiated a series of so-called rack and patch pictures, begun in 1879, and evidently influenced Harnett to paint a couple of similar examples at this time. On these flat boards or doors Peto painted letters, calling cards, photographs, and the like, held on by tape or tacked down. These were commissioned as forms of advertising for business establishments; an envelope label in the Ganz painting (fig. 97)

informs us that Christian Faser ran an art gallery on Arch Street in Philadelphia. There are other clues to the life of the artist and his patron: business cards, notes, and postcards, the folded letter and carte-de-visite photograph, and an almanac for 1881. Yet significantly, Peto does not reveal all. The letter is only partially visible, the photograph covered enough to obscure identification, and most provocatively, the orange envelope inscribed "Important Information Inside." Like Harnett's newspapers, these all help to fix time and place, yet Peto is different in concealing as much as revealing.

Actually, it is not so much that he wishes to hide information from us (though we do not know what is inside), as it is to force our contemplation along with his on the independent purity and beauty of art. In other words, the signs are legible enough to make this function as an office board, but illegible enough to make us see paint, and shape and color for themselves. Quite probably Peto has spelled a private joke in the emphatic capital I's on the orange envelope by attuning us to think of those other eyes by which we not only see but perceive. Thus, where Harnett assembles his fragments of existence mainly as antiquarian artifacts for study, Peto penetrates the surfaces of reality to ruminate on the substance of art.

These are highly personal visions which increasingly retreat from the outer world for Peto and into the private corners of his studio. In contrast to the wide traveling and continued commercial success of Harnett, Peto became more reclusive, and in 1889 actually withdrew to a revival community at Island Heights, New Jersey. There he played his cornet at camp meetings while continuing to work in a seclusion not unlike that Homer and Eakins drew about themselves in later years. Typically, Peto's cornet frequently appears in his paintings, an emblem of his person, so different from the more antiquarian presence of a piccolo or flute in Harnett. Likewise, paintings of single violins hanging against blank textured walls become for Peto pure shapes of aesthetic delight, let alone fellow agents for the making of harmonious art.

Peto's later office boards and paintings of his last years generally bear an increased sense of wear and tear, which we can read as an index of both the gathering difficulties in his own career and the larger uneasiness of America on the threshold of a new age. In the rack pictures of the nineties the tapes unravel, more cards are torn from their nails, pamphlet bindings are shredded, and everywhere is the melancholy evidence of time's deteriorations. No more moving embodiment of this sensibility is to be found than in one of Peto's last great series, again notably personal in its invention, namely, the bookshelves. Both for the rack pictures and here, there are occasional

Fig. 92   Albert Bierstadt, *Butterfly*, December 16, 1890

precedents for the subject in earlier American painting as well as in Dutch and German baroque art, but as with his best art Peto brings a new poignance and freshness to his form.

Old Companions (fig. 98) is also one of a series which preoccupied Peto around the turn of the century and which perhaps best serves as an analogue to Richardsonian romanesque architecture. For example, there are interesting parallels to be drawn between this painting and Richardson's finest libraries built in the early 1880s, such as the Crane Memorial Library in Quincy, Massachusetts. In both we have compositions which assemble a carefully modulated variety of geometric volumes, building up from a solid horizontal base to a compact mass above. Both artists exploit strong rhythmic contrasts of surface textures, silhouettes, and related shapes; both quietly orchestrate the interplay of bulk and surface. The shared result combines a sense of the monumental and the picturesque with compelling expressiveness. And of course there is the interest both artists hold for the library as a house for books and the

"important information inside" each. For Peto particularly, the book was yet another metaphor embodying the language of art.

Looking at the near disarray of Peto's shelf, we become further aware of his Richardsonian design of large asymmetries. But, where the architect's buildings served the expanding needs of informal education, the painter's still lifes evoke an additional feeling of order in tension with some threatened chaos. This is the distinction which places Peto's art at the turn of the century, when nostalgia for loss of the old one mingled with anxiety about the prospects of the new one. Henry Adams worried in his *Education* about the loosening of former absolutes as the new age promised uncertain and unfixed relationships. It is worth remembering that this key memoir was written just a year after *Old Companions* and that Peto might just as well have been speaking when Adams brooded, "Chaos was the law of nature; Order was the dream of man."[38] The seemingly random conjunction of objects in Peto's painting—hanging,

Fig. 97 John F. Peto,
Office Board for Christian Faser, 1881

Fig. 98 John F. Peto,
Old Companions, 1904

teetering, inclining uncomfortably—recalls another Adams apprehension about the "chance collision of movements."[39] For both men art was one means of salvaging a stay against confusion.

There is also a comparison in mood and manner to be drawn with the private, hermetic poems of Emily Dickinson, like Peto, reclusive in art and life, neither to be fully appreciated until the mid-twentieth century. Examining the shadowed corners of her mind, she too reflected on the exhilaration and exhaustion of her "small library":

Unto my books so good to turn
Far ends of tired days; . . .
I thank these kinsmen of the shelf;
Their countenances bland[40]

Her finely crafted lines and compact verses are independent artifices with an abstraction and subjectivity close to Peto's paintings, causing one to wonder if still lifes and poetry do not inherently bear natural affinities.

Certainly there are associations between the meditative visions of Peto and Dickinson and later nineteenth-century figure painting. From the Ganz collection it suffices to call attention to such diverse images as George W. Maynard's *A Geographer* (fig. 59), Winslow Homer's *Blackboard* (fig. 58), Francis Millet's *After the Festival* (fig. 76), Rhoda Nicholls's *After the Ball* (fig. 64), and Francis C. Jones's *Lady and Lyre* (fig. 66). The naturalist fevers and scientific ebullience of an earlier generation could produce equally the lush growths of Severin Roesen and William Mason Brown, the serene expanses of Fitz Hugh Lane and Sanford Gifford, and the dense foliages of Frederic Edwin Church and William Trost Richards. By contrast, for Peto and many of his contemporaries the subjects of art were increasingly inner landscapes. Peto himself literally made the ordinary things of his life around him into art: his "kinsmen on the shelf" formed the physical cosmos of his studio as well as the mental cosmos of his paintings. Painted in 1904, *Old Companions* brings us into the twentieth century in essence and in fact.

Beginning with Peale's *A Dessert* we have joined the growth of American still-life painting through the rich harvest of the nineteenth century, from the spirit of the eighteenth to that of our own.

Fig. 77   Peale, *A Dessert* (detail)

Notes

1.   Wolfgang Born, *Still-Life Painting in America* (New York, 1947); Alfred Frankenstein, *After the Hunt, William Harnett and Other American Still Life Painters, 1870–1900* (Berkeley and Los Angeles, 1969); William H. Gerdts and Russell Burke, *American Still-Life Painting* (New York, 1971).

2.   Gerdts and Burke, *Still-Life Painting*, 133.

3.   Frankenstein, *After the Hunt*, 31.

4.   The most influential recent argument on American realism is in Barbara Novak's *American Painting of the Nineteenth Century, Realism, Idealism, and the American Experience* (New York, 1969). See also John Wilmerding, *The Genius of American Painting* (New York and London, 1973), "Introduction," 13–23.

5.   Ingvar Bergstrom, *Dutch Still-Life Painting in the Seventeenth Century* (London, 1956), 1, 4, 40.

6.   Theodore E. Stebbins, Jr., *The Life and Works of Martin Johnson Heade* (New Haven and London, 1975), 114–115.

7.   Bergstrom, *Dutch Still-Life Painting*, 3.

8.   See Garry Wills, *Inventing America, Jefferson's Declaration of Independence* (Garden City, New York, 1978).

9.   William H. Pierson, Jr., *American Buildings and Their Architects: The Colonial and Neoclassical Styles* (Garden City, New York, 1970), Part II: "Neoclassicism in America."

10.   Pierson, *American Buildings*, 224.

11.   Pierson, *American Buildings*, 264.

12.   Pierson, *American Buildings*, 314.

13.   Pierson, *American Buildings*, 338.

14.   Pierson, *American Buildings*, 358, 382.

15.   Pierson, *American Buildings*, 383–384.

16.   Gerdts and Burke, *Still-Life Painting*, 60–61.

17.   Nathaniel Hawthorne, *The Marble Faun* (1860; reprint ed. Indianapolis and New York, 1971), 110.

18.   Hawthorne, *The Marble Faun*, 110.

19.   Hawthorne, *The Marble Faun*, 113.

20.   Hawthorne, *The Marble Faun*, 118.

21.   Hawthorne, *The Marble Faun*, 116–117.

22.   Horatio Greenough, quoted in Sylvia E. Crane, *White Silence, Greenough, Powers, and Crawford, American Sculptors in Nineteenth-Century Italy* (Coral Gables, Florida, 1972), 151.

23.   William H. Pierson, Jr., *American Buildings and Their Architects: Technology and the Picturesque, The Corporate and the Early Gothic Styles* (Garden City, New York, 1978), 270.

24.   Bergstrom, *Dutch Still-Life Painting*, 10, 154.

25.   Bergstrom, *Dutch Still-Life Painting*, 10, 13, 15, 154, 214.

26.   Stebbins, *Heade*, 116–117, 121, 124, 138, 142–143, 149, 167, 172.

27.   John Ruskin, "Proserpina," *Complete Works of John Ruskin*, ed. E. J. Cook and Alexander Wedderburn (London, 1899–1905), 25: 249.

28.   Ruskin, *Works*, 2: 300.

29.   See Ella Milbank Foshay, "Nineteenth Century American Flower

Painting and the Botanical Sciences" (Ph.D. diss., Columbia University, 1979), 220. This comprehensive thesis deals with the complementary influences of Ruskin and Darwin.

30.   Foshay, "Flower Painting," 206, 233. See also Gerdts and Burke, *Still-Life Painting,* Chapter 6, "Nineteenth-Century Flower Painters."

31.   *The Writings of Henry David Thoreau* (Walden ed., Boston, 1906), "Journal," 10: 325.

32.   Andrew Jackson Downing, *The Fruits and Fruit Trees of America,* 1845, quoted in William Pierson, *Technology and the Picturesque,* 350.

33.   See Pierson, *Technology and the Picturesque,* 297, 300, 408.

34.   Pierson, *Technology and the Picturesque,* 343.

35.   Stebbins, *Heade,* 138–149.

36.   See Bergstrom, *Dutch Still-Life Painting,* 10.

37.   See Frankenstein's argument on this in his *After the Hunt,* 58–59 ff.; and the demurrer by Gerdts and Burke in their *Still-Life Painting,* 142.

38.   Henry Adams, *The Education of Henry Adams* (1918; Sentry ed., Boston, 1961), 451.

39.   Adams, *Education,* 381.

40.   Emily Dickinson, *Selected Poems & Letters* (Anchor ed., Garden City, New York, 1959), 92.

Catalogue

❧

Biographies

John Lamb   Stephen Edidin

Deborah Chotner

❧

Entries

Stephen Edidin

THE CATALOGUE CONSISTS of artists' biographies and individual entries on each work in the collection. These are arranged alphabetically by artist, with entries placed chronologically within each artist's career. Each catalogue entry has a reference photograph of the object, accompanied by a figure number which refers to the larger illustration in the essay discussion. In the provenance listings, brackets indicate the work was with a commercial dealer. In all measurements height precedes width.

In addition to those mentioned in the Preface, the National Gallery wishes to express its great appreciation to the following individuals who contributed helpful information to the catalogue: Helen Cooper, Stuart P. Feld, Linda Ferber, Jack Gyer, Anthony F. Janson, Joan B. Morgan, M. P. Naud, Michael Quick, Millard F. Rogers, Jr., Robert C. Vose, Jr., H. Barbara Weinberg, Ila Weiss, Richard N. Wright, and Richard P. Wunder.

Fig. 7   Lane, *Boston Harbor: Sunset* (detail)

Albert Bierstadt (1830–1902)

Born in Solingen, Germany (near Düsseldorf) in 1830, Albert Bierstadt was brought to New Bedford, Massachusetts, by his parents at age two. In 1853 he returned to Europe, studying for three years in the Düsseldorf studio of the American painter Worthington Whittredge (q.v.) and taking summer sketching tours in the German countryside. During the fourth year of his European training he worked in Italy with Whittredge and Sanford R. Gifford (q.v.) before returning to New Bedford in August 1857. Twenty months later, Bierstadt headed west with an army exploring expedition, sent to find a route through the Rocky Mountains to the West Coast. Leaving the expedition at mid-journey, he spent the summer of 1859 sketching in the Wind River Mountains of Wyoming. Upon his return east, he began painting a series of large canvases in which he sought to portray the grandeur of the American West. These paintings quickly established Bierstadt's reputation.

In 1867 he was awarded the French Legion of Honor. Social prominence accompanied his artistic success. During the 1860s and seventies, Bierstadt made several extended tours of Europe, spending as much as two years at a time there. He also traveled to California in 1863 (when he visited the Yosemite Valley), again in 1871 (for a period of two years), and in 1880. In the mid-1870s, however, Bierstadt had begun to experience a gradual loss in popularity, and in 1895 he was forced to declare bankruptcy. He died in New York in 1902.

Albert Bierstadt
Yosemite Valley
1866, Oil on canvas
38 x 60 in. (96.5 x 152.4 cm.)
Signed (lower right): *ABierstadt / 66*. (AB in monogram)
(fig. 26)

PROVENANCE
James M. Cowan, Aurora, Ill.
Mrs. Minnie C. Havron, Nashville, 1930 (by inheritance, sister)
Roger A. Watkins, Aurora, Ill., 1944
Aurora College, Aurora, Ill., 1944
[Hirschl & Adler Galleries, New York, 1976]
Jo Ann and Julian Ganz, Jr., 1977

EXHIBITED
The Old Second National Bank, Aurora, Ill., *Public Exhibition of Yosemite Valley*, July 6–10, 1976 (broadside).
Hirschl & Adler Galleries, New York, *The American Experience*, October 27–November 27, 1976, no. 35 (illus.), n.p.
————, *A Gallery Collects*, October 19–November 19, 1977, no. 30 (illus.), n.p.

BIBLIOGRAPHY
In Memory of Roger A. Watkins, Aurora, Ill.: Aurora College, 1978, n.p. (illus.).

This view of Yosemite Valley is taken from the north bank of the Merced River in the west end of the valley. In the middle distance are Sentinel Rock on the right, Royal Arches, Washington Column, and North Dome partially obscured.

Bierstadt took certain liberties with the setting: what is probably Cloud's Rest in the center background is not located there in reality, and the two foreground trees are not the indigenous black oaks, but rather valley oaks.[1] The work was painted from sketches made by Bierstadt on his first visit to Yosemite Valley in August and September of 1863. The view was one of a series of Yosemite scenes painted in 1866 after the successful showing of *Looking Down Yo Semite Valley, Cal.* (c. 1865, approx. 8 x 11 feet, location unknown) at the 1865 Annual Exhibition of the National Academy of Design. *Looking Down Yo Semite Valley* was in the possession of the Crosby Opera House Association of Chicago in 1866, passing to the private collection of Uranus H. Crosby in 1867. It was exhibited by his descendants at the Art Institute of Chicago's Second Annual Exhibition in 1884, and again at the opening of the Institute's new art museum in 1887, a year before James M. Cowan moved to Chicago. It may, therefore, have acted as an inducement for Mr. Cowan's purchase of *Yosemite Valley*, as the latter work was intended for the Art Institute of Aurora, Illinois, which, due to lack of funds, never progressed beyond the planning stage.[2]

1. Information supplied by Jack Gyer, curator, Yosemite National Park Museum, Yosemite National Park, California.
2. For a discussion of the Cowan Collection see Lee Minton and A. Everette James, "The James M. Cowan Collection of American paintings in the Parthenon, Nashville, Tennessee," *The Magazine Antiques*, 118 (November, 1980): 988–997.

Albert Bierstadt

Butterfly
December 16, 1890, Oil and pencil on paper
5¹³⁄₁₆ x 7⅞ in. (14.76 x 20 cm.), sight
Signed (lower right): *Albert Bierstadt / Dec 16 / 90*
(fig. 92)

PROVENANCE
[Terry DeLapp, Los Angeles, 1974]
Jo Ann and Julian Ganz, Jr., 1974

Bierstadt's butterflies were made as souvenirs for lady visitors to his New York studio, although the date of this particular example suggests that it might have served as a Christmas gift. A visitor in May 1892 described Bierstadt's method of creating these butterflies:

. . . he took out a palette, a knife and some large slips of cartridge paper. Two or three daubs of pigment on the paper, a quick fold, and holding it still folded against a pane of glass, he made two or three strokes on that wizard-like palette knife on the outside, and hey, presto! a wonderful Brazillian [*sic*] butterfly or moth, even the veining on the wings complete! A pencil touch added to the antennae, the artist's autograph was added to the corner, and now each of us own [*sic*] a painting by Bierstadt.[1]

1. *The Detroit Free Press*, May 15, 1892, quoted in Gordon Hendricks, *Albert Bierstadt, Painter of the American West* (New York: Harry N. Abrams, Inc., 1974), 302–303; and in Carol L. Troyen, *A Private Eye: Fifty Nineteenth-Century American Paintings, Drawings, & Watercolors from the Stebbins Collection* (Huntington, New York: The Heckscher Museum, 1977), 18.

Alfred Thompson Bricher (1837–1908)

Born in Portsmouth, New Hampshire, in 1837, Alfred Thompson Bricher was largely a self-taught artist. He established a studio in Newburyport, Massachusetts, in 1858 and one in Boston the following year, painting New England and Hudson River Valley landscapes. Moving to New York following his marriage in 1868, Bricher started to paint in watercolor as well as in oil. Beginning in the 1870s, he exhibited with the National Academy of Design, the Artists' Fund Society, the Brooklyn Art Association, and the American Society of Painters in Water Colors, to whose board he was elected in 1874. Marine subjects—especially coastal scenes—began to play an increasingly significant role in his work, and Bricher made periodic sketching trips to New Brunswick and Nova Scotia, as well as to the offshore islands of Maine and the shorelines of New Jersey, Rhode Island, Massachusetts, and Long Island.

Bricher's paintings caught the attention of Springfield, Massachusetts art collector George Walter Vincent Smith who eventually owned fifteen of his works. Alfred Bricher exhibited regularly and continued painting up to his death in 1908 at his home on Staten Island.

Alfred Thompson Bricher

Beach at Little Boar's Head, New Hampshire
1870s, Watercolor and gouache on paper
10⅞ x 21¾ in. (27.6 x 55.3 cm.), sight
Signed (lower left): *ATBricher.* (ATB in monogram)
(fig. 11)

PROVENANCE
Mr. and Mrs. Cecil A. Comfort, Kensington, N. H.

[Sotheby Parke Bernet, Inc., New York (*American 18th, 19th & 20th Century Paintings, Drawings, Watercolors & Sculpture*, Sale No. 3865, Lot No. 49) April 29, 1976; Hirschl & Adler Galleries, New York, as agent]
Jo Ann and Julian Ganz, Jr., 1976

Although Bricher usually dated his works in the 1870s,[1] this undated work bears a very close relationship to a sketch done at Narragansett, Rhode Island, on June 27, 1871 (*Bricher Sketch Books*, Archives of American Art, roll no. 911, frame no. 962) and may be related to it.

1. See Jeffrey R. Brown, *Alfred Thompson Bricher 1837–1908* (Indianapolis: Indianapolis Museum of Art, 1973), 29.

Alfred Thompson Bricher

Indian Rock, Narragansett Bay
1871, Oil on canvas
27 x 50⅛ in. (68.6 x 127.3 cm.)
Signed (lower left): *A.T.Bricher. 1871*
Inscribed (on back of canvas in paint, now obscured): *Indian Rock / A. T. Bricher 1871 / Indian Rock / Narragansett Pier / RI*
(fig. 12)

PROVENANCE
[Vose and Gillespie, Providence, R. I., c. 1871 (see below)]
[Richard Mills, Exeter, N. H., 1967]
[Vose Galleries of Boston, Mass., 1967]
Private Collection, 1967
[Hirschl & Adler Galleries, New York, 1981]
Jo Ann and Julian Ganz, Jr., 1981

EXHIBITED
The Metropolitan Museum of Art, New York, *19th-Century America, Paintings and Sculpture: An Exhibition in Celebration of the Hundredth Anniversary of The Metropolitan Museum of Art,*

April 16–September 7, 1970, no. 153 (illus.), n.p.

Indianapolis Museum of Art, Indianapolis, *Alfred Thompson Bricher 1837–1908*, September 12–October 28, 1973; George Walter Vincent Smith Art Museum, Springfield, Mass., November 25, 1973–January 13, 1974, no. 28, pp. 19, 53 (illus.).

The Museum of Modern Art, New York, *The Natural Paradise: Painting in America 1800–1950*, October 1–November 30, 1976, pp. 10, 152 (illus.).

BIBLIOGRAPHY

John Wilmerding, *A History of American Marine Painting* (Salem, Mass.: The Peabody Museum; Boston: Little, Brown and Company, 1968), 77, 202 (fig. 137), 203.

Jeffrey R. Brown, "Alfred Thompson Bricher," *American Art Review*, 1 (January–February, 1974): 70 (illus.), 71.

A label originally attached to the stretcher indicated that the picture passed through the firm of Vose and Huxford, Providence, Rhode Island. Since this firm was extant from c.1862 to 1867, when it was superceded in c.1868 by the short-lived firm of Vose and Gillespie, it is probable that Vose and Huxford labels were used after 1867 and that the picture entered the gallery shortly after it was completed.[1] The work was based upon sketches made in June and July, 1871 (*Bricher Sketch Books*, May–July, 1871, Archives of American Art, roll no. 911). A sketch of the opposite side of Indian Rock is inscribed "Twilight (and) The color of water and wet / Beach just the same— / The water advancing in Bluish lines" (roll no. 911, frame no. 968). A sketch of one standing and two sitting young girls with featureless faces, inscribed "Miss Helen Calder—Miss Anna Boynton" and "Narragansett Pier July 4th 1871" was the basis for the depiction of the two girls in the painting (roll no. 911, frame no. 971, reproduced in Indianapolis, *Bricher* p. 52). The seated woman and child in the foreground and the couple in the left middle distance also appear in *Morning at Narragansett—The Turn of the Tide* (1871, oil on canvas, 20½ x 41 in., Mr. and Mrs. Walter H.

Rubin Collection, reproduced in Indianapolis, *Bricher*, p. 52).

1. Information supplied by Robert C. Vose, Jr., Vose Galleries of Boston.

Alfred Thompson Bricher

On the Meadows of Old Newburyport
1873, Watercolor and gouache on paper
12½ x 25½ in. (31.8 x 64.8 cm.), sight
Signed (lower left): *A T Bricher. 1873*
(fig. 10)

PROVENANCE
John F. Norton, Pueblo, Colo.
[Hirschl & Adler Galleries, New York, 1969]
Jo Ann and Julian Ganz, Jr., 1969

EXHIBITED
Sixth Annual Exhibition of the American Society of Painters in Water Colors, included in the *Sixth Winter Exhibition, National Academy of Design*, New York, 1873, no. 85, p. 12.

Brooklyn Art Association, Brooklyn, New York, *Spring Exhibition*, March 18–22, 1873, no. 174, p. 15.

Santa Barbara Museum of Art, Santa Barbara, California, *American Paintings, Watercolors and Drawings from the Collection of Jo Ann and Julian Ganz, Jr.*, June 23–July 22, 1973, no. 9, n.p.

Indianapolis Museum of Art, Indianapolis, *Alfred Thompson Bricher 1837–1908*, September 12–October 28, 1973; George Walter Vincent Smith Art Museum, Springfield, Mass., November 25, 1973–January 13, 1974, no. 32 (illus.), pp. 17–18, 56.

BIBLIOGRAPHY
The New York Times, vol. 22, February 4, 1873, p. 5, col. 2. "The last [Bricher] has a very notable work in the north room [of the National Academy of Design] (No. 85) 'On the Meadows of Old Newburyport,' which is an advance on any of his previous efforts. It is certainly a little hard and metallic, but a picture which will bear inspection."

The marshy area depicted is actually outside of Newburyport proper, which had no marshes. Like Martin Johnson Heade, Bricher used the words "marshes" and "meadows" interchangeably when referring to this area.[1]

1. See Theodore E. Stebbins, *The Life and Works of Martin Johnson Heade* (New Haven and London: Yale University Press, 1975), 52.

 John George Brown (1831–1913)

Born in Durham, England, John George Brown emigrated to the United States in 1853 at the age of twenty-two. He worked briefly making sketches for stained glass and studied with portraitist Thomas Seir Cummings. In 1855 he established a painting studio in Brooklyn, and in 1860 Brown took a studio in the 10th Street Studio Building in New York. In 1863 he was elected an academician of the National Academy of Design, later serving as its vice president. He also was one of the original members of the American Water Color Society and its president from 1887 to 1904. He was appointed chairman of the National Art Committee and a member of the jury of award for the 1893 Columbian Exposition in Chicago.

During the 1860s and seventies, Brown's work reached new creative levels with his rural genre scenes, such as the 1872 *Children at the Gate*. With these and his portraits and well-known images of poor city children, Brown became one of the most successful artists of his time. His patrons included John Jacob Astor III and William H. Vanderbilt, and he exhibited his work in Europe as well as in the United States. He died in New York City in 1913 at the age of eighty-two.

John George Brown
The Fur Muff
1864, Oil on canvas
15 x 9½ in. (38.2 x 24.1 cm.)
Signed (lower left): *J. G. Brown / 1864*
(fig. 99)

PROVENANCE
[Christie, Manson & Woods International, Inc.,
  New York (*American Paintings, Drawings, and
  Sculpture of the 18th, 19th and 20th Centuries,*
  Sale "JOY-5049," Lot no. 42, p. 39 (illus.),
  April 24, 1981; Hirschl & Adler Galleries, New
  York, as agent]
Jo Ann and Julian Ganz, Jr., 1981

John George Brown
John Jacob Astor III
c. 1860, Oil on canvas
6½ x 5 in. (16.51 x 12.7 cm.), oval
Signed (lower right): *J. G. Brown*
(fig. 43)

PROVENANCE
[Schweitzer Gallery, New York]
Jo Ann and Julian Ganz, Jr., 1972

EXHIBITED
Santa Barbara Museum of Art, Santa Barbara,
  Calif., *American Paintings, Watercolors and
  Drawings from the Collection of Jo Ann and Julian
  Ganz, Jr.,* June 23–July 22, 1973, no. 12 (illus.),
  as *John Jacob Astor II,* n.p.

John Jacob Astor III (1822–1896) was the son of
William Backhouse Astor and Margaret Arm-
strong Astor and a patron of Brown. The artist
also painted *John Jacob Astor in Hunting Costume*
(1864, oil on canvas, 16 x 12 in., with Kennedy
Galleries, New York, 1975) which, itself, was
a study for *Claiming the Shot—A Group of Portraits
after the Hunt in the Adirondacks* (1865, oil on
canvas, 32 x 50 in., Detroit Institute of Arts),
exhibited as no. 435 at the Fortieth Annual Exhibition of the National Academy of Design in
1865. The portraits are all from the same period,
although Astor's beard is shorter in the Ganzes'
oval portrait than in the other two versions.

John George Brown
Resting in the Woods (Girl under a Tree)
1866, Oil on canvas
18⅜ x 12⅛ in. (46.67 x 30.8 cm.)
Signed (lower right): *J. G. Brown / 1866*
Imprinted (on back): *GOUPIL(S) / 772 / BROAD-
WAY* (words in a circle around number)
(fig. 44)

PROVENANCE
Hermann Warner Williams, Washington, D.C.,
  late 1930s
[George P. Guerry, New York]
Mr. and Mrs. Ferdinand H. Davis, New York
Lee B. Anderson, New York
[Robert Mann, Miami, Fla.]

[Hirschl & Adler Galleries, New York, 1973]
Jo Ann and Julian Ganz, Jr., 1973

EXHIBITED (as *Girl under a Tree*)
M. Knoedler and Co., Hirschl & Adler Galleries,
  Paul Rosenberg and Co., New York, *The
  American Vision, Paintings 1825–1875,* October
  8–November 2, 1968, no. 65 (illus.), n.p.
Museum of Fine Arts, St. Petersburg, Fla., *The
  Good Life, An Exhibition of American Genre Paint-
  ing,* September 28–October 24, 1971; Loch
  Haven Art Center, Orlando, Fla., November
  3–28, 1971, no. 6 (illus.), p. 40.

Whitney Museum of American Art, New York,
  *18th and 19th Century Paintings from Private
  Collections,* June 27–September 11, 1972, no.
  7, n.p.
Santa Barbara Museum of Art, Santa Barbara,
  Calif., *American Paintings, Watercolors and
  Drawings from the Collection of Jo Ann and Julian
  Ganz, Jr.,* June 23–July 22, 1973, no. 12 (illus.),
  n.p.
Meredith Long & Company, Houston, Texas,
  *Tradition and Innovation, American Paintings
  1860–1970,* January 10–25, 1974, no. 3 (illus.),
  p. 15.
National Academy of Design, New York, *A Cen-
  tury and a Half of American Art,* October
  10–November 16, 1975, pp. 37–38 (illus.).

BIBLIOGRAPHY (recorded as *Girl under a Tree*)
Donelson Hoopes, "The Jo Ann and Julian Ganz, Jr. Collection," *American Art Review*, 1 (September–October, 1973): 52 (illus.).
The Art Gallery "Scene" (January, 1974): 25 (illus.)

This work was probably exhibited as No. 563, *Resting in the Woods,* at the Forty-Second Annual Exhibition of the National Academy of Design in 1867. *Resting in the Woods* was noted for its "expressive merit" in Henry T. Tuckerman, *Book of the Artists: American Artist Life* (New York: G. P. Putnam & Son; London: Sampson Low & Co., 1867), 487. The model for this work may have been Brown's sister-in-law, Emma, who was twenty-seven at the time of the June 1880 census and who became his second wife in 1871.

John George Brown
Among the Trees
mid-1870s, Oil on canvas
23½ x 15 in. (59.69 x 38.1 cm.)
Signed (lower left): *J.G. Brown N.A.*
(fig. 45)

PROVENANCE
Estate of Ethel Ratnoff Mayorga-Rivas
[Sotheby Parke Bernet, New York (Sale No. 4435M, *American 18th Century, 19th Century & Western Paintings, Drawings, Watercolors & Sculpture,* Lot No. 143, illus.), October 17, 1980]
[Hirschl & Adler Galleries, New York, 1980]
Jo Ann and Julian Ganz, Jr., 1980

The work is dated on the basis of costume.

John George Brown
Children at the Gate
1872, Oil on canvas
18⅛ x 14⅛ in. (46.04 x 35.88 cm.)
Signed (lower left): *J. G. Brown / 1872*
(fig. 46)

PROVENANCE
[Sloan and Roman, Inc., New York, 1969]
Jo Ann and Julian Ganz, Jr., 1969

EXHIBITED
Los Angeles County Museum of Art, *Chosen Works of American Art 1850–1924 from the Collection of Jo Ann and Julian Ganz, Jr.,* October 1–November 16, 1969, no. 10 (illus.), n.p.
Santa Barbara Museum of Art, Santa Barbara, Calif., *American Paintings, Watercolors and Drawings from the Collection of Jo Ann and Julian Ganz, Jr.,* June 23–July 22, 1973, no. 14 (illus.), n.p.

BIBLIOGRAPHY
Henry J. Seldis, "Accent on American: Ganz Collection at Museum," *Los Angeles Times,* October 6, 1969, part 4, p. 10.
Santa Barbara Museum of Art, Santa Barbara, Calif., *Bulletin* (June, 1973): n.p. (illus.).
Linda S. Ferber, "Ripe for Revival: Forgotten American Artists," *Art News,* 79 (December, 1980): 3 (illus.), 71 (illus.), 72.

Although the country boy is unidentified, the city girl may be Brown's eldest child, Charlotte, who is depicted with the same earrings at the age of fourteen in *Portrait of Lottie Brown* (1874, pencil on paper, Collection of Mr. and Mrs. George J. Arden, New York).[1] The picture may have been exhibited as No. 348, *Touch Him Again If You Dare,* at the Forty-Seventh Annual Exhibition of the National Academy of Design in 1872.

1. Incorrectly dated as 1871 in *John George Brown 1831–1913: A Reappraisal,* The Robert Hull Fleming Museum, The University of Vermont, Burlington, April 14–May 10, 1975, no. 7 (illus.), n.p. Although the downward strokes of the last numeral are disconnected in the reproduction, they appear to form a 4. As the work is inscribed, "Lottie Brown / Age 14 years" and dated "Dec. 4th 187(4)," this must be the case, for Lottie Brown was nineteen years old in June, 1880, according to the census of that year.

John George Brown
Picnic Party in the Woods (Waiting for a Partner)
1872, Oil on canvas
24 x 44 in. (60.96 x 111.76 cm.)
Signed (lower left): *J. G. Brown. / N.Y. 1872.*
(fig. 47)

PROVENANCE
Mr. and Mrs. Henry H. Baxter, New York, 1870s?
Hugh H. Baxter, New Rochelle, N.Y. (by inheritance, son)
Mrs. Hugh H. Baxter, New Rochelle, N.Y. (by inheritance)
[Plaza Art Galleries, New York (*Auction Sale On the Premises of Knoll House, the Estate of the late Mrs. Hugh H. Baxter, Premium Point, New Rochelle,* Public Sale No. 3520, Lot No. 479), October 5–6, 1954] as *Sunday Picnic*
[Williams Antique Shop, Old Greenwich, Conn., 1954]
[Herbert Roman, New York]
[Max Saffron, New York]

[Graham Gallery, New York]
Alan Funt, Croton-Harmon, N.Y.
[Coe-Kerr Gallery, Inc., New York, 1972]
Jo Ann and Julian Ganz, Jr., 1972

EXHIBITED (as *Waiting for a Partner*)
Santa Barbara Museum of Art, Santa Barbara, Calif., *American Paintings, Watercolors and Drawings from the Collection of Jo Ann and Julian Ganz, Jr.*, June 23–July 22, 1973, no. 15 (illus.), n.p.
Los Angeles County Museum of Art, *American Paintings from Los Angeles Collections*, May 7–June 30, 1974, n.p.
———, *American Narrative Painting*, October 1–November 17, 1974, no. 66 (illus.), pp. 20, 140–141.
William Rockhill Nelson Gallery, Kansas City, Mo., *Kaleidoscope of American Painting, Eighteenth and Nineteenth Centuries*, December 2, 1977–January 22, 1978, no. 72 (illus.), p. 60.

BIBLIOGRAPHY (recorded as *Waiting for a Partner*)
Henry J. Seldis, "Collecting an Adventure for Jo Ann and Julian Ganz," *Los Angeles Times*, July 8, 1973, p. 63.
Donelson F. Hoopes, "The Jo Ann and Julian Ganz, Jr. Collection," *American Art Review*, 1 (September–October, 1973): 53, 57–58 (illus.).
Henry J. Seldis, "Palette of the American Experience," *Calendar, Los Angeles Times*, June 2, 1974, p. 64.
Donelson F. Hoopes, "American Narrative Painting," *The Magazine Antiques*, 106 (November, 1974): 819, 824 (illus.).

This is probably the same work exhibited as *Picnic Party in the Woods* at Rufus Ellis Moore's Art Rooms in 1874 (*Notes On What Is Art and Catalogue of American Paintings On View And For Sale*, Moore's Art Rooms, Union Square, New York, copyright 1874, p. 22). Moore also placed the work on sale as no. 361 *Picnic Party* at the Spring Exhibition of the Brooklyn Art Association, Brooklyn, N.Y., April 27–May 9, 1874. The family group on the right, although unidentified, may allude to Brown, his second wife Emma, and their first child and the artist's first son, Arthur G. Brown, who was seven years old in June, 1880, when the census was taken.

William Mason Brown (1828–1898)

William Mason Brown was born in Troy, New York, and was active as a landscape painter in Newark, New Jersey, between 1850 and 1858. That year he moved to Brooklyn, where he lived until his death. By 1865 Brown had switched from romantic landscapes to sharply defined still lifes. He achieved a great deal of success as a still-life artist and was principally known for his paintings of fruit, such as *Bounties of Nature*. Brown exhibited his work annually at the National Academy of Design from 1859 to 1891 and at the Brooklyn Art Association from 1865 to 1886. A series of his paintings was reproduced, for popular consumption, by the chromolithograph process, including a painting of apples which was published by the lithographic firm of Currier and Ives in 1868. He died in Brooklyn in 1898.

William Mason Brown
The Bounties of Nature
c. 1867, Oil on canvas
15 x 24½ in. (38.1 x 62.23 cm.)
Signed (lower left): *WMBrown.*
Printed (on piece of paper attached to lower edge of painting):
Entered according to Act of Congress, in the year 1867, by Wm. M. Brown, in the Clerk's Office of the District Court of the United States for the Southern District of New York

Label (under glassine on top of the stretcher on the back, partially torn off on the right-hand side):
(top left corner): illegible Goupil imprint with "BROADWAY" only word visible, followed by illegible script

(second and third lines of label in brown script):
W.M. Brown of . . . / bought of Goupil
(fig. 79)

PROVENANCE
Private Collection, New York
[Hirschl & Adler Galleries, New York, 1975]
Jo Ann and Julian Ganz, Jr., 1975

It is not known whether a chromolithograph of *The Bounties of Nature* was made. However, there may have been more than one version of the painting, as it is closely related to the chromolithograph *Autumn Fruits* (1868, printed by Fabronius, Gurney and Son, New York; Prints and Photographs Division, Library of Congress, Washington, D.C.) by Dominique C. Fabronius after a painting by Brown.[1]

1. Peter C. Marzio, *The Democratic Art: Pictures for a 19th-Century America* (Boston: David R. Godine, Publisher, 1979), 44, 293, plate 34.

George de Forest Brush (1855–1941)

George de Forest Brush was born in Shelbyville, Tennessee, in 1855 and spent his youth in Connecticut. Encouraged by his mother, an amateur portraitist, Brush enrolled at the National Academy of Design in 1871. In 1874 he traveled to Paris where he worked for nearly six years with Jean-Léon Gérôme at the Ecole des Beaux-Arts. On his return to America in 1880, Brush was elected to the Society of American Artists. Through the 1880s he painted the Indians of the western frontier and Florida.

He taught at the Art Students League and exhibited widely, winning many prizes. He was elected an associate of the National Academy in 1888, won the academy's Hallgarten prize that year, and became an academician in 1901. He also was a charter member of the National Institute of Arts and Letters. Brush married in 1886 and returned to Europe in 1889, beginning a series of mother and child paintings that would serve as his primary theme for the remainder of his career. From 1892 to 1898 he was in New York but then began spending part of nearly every year (until the outbreak of World

War I) in Florence, where Italian Renaissance art influenced his style and subject matter. From 1901 until 1937 he worked mainly on his farm in Dublin, New Hampshire. He died in Hanover, New Hampshire, in 1941.

George de Forest Brush
The Indian Hunter
1890, Oil on wood panel
13 x 9⅜ in. (33.02 x 23.81 cm.)
Signed (lower right): *Geo. De.F. Brush/.1890*
(fig. 69)

PROVENANCE
William T. Evans, New York
[American Art Galleries, New York (*American Paintings Belonging to William T. Evans*, Lot. No. 210), January 31, February 1 and 2, 1900]
George G. Heye, New York
[Plaza Art Galleries, Inc., New York (*Important Diamond and Gold Jewelry, Furniture and Decorations, Bronzes, Oil Paintings From the Estates of Grace M. Ranny, Rebecca Neumann, George G. Heye, and from others*, Public Sale No. 4257, Lot. No. 106), June 13, 1957]
[Hirschl & Adler Galleries, New York, 1957, co-owned with M. Knoedler & Co., New York]
Private Collection, 1971
[Hirschl & Adler Galleries, New York, 1978]
Jo Ann and Julian Ganz, Jr., 1978

EXHIBITED
M. Knoedler & Co., New York, *The American Indian Observed*, November 30–December 31, 1971, no. 21, p. 19 (illus.).

BIBLIOGRAPHY
Mina C. Smith, "George de Forest Brush," *The International Studio*, 34 (April, 1908): 54 (illus.), with George G. Heye Collection.
Lula Merrick, "Brush's Indian Pictures," *The International Studio*, 76 (December, 1922): 190 (illus.) with George G. Heye Collection.

The work may depict a Florida Indian since the same Indian is depicted in *The Indian and the Lily* (private collection) which is signed and dated, "Geo. De F. Brush / Florida 1887." (A replica of this latter work, location unknown, is signed and dated, "Geo de Forest Brush 1930.") Brush is known to have met with several Indian tribes including the Seminoles while in Florida. However, the moccasins are problematic and may be adaptations of Plains Indian moccasins.[1]

1. Information supplied by Joan B. Morgan, Rochester, New York.

George de Forest Brush
Orpheus
1890, Oil on wood panel
12 x 20 in. (30.48 x 50.80 cm.)
Signed (upper left): *Geo.de.F. Brush 1890*
(fig. 68)

PROVENANCE
Paul Rich, Marlow, England
[Tillou Gallery, Litchfield, Conn.]
Theodore E. Stebbins, Jr., Branford, Conn., 1972
Jo Ann and Julian Ganz, Jr., 1980

EXHIBITED
Sixty-Fifth Annual Exhibition of the National Academy of Design, 1890, no. 659, submitted in competition for the Thomas B. Clarke Prize.
The Heckscher Museum, Huntington, New York, *A Private Eye: Fifty Nineteenth Century American Paintings, Drawings & Watercolors from the Stebbins Collection*, September 30, 1977–November 6, 1977; The George Walter Vincent Smith Art Museum, Springfield, Mass., November 22, 1977–January 8, 1978, no. 9 (illus.), pp. 26–27.

Painted in Morocco, but perhaps conceived in the United States, the work depicts Orpheus charming wild hares while playing his lyre.[1] The use of hares may have been inspired by versions of Elihu Vedder's (q.v.) *Marsyas*, but the composition is probably borrowed from Gérôme's *Diogenes* (1860, oil on canvas, Walters Art Gallery, Baltimore). The moment depicted in the Orphic legend is not specific. Orpheus wears the laurel crown, the symbol of victory in contests of poetry and song, but the oak leaves to the left suggest the period after his death, referring either to the trees who shed their leaves in mourning for him or the metamorphosis of the Maenads into oak trees in punishment for Orpheus's murder (see Troyen, *A Private Eye*, 26). *A Celtic Huntress*, also exhibited at the 1890 National Academy Annual Exhibition as No. 495, may have been meant as a thematic pendant to this work.

1. The Clarke Prize was intended for works painted by American citizens in the United States, but the latter part of this rule was not strictly enforced.

Samuel S. Carr (1837–1908)

Born in England, Samuel S. Carr studied drawing at the Royal School of Design, Chester. He emigrated to the United States in 1863 and studied mechanical drawing at the Cooper Union in New York in 1865. After 1870 he lived in Brooklyn where he shared a studio with landscape painter Clinton Loveridge. Carr was active in Brooklyn art circles, exhibiting at the Brooklyn Art Association and the Brooklyn Art Club. He also exhibited at the National Academy of Design in the 1890s.

Carr's naturalistic approach and freshness of color and light are well applied to his scenes of children at play or sheep grazing (popular in the 1890s). However, his most interesting works are those which depict the activities of visitors to the beach (almost certainly Coney Island), painted around 1880.

Samuel S. Carr
The Beach at Coney Island
c. 1879, Oil on canvas
6¼ x 10⅛ in. (15.88 x 25.72 cm.)
Signed (lower left): *S S CARR.*
(fig. 48)

PROVENANCE
The Tucker Family, New York
[Newhouse Galleries, New York, 1979]
Jo Ann and Julian Ganz, Jr., 1979

RELATED BIBLIOGRAPHY
Deborah Chotner, *S. S. Carr (American, 1837–1908)*, Smith College Museum of Art, Northampton, Mass., April 2–May 30, 1976.

In 1879 and 1880 Carr painted a series of Coney Island beach scenes in which the same people were repositioned in the same setting.[1] The works function much as a series of snapshots would and may have been based on photographs, although Carr himself was not known to be a photographer. This particular scene is most closely related to *Beach Scene* (c. 1879, oil on canvas, 12 x 20 in., Smith College Museum of Art) and may have served as a study for it because of the difference in size. The family being photographed is the Tucker family, in whose possession the work descended.

1. Such scenes were popular in this period, and one of A. T. Bricher's (q.v.) few figure paintings, *Baby as King* (1880, oil on canvas, Fine Arts Museums, San Francisco), is similar to Carr's series.

Frederic Edwin Church (1826–1900)

Frederic Edwin Church was born in 1826 in Hartford, Connecticut. He studied for two years with Thomas Cole (q.v.), enjoying the distinction of being Cole's sole pupil. In 1846 he opened a studio in New York and began to exhibit landscapes at the National Academy of Design and the American Art Union. His talent was recognized early, for he became an academy associate at age twenty-two and an academician at twenty-three. Church traveled extensively, visiting the upper Mississippi (1851), Mount Desert Island and the Katadn region in Maine (1850, 1851, and 1852), and Grand Manan Island in Canada (1852). In 1853, inspired by the writings of German naturalist Alexander von Humboldt, he made the first of two trips to South America, from Colombia to Ecuador, and began to paint a series of cosmological landscapes, including *The Cordilleras: Sunrise*. Church was the first major American artist to visit South America, and these paintings, along with his American landscapes such as the 1857 *Niagara*, caused a sensation. In 1859 the crowd coming to see his *Heart of the Andes* (which was exhibited in Church's studio) was so large that two policemen were stationed on the sidewalk.

During the late 1850s and 1860s Church continued to visit exotic locales, including a second visit to Ecuador in 1857, Labrador in 1859, Jamaica in 1865, and Greece, Lebanon, and Syria in 1868. His output slackened, however, in the eighties and nineties, and in the last decades of his life, Church spent most of his time at his Moorish villa, "Olana," above the Hudson River in the Catskills. He died there in 1900.

Frederic Edwin Church
The Cordilleras: Sunrise
1854, Oil on canvas
28½ x 43 in. (72.39 x 109.22 cm.)
Signed (lower center): *F. E. CHURCH / 1854*
(fig. 25)

PROVENANCE
Jonathan Sturges, New York
Mrs. Dudley Parker, Morristown, N. J.
[Robert Weimann, Ansonia, Conn.]
Private Collection, New Hampshire, 1967.

[Hirschl & Adler Galleries, New York, 1977]
Jo Ann and Julian Ganz, Jr., 1977

EXHIBITED
National Academy of Design, New York, *Thirtieth Annual Exhibition of the National Academy of Design 1855*, no. 49, p. 19, Jonathan Sturges Collection, N. Y.

BIBLIOGRAPHY
"Sketchings," *The Crayon*, 1 (March 21, 1855): 186.
"Fine Arts. The National Academy of Design," *The Albion or British, Colonial, and Foreign Weekly Gazette*, 14 (March 24, 1855): 141, cols. 1–2.
"Sketchings: The Academy Exhibition—No. 1," *The Crayon* (March 28, 1855): 203.
"National Academy of Design," *New-York Daily Times*, April 12, 1855, p. 4, col. 4.
R.T., "Exhibition of the National Academy of Design. Third Article," *New-York Daily Tribune*, May 7, 1855, pp. 6 (col. 6) –7 (col. 1).
"Sketchings: Our Private Collections—No. 2," *The Crayon*, 3 (February, 1856): 58, Jonathan Sturges Collection, N.Y.
Henry T. Tuckerman, *Book of the Artists* (New York: G. P. Putnam & Son; London: Sampson Low & Co., 1867), 384 as *Morning on the Cordilleras*, 627 as *Morning in the Cordilleras*, with Jonathan Sturges Collection, N. Y.
George W. Sheldon, *American Painters: With One Hundred and Four Examples of Their Work Engraved on Wood*, enlarged edition (New York: D. Appleton and Company, 1881), 12, as *The Great Mountain-Chain of New Granada*?

George Templeton Strong, *The Diary of George Templeton Strong*, Alan Nevins and Milton Halsey Thomas, eds., 4 vols. (New York: The Macmillan Company, 1952), vol. 2, *The Turbulent Fifties 1850–1859*, 215–216.

David C. Huntington, "Frederic Edwin Church, 1826–1900, Painter of the Adamic New World Myth" (Ph.D. diss., Yale University, 1960), 45, 47.

———, "Landscape and Diaries: The South American Trips of F. E. Church," *The Brooklyn Museum Annual*, 5 (1963–1964): 84–85, diary entry for August 21?–August 30, 1853.

———, *The Landscapes of Frederic Edwin Church: Vision of an American Era* (New York: George Braziller, Inc., 1966), 43, with Mrs. Dudley Parker, Morristown, N.J.

National Collection of Fine Arts, Washington, D. C., *Frederic Edwin Church: An Exhibition Organized by the National Collection of Fine Arts* (Washington, D. C.: Smithsonian Institution, 1966), 30–31, with Mrs. Dudley Parker, Morristown, N.J.

National Academy of Design, New York, *Next to Nature: Landscape Paintings from the National Academy of Design* (New York: National Academy of Design, 1980), 108.

The work evolved from sketches made on August 26, 1853. Church began a diary on August 24 of that year and, on the 25th he noted that he and Cyrus Field crossed "the river which separates New Granada from Equador [*sic*]." One of the highlights of the 1853 trip occurred on his second day in Ecuador:

After a disagreeable journey across an elevated plain with a cold piercing wind and a sprinkling of rain we finally came to the edge of an eminence which overlooked the valley of Chota. And a view of such unparalleled magnificence presented itself that I must pronounce it one of the great wonders of Nature. I made a couple of feeble sketches this evening in recollection of the scene. My ideal of the Cordilleras is realized.[1]

1. Huntington, "Landscape and Diaries," *Brooklyn Museum Annual*, 84–85.

 ## Thomas Cole (1801–1848)

One of the founders of the Hudson River School of landscape painting, Thomas Cole was born in England in 1801. He came to the United States with his family at the age of nineteen, having been trained as an engraver. With the encouragement of an artist named Stein, Cole decided around 1820 to become a painter. The first years of his career were spent as an itinerant portraitist in Ohio, but in 1823 he went east to Philadelphia, where he studied intermittently at the Pennsylvania Academy of the Fine Arts. By 1825, when he settled in New York, Cole had begun to paint landscapes that caught the attention of the leading artists of the day, notably Asher B. Durand and John Trumbull. With a growing reputation, Cole in 1826 helped to found the National Academy of Design. Beginning in 1829, he traveled abroad, visiting London, Paris, Rome, and Florence. Upon his return to the United States in late 1832, Cole painted landscapes composed from sketches he made on his numerous trips to the Catskills.

Cole was especially impressed with the force of nature manifested by the untamed aspect of the American wilderness. Even his landscapes that depict a recognizable location often have an allegorical or religious aspect to them. In 1834 Cole painted his first series of allegorical paintings, *The Course of Empire*. The great success of these five works encouraged him to undertake another series, *The Voyage of Life*, which was reproduced in engravings and established his popularity throughout the country. Cole considered these allegorical paintings the most serious and important of his works, although he continued to accept commissions for landscapes depicting actual locations in Italy and America and romanticized landscapes such as *The Old Mill at Sunset*. He died in 1848 at Catskill, New York.

Thomas Cole
The Old Mill at Sunset
1844, Oil on canvas
26⅛ x 36 in. (66.36 x 91.44 cm.), oval
Signed (lower center): *T Cole / 1844*.
Inscribed (in pencil, on back, lower center):
Thomas N. Howitt / Canadaegua / 1844
(fig. 1)

PROVENANCE
H. S. Mulligan, commissioned from the artist
Mark Finley
The Brooklyn Museum, 1911, Mark Finley bequest
[Hirschl & Adler Galleries, New York, 1976]
Jo Ann and Julian Ganz, Jr., 1976

EXHIBITED
National Academy of Design, New York, *Twentieth Annual Exhibition of the National Academy of Design 1845*, no. 178, with H. S. Mulligan, p. 16.
Macbeth Gallery, New York, *Paintings of the Hudson River School*, January 25–February 13, 1932, no. 6 (illus.), n.p.
Century Association, New York, *Fifty Years of American Landscape and Genre Painting, 1825–1875*, March 3–31, 1940, no. 9, n.p.
Art Institute of Chicago, *The Hudson River School*, February 15–March 25, 1945; Whitney Museum of American Art, New York, April 17–May 18, 1945, no. 62, p. 118.
Wadsworth Atheneum, Hartford, Conn., *Thomas Cole 1801–1848: One Hundred Years Later, A Loan Exhibition*, November 12, 1948–January 2, 1949; Whitney Museum of American Art, New York, January 8–31, 1949, no. 42, plate 16, pp. 32–33.
Society of the Four Arts, Palm Beach, Fla., *From Plymouth Rock to the Armory*, February 9–March 5, 1950, no. 25, n.p.
Stedelijk Museum, Amsterdam, The Netherlands, *Amerika Schildert*, Catalogue 74, June 16–September 25, 1950, no. 7 (illus.), pp. 2, 6, 38 as *De oude molen bij zonsondergang*.

Vancouver Art Gallery, B.C., *Two Hundred Years of American Painting*, March 8–April 3, 1955, no. 15.

The Brooklyn Museum, Brooklyn, N.Y., *Victoriana, An Exhibition of the Arts of the Victorian Era in America*, April 7–June 5, 1960, no. 186, n.p.

Baltimore Museum of Art, *Thomas Cole, Paintings of an American Romanticist*, January 26–February 28, 1965, no. 23, p. 123.

Hirschl & Adler Galleries, New York, *The American Experience*, October 27–November 27, 1976, no. 24 (illus.), n.p.

BIBLIOGRAPHY

Louis Legrand Noble, *The Course of Empire, Voyage of Life, and Other Pictures of Thomas Cole, N.A., With Selections from His Letters and Miscellaneous Writings: Illustrative of his Life, Character, and Genius* (New York: Cornish, Lamport & Company, 1853), 358–359, 381, as *Mill at Sunset*. Reprinted: Elliot S. Vesell, ed., *The Life and Works of Thomas Cole* (Cambridge, Mass.: The Belknap Press of Harvard University Press, 1964), 268–269, 286, as *Mill at Sunset*.

Royal Cortissoz, "The Hudson River and Barbizon Men," *New York Herald Tribune*, January 31, 1932, section 7, p. 9 (illus.).

———, "The Pioneers in Our Landscape Art," *New York Herald Tribune*, March 10, 1940, section 6, p. 8 (illus.).

"The Genesis of American Landscape," *Bulletin of the Brooklyn Institute of Arts and Sciences*, 41 (October 17, 1936): 54 (illus.).

Margit Varga, "The Rise of American Art," *The Studio*, 125 (April–May, 1943): 113 (illus.).

William Gerdts, "Cole's Painting 'After the Temptation'," *Studies on Thomas Cole, An American Romanticist* (*Annual II*) (Baltimore: The Baltimore Museum of Art, 1967), 103. See also 1965 exhibition checklist reprint, "Thomas Cole, Paintings of an American Romanticist," 123.

John C. Riordan, "Thomas Cole: A Case Study of the Painter-Poet Theory of Art in American Painting from 1825–1850" (Ph.D. diss., Syracuse University, 1970), 568.

Henry H. Glassie, "Thomas Cole and Niagara Falls," *The New-York Historical Society Quarterly*, 58 (April, 1974): 109.

Grace Glueck, "Brooklyn Museum Gets Huge Canvas," *New York Times*, July 6, 1976, p. 27.

Earl A. Powell, III, "Thomas Cole's 'Dream of Arcadia,'" *Arts Magazine*, 52 (November, 1977): 115.

Sketches of the mill and other details of the painting are in the *Thomas Cole Sketch Book—1839–18??*, Princeton University Art Museum, Princeton, New Jersey, nos. 40–85.

 Charles Caryl Coleman (1840–1928)

Charles Caryl Coleman, an expatriate artist, was born in Buffalo, New York, in 1840 and first studied art there under William H. Beard. In 1859, at the age of nineteen, he went to Paris to study with Thomas Couture. He returned to the United States in 1862 to serve in the Civil War but went to Europe again in 1866 with his artist friends William Hunt and Elihu Vedder (q.v.). Coleman remained in Europe for the rest of his life, dividing his time between Capri, where he was Vedder's neighbor, and Rome. Early in his career Coleman had painted portraits and figure paintings, but he later turned to landscapes and architectural pieces. He exhibited with the National Academy of Design (where he became an associate in 1865), the Boston Athenaeum, the Brooklyn Art Association, and galleries in England. Shortly after his death in Capri in 1928, the Brooklyn Museum honored him with a memorial exhibition.

Charles Caryl Coleman
Vintage Time in a Capri Garden
1889, Oil on wood panel
9½ x 16 in. (24.13 x 40.64 cm.)
Signed (lower right): *CCC (in monogram) / Roma / 1889.*
Incised (painted over, lower left end of bench): *CCC (in monogram) / Roma*
(fig. 74)

PROVENANCE
[Park Avenue Gallery, New York]
[Kennedy Galleries, New York, 1966]
Jo Ann and Julian Ganz, Jr., 1978

Because the tambourine suggests a vintage festival, and the fallen grape leaves and jar suggest vintage time, the work is identical in subject matter with *Vintage Time in a Capri Garden*, no. 6 in *Catalogue of an Exhibition of Paintings by Charles Caryl Coleman*, The Buffalo Fine Arts Academy—Albright Art Gallery, February 9–27, 1916, and is probably the same painting. The work is related to no. 64 in the same exhibition, *Capri Terrace with Capri girls, Vesuvius in the Distance*, which was illustrated in "Exhibition of Works by Charles Caryl Coleman at the Albright Art Gallery," *Academy Notes* (Buffalo Fine Arts Academy), 11 (April, 1916): 59.

 John Singleton Copley (1738–1815)

John Singleton Copley, America's leading colonial artist, was born in Boston in 1738. He studied painting and engraving with his stepfather, the artist and teacher Peter Pelham, and by the age of nineteen was a well-established painter of portraits and miniatures. His more than 275 oil and pastel portraits of Boston's elite were admired for their realism, sophistication, and elegance. By 1767, Copley was able to write that he made "as much as if I were a Raphael or Correggio."

In 1766 Copley had sent his *Boy with a Squirrel* to London, where it drew praise from Sir Joshua Reynolds and Benjamin West, who urged Copley to move abroad. Although he was elected a fellow of the Society of Artists of Great Britain and continued to send paintings to London, Copley decided to remain in the colonies. However, in 1774, the economic unrest that preceded the American Revolution, together with the fact that his father-in-law was a prominent Tory, led Copley to leave America. He spent a year studying the Old Masters in Paris and Rome before settling permanently in London. There Copley embraced a style of more complex compositions, ornate settings, and looser brushwork. He began to produce historical and religious paintings as well as portraits and became a member of the Royal Academy in 1776. His paintings of events from modern history, such as *Watson and the Shark* and *Death of the Earl of Chatham,* were among his most notable successes. He died in London in 1815.

John Singleton Copley
Sketch for "The Copley Family"
1776, Oil on canvas en grisaille
15½ x 13½ in. (39.37 x 34.29 cm.), oval
Unsigned
(fig. 28)

PROVENANCE
John Singleton Copley Greene (great-grandson of J. S. Copley)
Miss Mary Amory Greene
Mrs. Henry Copley Greene, Cambridge, Mass.
Mrs. Gordon Sweet, Mount Carmel, Conn. (by inheritance)
[Hirschl & Adler Galleries, New York, 1978]
Jo Ann and Julian Ganz, Jr., 1980

EXHIBITED
Museum of Fine Arts, Boston, *John Singleton Copley 1738–1815, Loan Exhibition of Paintings, Pastels, Miniatures and Drawings,* February 1–March 15, 1938, no. 24, p. 22, as *The Copley Family (Sketch),* Mrs. Henry Copley Greene Collection.
Vassar College, Poughkeepsie, N.Y., *Centennial Loan Exhibition, Drawings & Watercolors from Alumnae and Their Families,* May 19–June 11, 1961; Wildenstein & Co., Inc., New York, June 14–September 9, 1961, no. 68 (illus.), n.p., as *Study of Lord Lyndhurst and Mother (for The Copley Family),* Mrs. Henry Copley Greene Collection.
Hirschl & Adler Galleries, New York, *Recent Acquisitions of American Art 1769–1938,* March 3–31, 1979, frontispiece and no. 3 (illus.), n.p.

ON DEPOSIT
Museum of Fine Arts, Boston, 1894–1932, 1933–1964, 1965–1972.
Yale University Art Gallery, New Haven, Conn., 1972–1978.

BIBLIOGRAPHY
Augustus Thorndike Perkins, *A Sketch of the Life and a List of Some of the Works of John Singleton Copley* (Boston: James R. Osgood & Company, 1873); also (Boston: Privately Printed, 1873), 48 as *Mrs. Copley and her two children.*
Frank W. Bayley, *The Life and Works of John Singleton Copley Founded on the work of Augustus Thorndike Perkins* (Boston: The Taylor Press, 1915), 85, 102, as *Mrs. Copley and her two children,* Miss Mary Amory Greene Collection.
Theodore Bolton and Harry Lorin Binsse, "John Singleton Copley," *The Antiquarian,* 15 (December, 1930): 116, as *Mrs. John Singleton Copley and her son John.*
Jules David Prown, *The Ailsa Mellon Bruce Studies in American Art: John Singleton Copley,* 2 vols., *Volume II: John Singleton Copley: In England 1774–1815* (Cambridge, Mass.: Published for the National Gallery of Art, Washington, D. C., by Harvard University Press, 1966), vii, 262–263, 415, pl. 345 (n.p.), Mrs. Gordon Sweet Collection.

Carol Troyen, *The Boston Tradition: American Paintings from the Museum of Fine Arts, Boston* (New York: American Federation of the Arts, 1980), 66 (under related works for cat. no. 12, *The Copley Family*) as *Head of Mrs. Copley, John Jr., and Susannah.*

John Singleton Copley, Jr. (1772–1863), later Lord Lyndhurst, Lord Chancellor of England, stands to the left of Mrs. Copley, the former Susanna Farnum Clarke (1745–1836) who married Copley in 1769. Miss Mary Copley (1773–1868), Lord Lyndhurst's unmarried sister, stands to the right. This sketch is a study for the right side of *The Copley Family* (1776, oil on canvas, National Gallery of Art, Washington, D. C.). An oil sketch after the finished painting also descended in the Greene family and is now in the Museum of Fine Arts, Boston (*The Copley Family,* grisaille study, 1780s, oil on canvas, 20¾ x 26¼ in.).

Jasper Francis Cropsey (1823–1900)

Jasper Francis Cropsey, known as the "painter of the American autumn," was born on Staten Island in 1823, the grandson of a Dutch immigrant. Apprenticed to an architect, Cropsey took lessons in watercolor in his free time and also began to paint in oil. In 1843, after moving to New York City where he continued his architectural practice, Cropsey exhibited several landscapes at the American Art Union and the National Academy of Design, where he was elected an associate in 1844—one of the youngest associate members in its history. In 1847 Cropsey traveled through England and Scotland and then spent more than a year in Rome, sending his paintings of English and Italian scenes to the United States for exhibition. Following his return to America in late 1849, Cropsey devoted almost all of his time to painting and took a studio in New York where he worked between sketching trips.

In 1856 Cropsey again went to England, staying there until 1863, when he returned to New York. Many of Cropsey's best-known American landscapes, including his *Niagara Falls,* were in fact painted while he was abroad. Cropsey exhibited his landscapes both in England and in the United States and achieved great popularity, particularly with his vibrantly colored scenes of American autumn which amazed his British audiences. Cropsey enjoyed success through the 1870s, but by the 1880s his appeal had begun to decline. Nonetheless, Cropsey continued to exhibit landscapes painted in his traditional manner until his death in 1900 at his home in Hastings-on-Hudson, New York.

Jasper Francis Cropsey
Niagara Falls
1860, Oil on canvas
36 x 25⅜ in. (91.4 x 64.5 cm.), arched top
Signed (lower left): *J. F. Cropsey 1860*
(fig. 2)

PROVENANCE
J. A. H. Bell, May 20, 1862
The Brooklyn Museum, Brooklyn, N.Y., 1898 / 1899[1]
[Hirschl & Adler Galleries, New York, 1976]
Jo Ann and Julian Ganz, Jr., 1976

EXHIBITED
Whitney Museum of American Art, New York, *A Century of American Landscape Painting 1800–1900*, January 19–February 25, 1938, no. 28, p. 27.

Springfield Museum of Fine Arts, Springfield, Mass., *A Century of American Landscape Painting 1800–1900*, March 8–28, 1938, no. 23, p. 27.
Department of Fine Arts, Carnegie Institute, Pittsburgh, Pa., *Century of American Landscape Painting 1800–1900*, March 22–April 30, 1939, no. 5, p. 25.
Art Institute of Chicago, *Hudson River School*, February 15–March 25, 1945; Whitney Museum of American Art, April 17–May 18, 1945, no. 78, p. 118.
Vancouver Art Gallery, B.C., *Two Hundred Years of American Paintings*, March 8–April 3, 1955, no. 18.
The Buffalo Fine Arts Academy—Albright-Knox Art Gallery, Buffalo, N.Y., *Three Centuries of Niagara Falls: Oils, Watercolors, Drawings, Prints*, May 2–September 7, 1964, no. 25, p. 20 (illus.).

BIBLIOGRAPHY
"Art Items," *The New-York Daily Tribune*, January 31, 1861, p. 7, col. 1.
Brooklyn Institute of Arts and Sciences, Brooklyn, N.Y., *Annual Report*, 1898–1899, 261.
C. J. Bulliet, "Chicago Surveys the Hudson River School in Major Exhibition," *The Art Digest*, 19 (March 1, 1945): 5 (illus.).
David C. Huntington, "Frederic Edwin Church, 1826–1900, Painter of the Adamic New World Myth" (Ph.D. diss., Yale University, 1960), 91.
———, *The Landscapes of Frederic Edwin Church: Vision of an American Era* (New York: George Braziller, Inc., 1966), 3–4.
William S. Talbot, "Jasper F. Cropsey 1823–1900" (Ph.D. diss., Institute of Fine Arts, New York University, 1972), no. 129, fig. 122, p. 417–418.
Kynaston McShine, ed., *The Natural Paradise: Painting in America 1800–1950* (New York: Museum of Modern Art, 1976), 98 (illus.).

The figures are situated on Goat Island with Horseshoe Falls and the Canadian side in the background. The *Tribune* noted that because Niagara formed "only a subordinate part of the composition," the work was a "novel view of that very hackneyed subject, Niagara Falls." This suggests that the work may have been painted in reaction to Frederic Edwin Church's

(q.v.) overwhelming view of *Niagara* (1857, oil on canvas, Corcoran Gallery of Art, Washington, D.C.; see Huntington, "Church," 91 and *Landscapes,* 3–4). Cropsey first visited Niagara in 1852, and later in 1855. This work is preceded by two more typically dramatic scenes of Niagara, both entitled *Niagara Falls from the Foot of Goat Island* (1856, c. 10 x 16 in., Mrs. James H. Dempsey, Jr., Cleveland and 1857, 15¼ x 24 in., Museum of Fine Arts, Boston).

1. The assumption based upon ambiguous reports in *The Brooklyn Daily Eagle*, March 14, 1899, p. 6 and the Brooklyn *Daily Standard Union* and *Daily Times* of the same date that the work was not a gift of J. A. Bell to the Museum, is incorrect.

S. S. David (1847–1898)
(pseudonym of De Scott Evans)

Evans was born in Boston, Indiana, the son of Dr. David S. Evans. He attended Miami University, Miami, Ohio, and served as an instructor of music and art at local Ohio colleges between 1872 and 1874, before opening a studio in Cleveland around 1875. In 1877 he studied in Paris with William Adolphe Bouguereau (1825–1905). After his return to Cleveland in 1878, he became an instructor and codirector of the Cleveland Academy of Fine Arts. Evans moved to New York in 1887 and maintained a studio there until 1898 when he was lost at sea on his way to decorate a ceiling in Paris. A frequent exhibitor at the National Academy of Design, Evans developed a reputation primarily for his depictions of upper-middle class young women. His still-life career was probably incidental to his genre career, beginning only after his move to New York and involving the use of pseudonyms in many cases.

ically acclaimed for his deceptively realistic depictions of elegantly textured draperies. In his still lifes Evans kept the sense of deceptive realism, but chose objects—such as rough-hewn wood and broken glass—of a much less elegant nature.

1. See William H. Gerdts and Russell Burke, *American Still-Life Painting* (New York: Praeger Publishers, 1971), 167–168.
2. No Stanley S. David is listed in the *New York City Directories* of the 1880s and 1890s. The peanut paintings are all signed S. S. David.

S. S. David

A New Variety
after 1887, Oil on canvas
12 x 10 in. (30.48 x 25.4 cm.)
Signed (on card, upper right): *A New Variety/ S. S. David-*
(fig. 94)

PROVENANCE
Paul F. Mohr
Lars Branstad, Chicago, Ill. and Oakland, Calif.
Miss Una Lucile Burke, Carmel, Calif. (by inheritance, granddaughter)
[James Maroney, Inc., New York, 1980]
Jo Ann and Julian Ganz, Jr., 1980

Evans painted a closely related series of peanut still lifes (Portland Art Museum, Portland, Ore.; Noah Goldowsky Collection, New York; Dr. and Mrs. Laslo Galdonyi Collection, Detroit, Mich.; Russell Carrell Collection, Salisbury, Conn.; Jack Lowrance Collection, Los Angeles) which, because of this work's title, probably predated *A New Variety*. Another nearly identical almond still life (oil on canvas, c. 12³⁄₁₆ x 10¼ in., Private Collection), containing nineteen almonds and a card in the upper left signed, "Stanley S. David/New York," may have been intended as a pendant.[1] Although christened David Scott, Evans changed his name to De Scott after his return from Paris. The reversal of his Christian name in some of his trompe l'oeil fruit paintings, which were simply signed Scott David, together with its further modification in the nut paintings, may have been intentional.[2] Throughout his career, he was crit-

Joseph Decker (1853–1942)

Born in Würtemburg, Germany, Decker emigrated to the United States in 1867 and took up residence in Brooklyn where he became a house and sign painter. For three years he studied evenings at the National Academy of Design and finished training in Munich, 1878–80, returning to Germany periodically for many years thereafter.

Decker exhibited regularly at the Society of American Artists, the Brooklyn Art Association, and the National Academy of Design throughout the 1880s, gaining the attention of the important American art patron Thomas B. Clarke, for whom he also worked as a porcelain restorer. Perhaps responding to negative criticism of his rather bold colors, crisp style, and unconventional choice of compositions (such as the close-up views of fruit on the bough), Decker turned, in the 1890s, to still lifes of fruit on tabletops, painted in a softer, more atmospheric style. In addition, Decker also did a number of landscapes. These later works appear not to have been exhibited, and Decker probably did little work after the turn of the century. Upon his death in Brooklyn in 1924 his death certificate listed him as "laborer."

Joseph Decker

Their Winter Hoard (The Gluttons)
c. 1889, Oil on canvas
11½ x 17½ in. (29.21 x 44.45 cm.)
Signed (upper left): *J DECKER.*
(fig. 82)

PROVENANCE
[Fifth Avenue Art Galleries (*Catalogue of the Private Collection of Modern Paintings belonging to Mr. Richard Butler of this City, with additions from other sources*, Lot No. 103, *The Gluttons*), March 20–21, 1890][1]
Thomas B. Clarke, New York
[American Art Galleries, New York (*Thomas B. Clarke Sale*, Lot No. 176, *The Gluttons*) February 14–18, 1899]
E. H. Bernheimer
Mr. and Mrs. Ferdinand H. Davis, New York
[Hirschl & Adler Galleries, New York, 1971]
Jo Ann and Julian Ganz, Jr., 1973

EXHIBITED
National Academy of Design, New York, *Sixty-Fourth Annual Exhibition of the National Academy of Design*, 1889, no. 53, as *The Gluttons*, p. 15.
Pennsylvania Academy of the Fine Arts, Philadelphia, *Thomas B. Clarke Collection of American Pictures*, October 15–November 28, 1891, no. 55, as *Their Winter Hoard*.
University Art Museum, Berkeley, Calif., *The Reality of Appearance: The Trompe L'Oeil Tradition in American Painting*, July 15–August 31, 1970; National Gallery of Art, Washington, D.C., March 21–May 3, 1970; Whitney Museum of American Art, New York, May 19–July 5, 1970; California Palace of the Legion of Honor, San Francisco, July 15–August 31, 1970; The Detroit Institute of Arts, September 15–October 31, 1970, no. 91, pp. 138–139 (illus.), as *Their Winter Hoard*.
Hirschl & Adler Galleries, New York, *American Still Lifes of the Nineteenth Century*, December 1–31, 1971, no. 9, p. 10 (illus.), as *Their Winter Hoard*.

Santa Barbara Museum of Art, Santa Barbara, Calif., *American Paintings, Watercolors and Drawings from the Collection of Jo Ann and Julian Ganz, Jr.*, June 23–July 22, 1973, no. 25 (illus.), n.p., as *Their Winter Hoard*.

BIBLIOGRAPHY

H. Barbara Weinberg, "Thomas B. Clarke: Foremost Patron of American Art from 1872 to 1899," *The American Art Journal*, 8 (May, 1976): 73.

Helen A. Cooper, "The Rediscovery of Joseph Decker," *The American Art Journal*, 10 (May, 1978): 57n., 67, 69 (illus.).

Decker's pet squirrel, Bonnie, served as the model for this and several other squirrel pictures by the artist (see Cooper, "Rediscovery," 69).

1. The 1890 sale is problematic. It is not known whether the work was owned by Richard Butler, an anonymous owner, or Thomas Clarke, who may have had a number of works in this sale which he bought in.

Thomas Wilmer Dewing (1851–1938)

A native of Boston, Thomas Wilmer Dewing began his artistic studies there at the School of the Museum of Fine Arts. He worked briefly as a lithographer and chalk portraitist and then, from 1876 to 1879, studied at the Académie Julian in Paris under Gustave Boulanger and Jules Lefebvre and in Munich with Frank Duveneck. Upon his return from Europe, he set up a studio in Boston, but in 1881 settled permanently in New York City, where he taught at the Art Students League until 1888. He was elected an associate of the National Academy of Design in 1887 and an academician the following year. He was elected to the Society of American Artists in 1880 and exhibited with that group until 1897. In 1898 Dewing resigned his membership to align himself with a group of Boston and New York artists who called themselves Ten American Painters. While most of The Ten were American impressionists, Dewing's style has been more accurately described as tonalist. His quiet, idealized paintings of beautiful, refined women were greatly appre-

ciated by such noted collectors as Charles L. Freer of Detroit and John Gellatly of New York. Dewing was married to an artist, Maria Oakey (1845–1938), and had an active interest in the theater, especially through his involvement with the Players' Club in New York. Dewing painted little during his last ten years. He died in New York in 1938 at the age of eighty-seven.

Thomas Wilmer Dewing
Woman with Violin
1891, Oil on wood panel
9½ x 7½ in. (24.13 x 19.05 cm.)
Signed (lower left): *T. W. Dewing/91*
(Frame by Stanford White, 1853–1906)
(fig. 65)

PROVENANCE
William Cheney, Hartford, Conn.
Frank Platt (by inheritance)
Estate of Charles A. Platt
[E. and A. Milch, Inc., New York]
Jo Ann and Julian Ganz, Jr., 1972

EXHIBITED
Santa Barbara Museum of Art, Santa Barbara, Calif., *American Paintings, Watercolors and Drawings from the Collection of Jo Ann and Julian Ganz, Jr.*, June 23–July 22, 1973, no. 26 (illus.), n.p.

 Frederick Dielman (1847–1935)

Born in Hannover, Germany, Dielman emigrated to Baltimore as a child. There he attended Calvert College and after graduation served as a cartographer and draftsman in the U.S. Corps of Engineers. He then went to Munich, where he studied at the Royal Academy with Wilhelm von Diez, before opening a studio in New York in 1876. In 1883 Dielman was elected an academician of the National Academy of Design and from 1889 until 1909 served as its first foreign-born president. Dielman's wide-ranging skills included illustration, figure painting, stained glass, and mural painting, but he is best remembered for his specialization—the designing of large-scale mosaics for public spaces, including the panels *Law* and *History* in the Library of Congress, Washington.

Frederick Dielman
Personification of Peace (Girl with Wreath)
1902, Watercolor and gouache on paper
13¹³⁄₁₆ x 11¹³⁄₁₆ in. (35.4 x 30.0 cm.), sight
Signed (upper right): *Frderick Dielman-./1902*
(fig. 71)

PROVENANCE
[Hirschl & Adler Galleries, New York, 1976]
Jo Ann and Julian Ganz, Jr., 1979

EXHIBITED (as *Girl with Wreath*)
Hirschl & Adler Galleries, New York, *100 American Drawings and Watercolors from 200 Years*, December 4–30, 1976, no. 28, n.p.

Whitney Museum of American Art, New York, *Turn-of-the-Century-America: Paintings, Graphics, Photographs, 1890–1900*, June 30–October 2, 1977; St. Louis Art Museum, St. Louis, December 1, 1977–January 12, 1978; Seattle Art Museum, Seattle, February 2–March 12, 1978; The Oakland Museum, Oakland, Calif., April 4–May 28, 1978, p. 20, fig. 7 (illus.).

Hirschl & Adler Galleries, New York, *American Drawings and Watercolors*, October 6–29, 1979, no. 29, n.p.

This three-quarter right profile head is based upon the three-quarter left profile head of *Peace* in the mosaic mural *Law* (copyright 1896), one of two murals Dielman designed for the House Reading Room in the new Library of Congress building. The olive wreath symbolizes peace. Dielman later used a variation of the Library of Congress head in three-quarter right profile for the head of *Moderation*, who performs the peacekeeping function in *The Editorial Function*, one of seven mural paintings (copyright 1900, destroyed) the artist created for the business office of the new *Evening Star* building in Washington, D.C. This watercolor variation may commemorate the unveiling of the *Evening Star* murals in 1902.

Charles Temple Dix (1838–1873)

Dix was born in Albany, New York, the youngest son of the distinguished statesman and soldier, John Adams Dix (1798–1879). Having already visited Europe as a child, Dix returned with his family to Italy from 1853 to 1855, where the sculptor Thomas Crawford (c. 1813–1879) was among the family's friends. Dix's decision to become a marine painter was enthusiastically supported by his father, and after graduation from Union College, Schenectady, Dix continued his art studies in New York City in the late 1850s. Although he was elected an associate of the National Academy of Design in 1861, he did not submit the diploma painting required for qualification. A promising career was interrupted by the Civil War, during which Dix served as his father's aide-de-camp. In March

1865, at the close of the war, Dix left for Europe, spending the winter in Rome and visiting England sometime thereafter. In 1868 he married Camilla Ottilie Watson, niece of the art historian, Mrs. Anna Brownell Jameson (1794–1860), in London. His brief married life was spent in Rome where he died, having never fully recovered his health after the Civil War.

Charles Temple Dix
Marina Grande—Capri
1866, Oil on canvas
18⅛ x 30⅛ in. (46.04 x 76.52 cm.)
Signed (lower left): *CTD* (in monogram) / '66.
Signed (on back): *Marina Grande-Capri C.T. Dix / Rome 1866*
(fig. 24)

PROVENANCE
[Hirschl & Adler Galleries, New York, 1980]
Jo Ann and Julian Ganz, Jr., 1980

Located on the northern side of the island, the Marina Grande was the chief port on Capri. Dix exhibited a *Scene at Capri* at the Forty-Fifth Annual Exhibition of the National Academy of Design, New York in 1870 (no. 343, p. 23), and a work entitled *Sunset at Capri* was mentioned as one of his "better known" works in Clara Erskine Clement (Waters) and Laurence Hutton, *Artists of the Nineteenth Century and Their Works*, 2 vols. (Boston: Houghton, Osgood and Company, 1879), 1, p. 209. The island was probably appreciated by Dix for reasons of health as well as aesthetics.

Charles Loring Elliott (1812–1868)

Charles Loring Elliott, considered to be New York's leading portraitist in the 1850s, is believed to have painted more than seven hundred portraits during his career. Born in Scipio, Cayuga County, New York, he studied briefly with John Trumbull and John Quidor and from 1830 to 1839 worked as an itinerant portrait painter in central New York State. Elliott returned to New York City in 1839 and began to exhibit his paintings at the National Academy of Design, where he became an associate in 1845 and an academician in 1846. Elliott's portraits found favor with the New York Knickerbocker society, and he received commissions from governors, novelists, merchants, and other notables of his day. Henry Tuckerman wrote that during the Civil War, when Elliott was at the height of his career, "he set up his easel in William Street, and dashed off upon canvas, at high prices, the cotton merchants who sat to him, in the hurried intervals of their restless speculations." Except for a few recorded landscapes and figure pieces, Elliott's work consisted entirely of portraits. Elliott resided chiefly in Hoboken, New Jersey, while working in New York City but moved to Albany in the last year of his life and died there at the age of fifty-six. Elliott was evidently held in high regard by his compatriots; he painted a number of his fellow artists and was painted many times by them.

Charles Loring Elliott
Self-Portrait
c. 1850, Oil on canvas
13 x 10 in. (33.02 x 25.4 cm.)
Unsigned
(fig. 34)

PROVENANCE
Samuel P. Avery, New York, by 1861
[Sale of Samuel P. Avery's private collection of cabinet size paintings, New York, 1867]
Mrs. Arthur Corwin, Greenwich, Conn.
George Roche, Greenwich, Conn. (nephew of Mrs. Corwin)
[Newhouse Galleries, New York, 1946; with Harry MacNeill Bland, New York, holding a partial interest, c. late 1946–1947]
Jo Ann and Julian Ganz, Jr., 1972

EXHIBITED

Young Men's Association, Troy, N.Y., *Fourth Annual Art Exhibition*, 1861, no. 209, p. 10, S. P. Avery Collection.

Brooklyn Art Association, Brooklyn, N.Y., *Fifth Exhibition*, March 4–5, 1863, no. 33, p. 6, S. P. Avery Collection.

Santa Barbara Museum of Art, Santa Barbara, Calif., *American Paintings, Watercolors and Drawings from the Collection of Jo Ann and Julian Ganz, Jr.*, June 23–July 22, 1973, no. 28 (illus.), n.p.

BIBLIOGRAPHY

Henry T. Tuckerman, *Book of the Artists*, 2 vols. (New York: G. P. Putnam & Son; London: Sampson Low & Co., 1867), 2, p. 303.

Benson J. Lossing, *History of New York City*, 2 vols. (New York: The Perine Engraving and Publishing Co., 1884), 2, p. 841 (information supplied by Samuel P. Avery).

———, *Some Notes: On the History of the Fine Arts in New York City during the Past Fifty Years* (New York, revised by Samuel P. Avery, 1885), 2.

The Art Quarterly, 10, no. 2 (1937): 155 (illus.).

Theodore Bolton, "A Catalogue of the Portraits Painted by Charles Loring Elliott," *The Art Quarterly*, 5, no. 1 (Winter 1942): 87–88.

RELATED BIBLIOGRAPHY

Bibliotheca Dramatica Catalogue of the Theatrical and Miscellaneous Library of the late William E. Burton, the distinguished Comedian . . . To be sold at auction by J. Sabin & Co. . . . New York On Monday, October 8, 1860. . . . (A copy of the above was listed as Lot No. 639, p. 32 in *Catalogue of the entire Art Library of Mr. S. P. Avery . . . to be sold at auction on Wednesday afternoon, January 30, 1867 by Bangs, Merwin & Co., . . . New York*).

Col. T. B. Thorpe, *Reminiscences of Charles L. Elliott, Artist* (New York: Evening Post, October 2, 1868) (pamphlet reprinted from the September 30 and October 1, 1868 editions of the *Evening Post*).

William L. Keese, *William E. Burton: Actor, Author and Manager* (New York & London: G. P. Putnam's Sons, The Knickerbocker Press, 1885), 179–180 ff.

In the early 1850s Elliott's appearance had gained a certain amount of notoriety, for he was commonly thought to resemble the accepted likenesses of Shakespeare. There is a distinct affinity between this portrait and the only possibly authentic likeness of Shakespeare in oil, the *Chandos Portrait* (National Portrait Gallery, London). Elliott would have known the *Portrait* probably from a copy which was exhibited in the United States during this period, but certainly from engravings of it in the collection of William E. Burton (1804–1860), the actor. Burton's library, which contained one of the major collections of Shakespeareana in the mid-nineteenth century, was a favorite meeting place for those interested in the theater, and Elliott was a frequent visitor. On one often-recounted occasion Burton and his guests had been overwhelmed by the similarity between Shakespeare and Elliott while the artist sat alone in Burton's library reading a rare folio under a copy of the *Stratford Memorial Bust*. It is not known whether the portrait was in Burton's collection prior to its entering Samuel P. Avery's private collection, but like the *Bust*, and unlike the *Chandos Portrait*, Elliott here wears a goatee. The Shakespearean similarity may have also helped account for the work having received the highest price, $800, among a group of 120 cabinet pictures belonging to Avery when they were sold at auction in 1867.

Elliott painted at least seven other self-portraits (Everson Museum of Art, Syracuse, N.Y.; National Academy of Design, New York; The Metropolitan Museum of Art, New York; Kennedy Galleries, New York, 1965; Walters Art Gallery, Baltimore; Hecksher Museum, Huntington, N.Y.; A. W. Mellon Educational and Charitable Trust, Washington, D.C.), which portray him at ages ranging from about twenty-five or thirty to about forty-eight.[1]

1. Information supplied by Richard N. Wright, president, Onondaga Historical Association, Syracuse, N.Y.

John F. Francis (1808–1886)

John F. Francis, born in Philadelphia, in 1808, spent his early career as an itinerant painter in central Pennsylvania, Ohio, and Tennessee. Although he eventually settled in rural Jefferson, Pennsylvania, Francis was listed as a resident of Philadelphia in 1840 and always maintained close ties with that city. In the 1840s and fifties, he exhibited his works there at the Artists' Fund Society and the Pennsylvania Academy of the Fine Arts. He began his career as a portrait painter but during the 1850s turned increasingly to still lifes, carrying on the tradition established in Philadelphia by the Peale family. Most of the fewer than one hundred paintings known to be by Francis are still lifes, ranging from elaborately set tables with wine, fruit, nuts, and cheeses, to more subdued paintings of fruit spilling out of a basket. Little is known about Francis's late career; no paintings dated after 1879 have been found. He died in Jefferson, Montgomery County, Pennsylvania in 1886.

Martha Hutson, "Nineteenth Century American Art Collections in Los Angeles," *American Art Review,* 2 (September–October, 1975): 71 (illus.).

Francis's still lifes fall into three major categories, the more complex "Dessert" and "Luncheon" varieties, and the fruit basket variety which, as in *Yellow Apples,* features common market-baskets indicative of the post-1850 democratization of American art.[1]

1. See William H. Gerdts and Russell Burke, *American Still-Life Painting* (New York: Praeger Publishers, 1971), 60–61.

John F. Francis

Still Life: Yellow Apples and Chestnuts Spilling from a Basket
1856, Oil on canvas
25 x 30 in. (63.5 x 76.2 cm.)
Signed (lower center): *J. F. Francis / pᵗ.1856*
(fig. 78)

PROVENANCE
Mr. and Mrs. Walter Reisch, Los Angeles
[Terry DeLapp, Los Angeles, 1974]
Jo Ann and Julian Ganz, Jr., 1974

EXHIBITED
Long Beach Museum of Art, Long Beach, Calif., *Mr. and Mrs. Walter Reisch Collection,* July 14–August 18, 1968, checklist no. 18 (illus.), as *Basket with apples and chestnuts,* n.p.
Phoenix Art Museum, Phoenix, Ariz., *Mr. and Mrs. Walter Reisch Collection,* December, 1968, checklist no. 37 (illus., on cover), n.p., as *Basket with apples and chestnuts.*
Los Angeles County Museum of Art, *American Paintings from Los Angeles Collections,* May 7–June 30, 1974, checklist, n.p.
The Hunt Institute for Botanical Documentation, Carnegie-Mellon University, Pittsburgh, *American Cornucopia: 19th Century Still Lifes and Studies,* April 5–July 30, 1976, no. 12 (illus.) pp. 14, 17.

BIBLIOGRAPHY
Alfred Frankenstein, "J. F. Francis," *The Magazine Antiques,* 59 (May, 1951): 377 (illus.), as *Still Life.*

Sanford Robinson Gifford (1823–1880)

Sanford Robinson Gifford was born in Greenfield, Saratoga County, New York, in 1823, the son of a successful owner of an iron works. After attending Brown University for two years, Gifford moved to New York City in 1844 to study drawing for two years with John Rubens Smith. In 1847 he began to exhibit his work at both the American Art Union and the National Academy of Design. In 1855 he made his first trip to Europe, where he remained for two years, traveling extensively, at times accompanying Worthington Whittredge (q.v.) and Albert Bierstadt (q.v.).

Returning to New York in 1857, Gifford established himself in the famous 10th Street Studio Building, which he occupied until his death. He served in the Union Army during the Civil War and then made a second trip abroad in 1868–69. This was followed in 1870 by a longer trip, with Whittredge and John Kensett (q.v.), to the Rocky Mountains, where Gifford joined the F. V. Hayden surveying expedition to Wyoming. In 1874 he made a final western trip. Throughout his career, Gifford continued to paint both European and American landscapes, working from sketches made during expeditions here and abroad and creating several versions of the same subject. He died in New York City in 1880 at the age of fifty-seven. Soon after his death, a major retrospective exhibition of his work was held at the Metropolitan Museum of Art.

Sanford Robinson Gifford

Lake Nemi
1856, Oil on canvas
10⅜ x 14¼ in. (26.35 x 36.2 cm.)
Signed (lower left): *SRG Rome Oct. 21, '56–*
Stamped (on back): *S.R. Gifford Sale*
(fig. 14)

PROVENANCE
Estate of the artist, 1881
[Hirschl & Adler Galleries, New York, 1971]
Jo Ann and Julian Ganz, Jr., 1971

EXHIBITED
Santa Barbara Museum of Art, Santa Barbara, Calif., *American Paintings, Watercolors and Drawings from the Collection of Jo Ann and Julian Ganz, Jr.,* June 23–July 22, 1973, no. 31 (illus.), n.p.

BIBLIOGRAPHY
A Memorial Catalogue of the Paintings of Sanford Robinson Gifford, N.A., with a biographical and critical essay by Prof. John F. Weir, of the Yale School of Fine Arts (New York: The Metropolitan Museum of Art, 1881; reprinted, New York: Olana Gallery, 1974), possible identification (see below), p. 17.
Catalogue of Valuable Oil Paintings, Works of the Famous Artist Sanford R. Gifford, N.A., Deceased, to be Sold Without Reserve, Part II April 28 and 29 (New York: Thomas E. Kirby and Co., 1881), possible identification (see below), p. 7.
Ila Weiss, *Sanford Robinson Gifford (1823–1880)* (Ph.D. diss., Columbia University, 1968; reprinted with a new preface, New York and London: Garland Publishing, Inc., 1977),

xii–xiii, xxxii–xxxiii,n. Related works (see below): pp. 145–150, fig. V E 1, n.p.

Susan E. Strickler, *The Toledo Museum of Art: American Paintings* (Toledo, Ohio: The Toledo Museum of Art, 1979), 54.

This is an oil sketch for *Lake Nemi* (1856–1857, oil on canvas, 40 x 60 in., The Toledo Museum of Art). Gifford first visited Lake Nemi on October 7, 1856. A possible second trip made later in the month is undocumented.[1] This may be the trip mentioned by Worthington Whittredge (q.v.) in which Whittredge, Gifford, William Stanley Haseltine (q.v.), and others shared a room in the inn from which this view was taken.[2] It seems likely that this work was included in the *Memorial Catalogue*, p. 17, with an incorrect date as, "101. *A Sketch of Lago di Nemi*. Dated October 23d, 1856. Size, 10 x 14½. Owned by the Estate"; and in the Gifford Estate Sale *Catalogue*, p. 7, as "10. *Lago Di Nemi* Dated October 23, 1856 [101] Size 10 x 14½."[3] The two other views of Lake Nemi included in the Gifford Estate Sale *Catalogue* bear marked dissimilarities either in dating or size to this work: "14. *Lago Di Nemi*, Dated October 7th 1856 [99] Size 10 x 14" (Part I, April 11th and 12th, p. 23); "37. *Shrine near Lago Di Nemi*, Dated October 23, 1856, [102] Size 8½ x 13" (Part II, p. 11).

1. Weiss, *Gifford*, 70, 145.
2. "The Autobiography of Worthington Whittredge 1820–1910," John I. H. Baur, ed., *Brooklyn Museum Journal* (1942), 38; referred to in Weiss, *Gifford*, 413n.
3. Weiss, *Gifford*, xxxiii,n.

Sanford Robinson Gifford

The Camp on Mansfield Mountain, Vermont
1858, Oil on canvas
7½ x 14⅛ in. (19.05 x 35.88 cm.)
Incised (lower left): *S R Gifford '58*
Stamped (on back): *S. R. GIFFORD* (in a circle)
SALE (inside circle)
(fig. 15)

PROVENANCE
Family of the artist
[Hirschl & Adler Galleries, New York, 1972]
Jo Ann and Julian Ganz, Jr., 1972

EXHIBITED
Santa Barbara Museum of Art, Santa Barbara, Calif., *American Paintings, Watercolors and Drawings from the Collection of Jo Ann and Julian Ganz, Jr.*, June 23–July 22, 1973, no. 32 (illus.), n.p.

BIBLIOGRAPHY
A Memorial Catalogue of the Paintings of Sanford Robinson Gifford, N.A., with a biographical and critical essay by Prof. John F. Weir, of the Yale School of Fine Arts (New York: The Metropolitan Museum of Art, 1881; reprinted, New York: Olana Gallery, 1974), probable identification (see below), p. 27. Related works (see below), pp. 19, 34.

Catalogue of Valuable Oil Paintings, Works of the Famous Artist Sanford R. Gifford, N.A., Deceased, to be Sold Without Reserve, Part II April 28 and 29 (New York: Thomas E. Kirby and Co., 1881), probable identification (see below), p. 24.

William C. Lipke and Philip N. Grimes, eds., *Vermont Landscape: Images 1776–1976* (Burlington, Vt.: The Robert Hull Fleming Museum, University of Vermont, 1976), 61 (illus.).

Ila Weiss, *Sanford Robinson Gifford (1823–1880)*, (Ph.D. diss., Columbia University, 1968; reprinted with a new preface, New York and London: Garland Publishing, Inc., 1977), xxxiv,n. Probable identification (see below), p. 438n. Related works (see below), pp. 176–180, 243–244, figs. VI D 1, VII E 7, n.p.

One of a series of views of the Mount Mansfield area made between 1858 and 1859, this work was probably listed in the *Memorial Catalogue*, p. 27, as "327. *The Camp on Mansfield Mountain, Vermont, A Sketch*. Not dated. Size, 7½ x 14. Owned by the Estate," and in the Gifford Estate Sale *Catalogue*, p. 24, as "106. *The Camp on Mans-*

field Mountain, Vermont."[1] It is an earlier daylight version of *Camping for the Night on Mansfield Mountain* (1868?, oil on canvas, 10⅛ x 16¾ in., The Adirondack Museum, Blue Mountain Lake, New York) which was probably listed as no. 469 in the *Memorial Catalogue*, p. 34.[2] It is closely related to *A Sketch of Mansfield Mountain* (1858, oil on canvas, 7 x 14 in. George Walter Vincent Smith Art Gallery, Springfield, Mass.) which was listed as no. 132 in the *Memorial Catalogue*, p. 19.[3]

1. Weiss, *Gifford*, xxxiv,n, 176–180.
2. Weiss, *Gifford*, xxxiv,n, 243–244, 438n, fig. VII E 7, n.p.
3. Weiss, *Gifford*, 176–77, fig. VI D 1, n.p. and Lipke, *Vermont*, 61 (illus.).

Sanford Robinson Gifford

Kauterskill Clove, in the Catskills
1862, Oil on canvas
12⅞ x 11¹¹⁄₁₆ in. (32.70 x 28.1 cm.)
Signed (lower left): *S R Gifford / 1862*
(fig. 16)

PROVENANCE
Robert Gordon, New York (from the artist)
Mrs. Lucy Tinker, New Milton Village, Hampshire, England
[Sotheby Parke Bernet, Inc., New York (*Fine Americana*, Sale no. 3947, Lot no. 654, as *Kauterskill Falls* (illus.), n.p.) January 26–29, 1977; Hirschl & Adler Galleries, New York, as agent]
Jo Ann and Julian Ganz, Jr., 1977

EXHIBITED

The Metropolitan Museum of Art, New York, *The Memorial Collection of the Works of the Late Sanford R. Gifford*, October 1880 to March 1881, as no. 18, *A Mountain Gorge, a study*, p. 5, Robert Gordon Collection.

BIBLIOGRAPHY

A Memorial Catalogue of the Paintings of Sanford Robinson Gifford, N.A., with a biographical and critical essay by Prof. John F. Weir, of the Yale School of Fine Arts (New York: The Metropolitan Museum of Art, 1881; reprinted, New York: Olana Gallery, 1974), as no. 264, *Kauterskill Clove, in the Catskills*, p. 25.

Ila Weiss, *Sanford Robinson Gifford (1823–1880)*, (Ph.D. diss., Columbia University, 1968; reprinted with a new preface, New York and London: Garland Publishing, Inc., 1977), 226, 434n. Related works (see below): pp. 225–230, figs. VII C 1–VII C 8, n.p.

This work is one of three smaller 1862 oil versions of the subject (*Memorial Catalogue* nos. 264, 265. *A Small Sketch of Kauterskill Clove*, 270. *Kauterskill Clove, a Study)*, probably related to *Kauterskill Falls* (1862, oil on canvas, 48 x 39⅞ in., The Metropolitan Museum of Art, New York).

Sanford Robinson Gifford
Riva—Lago di Garda
1863, Oil on canvas
10⅝ x 16¾ in. (26.99 x 42.55 cm.)
Signed (lower left): *S R Gifford 1863*
Signed (lower right): *S R Gifford1863*
Signed (on back): *Riva-Lago di Gard- / S. R. Gifford–1863–*
(fig. 17)

PROVENANCE

D. H. McAlpin, New York
Hillary Smart, Boston (by inheritance from his father)
[Vose Galleries, Boston]
Jo Ann and Julian Ganz, Jr., 1976

EXHIBITED

The Metropolitan Museum of Art, New York, *The Memorial Collection of the Works of the Late Sanford R. Gifford*, October 1880 to March 1881, as no. 44, *Lago Garda, Italy* (1863), p. 6, D. H. McAlpin Collection.

BIBLIOGRAPHY

A Memorial Catalogue of the Paintings of Sanford Robinson Gifford, N.A., with a biographical and critical essay by Prof. John F. Weir, of the Yale School of Fine Arts (New York: The Metropolitan Museum of Art, 1881; reprinted, New York: Olana Gallery, 1974), as no. 342, *Lago di Garda, Italy*, p. 28, D. H. McAlpin Collection.

Ila Weiss, *Sanford Robinson Gifford (1823–1880)*, (Ph.D. diss., Columbia University, 1968; reprinted with a new preface, New York and London: Garland Publishing, Inc., 1977), xxxii,n.

Sanford R. Gifford, *European Letters*, 3 vols., Archives of American Art. Related works (see below): vol. 2, p. 176, reel D21.

University of Texas Art Museum, Austin, Texas, *Sanford Robinson Gifford (1823–1880)*, October 25–December 13, 1970; The Albany Institute of History and Art, Albany, N.Y., December 28–January 31, 1971; Hirschl & Adler Galleries, New York, February 8–27, 1971. Related work: no. 24, pp. 25, 51 (illus.).

This work is a study for *Riva, Lago di Garda* (1863, oil on canvas, 20 x 32 in., Douglas and Webster Collins Collection, Longmeadow, Mass., 1970, in Texas, *Gifford*, no. 24, p. 25, illus., p. 51). Gifford took an Austrian steamer from Peschiera at the southern end of Lake Garda to Riva at the northwestern end on July 24, 1857, making sketches of Riva before leaving for Trent the next day.[1] These sketches are unlocated.[2] The town's chief medieval monuments are, on the left, the Torre Apponale, a fortress tower greatly altered into a clock tower, and,

on the right, the Antica Rocca, a Scaliger family castle, reconverted in 1850 into a garrison after having fallen into decay.

1. Gifford, *Letters*, vol. 2, p. 176.
2. Weiss, *Gifford*, xxxii,n.

Sanford Robinson Gifford
The Artist Sketching at Mount Desert, Maine
1864–1865, Oil on canvas
11 x 19 in. (27.94 x 48.26 cm.)
Signed (lower right): *S R Gifford / 1865 /* (faintly incised): *Mt. ——, / July 22, 1864*
(fig. 18)

PROVENANCE

[Lee Freedman, Southwest Harbor, Me. 1978]
[Thomas Colville, New Haven, Conn., 1979]
Jo Ann and Julian Ganz, Jr., 1979

BIBLIOGRAPHY

A Memorial Catalogue of the Paintings of Sanford Robinson Gifford, N.A., with a biographical and critical essay by Prof. John F. Weir, of the Yale School of Fine Arts (New York: The Metropolitan Museum of Art, 1881; reprinted, New York: Olana Gallery, 1974). Related work (see below), p. 30.

Ila Weiss, *Sanford Robinson Gifford (1823–1880)*, (Ph.D. diss., Columbia University, 1968; reprinted with a new preface, New York and London: Garland Publishing, Inc., 1977). Related work (see below): pp. 268, 443n.

The Magazine Antiques, 116 (November, 1979): 948 (illus.).

The work depicts Otter Cove from the summit of Green (Cadillac) Mountain, Mount Desert Island, Maine. It is either closely related to, or actually the work listed in the *Memorial Catalogue* as no. 385, *A View from Green Mountain, Mount Desert, Me.* (dated 1865, 12 x 19 in., Miss A. M. Williams, Augusta, Maine Collection, 1881), p. 30. A related sketch, *Green Mountain, Mt. Desert Island*, is dated July 15, 1864 (*Gifford Sketchbook 10*, Archives of American Art, roll no. 688, frame no. 403).[1] The July 18, 1865 date of another Mount Desert scene, *A Sketch of Mount Desert, Maine*[2] suggests that Gifford finished this work upon his return to its location exactly a year after he began the work. This may account for the picture within the picture in Gifford's paint box.

1. Attribution suggested by Ila Weiss.
2. *Memorial Catalogue*, no. 390, p. 30; Weiss, *Gifford*, 268, 443 n.

Sanford Robinson Gifford
A Home in the Wilderness
1865–1867, Oil on canvas
9⅛ x 14⅞ in. (23.18 x 37.78 cm.)
Signed (lower right): *S R Gifford*
Signed (on back): *S R Gifford Pinxit / 1865 / 67*
(fig. 19)

PROVENANCE
J. P. Waters, New York, 1867–1868
[Leavitt and Company, New York, before 1881]
[Hirschl & Adler Galleries, New York, 1971]
Jo Ann and Julian Ganz, Jr., 1971

EXHIBITED
Santa Barbara Museum of Art, Santa Barbara, Calif. *American Paintings, Watercolors and Drawings from the Collection of Jo Ann and Julian Ganz, Jr.*, June 23–July 22, 1973, no. 33 (illus.), n.p.
Hirschl & Adler Galleries, New York, *Retrospective of a Gallery*, November 8–December 1, 1973, no. 45 (illus.), n.p.
Meredith Long & Company, Houston, Texas, *Tradition and Innovation, American Paintings 1860–1870*, January 10–25, 1974, no. 10 (illus.), p. 22.

BIBLIOGRAPHY
A Memorial Catalogue of the Paintings of Sanford Robinson Gifford, N.A., with a biographical and critical essay by Prof. John F. Weir, of the Yale School of Fine Arts (New York: The Metropolitan Museum of Art, 1881; reprinted, New York: Olana Gallery, 1974), as no. 415, *A Home in the Wilderness, a Sketch*, p. 31.
William S. Talbot, "Landscape and Light," *The Bulletin of the Cleveland Museum of Art*, 60 (January, 1973): 10–11 (illus.), 20n.
Donelson F. Hoopes, "The Jo Ann and Julian Ganz, Jr. Collection," *American Art Review*, 1 (September–October, 1973): 58 (illus.).
Ila Weiss, *Sanford Robinson Gifford (1823–1880)*, (Ph.D. diss., Columbia University, 1968; reprinted with a new preface, New York and London: Garland Publishing, Inc., 1977), xviii–xix, xxxv,n. Related works (see below): pp. 256–260, 440n, figs. VII H 3, VII H 4, n.p.

The work was painted after pencil sketches of Mount Hayes, New Hampshire, dated August 27, 1865 (*Gifford Sketchbook*, Sept., 1865–Sept., 1866, Vassar College, Poughkeepsie, N.Y., on microfilm: Archives of American Art, roll no. D254, frame no. 104). It in turn served as an oil sketch for *A Home in the Wilderness* (1866, oil on canvas, 30½ x 54¼ in., Cleveland Museum of Art), although its dating suggests that it was reworked in 1867.

Sanford Robinson Gifford
The Desert at Assouan, Egypt
February, 1869, Oil on canvas
5⅞ x 13¼ in. (14.92 x 33.66 cm.)
Signed (lower right): *S R Gifford Assouan Feb. 69-*
(fig. 20)

PROVENANCE
Estate of the artist
[Thomas E. Kirby and Co., New York (*Catalogue of Valuable Oil Paintings, Works of the Famous Artist Sanford R. Gifford, N.A., Deceased, to be Sold Without Reserve, Part I*, probably as no. 119, *Assouan, Egypt*, p. 41) April 11–12, 1881] see below
W. S. Gurnee
Isabella Gurnee Thorndike
Preservation Society of Newport County, Newport, R.I.
[Vose Galleries, Boston, 1969]
Webster and Douglas Collins, Longmeadow, Mass., 1969
[Vose Galleries, Boston, 1972]
Jo Ann and Julian Ganz, Jr., 1972

EXHIBITED
The Metropolitan Museum of Art, New York, *The Memorial Collection of the Works of the Late Sanford R. Gifford*, October 1880 to March 1881, probably as no. 54, *Assouan, Egypt, a study*, p. 7 (see below).
University of Texas Art Museum, Austin, Texas, *Sanford Robinson Gifford (1823–1880)*, October 25–December 13, 1970; The Albany Institute of History and Art, Albany, N.Y., December 28, 1970–January 31, 1971; Hirschl & Adler Galleries, New York, February 8–27, 1971, no. 45, pp. 28, 67 (illus.), as *The Desert at Assouan*.
Santa Barbara Museum of Art, Santa Barbara, Calif. *American Paintings, Watercolors and Drawings from the Collection of Jo Ann and Julian Ganz, Jr.*, June 23–July 22, 1973, no. 34, n.p.

BIBLIOGRAPHY
A Memorial Catalogue of the Paintings of Sanford Robinson Gifford, N.A., with a biographical and critical essay by Prof. John F. Weir, of the Yale School of Fine Arts (New York: The Metropolitan Museum of Art, 1881; reprinted, New

York: Olana Gallery, 1974), probably as no. 524, *Assouan, Egypt, a Sketch*, p. 36 (see below).

Ila Weiss, *Sanford Robinson Gifford (1823–1880)*, (Ph.D. diss., Columbia University, 1968; reprinted with a new preface, New York and London: Garland Publishing, Inc., 1977). Related work (see below): pp. 305–306, fig. VIII F 4, n.p.

The size of this work suggests that it is more likely to be no. 54, *Memorial Collection*, no. 524, *Memorial Catalogue* (6 x 13½ in.), and no. 119, Gifford Estate Sale *Catalogue* (6 x 13½ in.), than is the closely related *Assouan, Egypt* (February, 1869, oil on canvas, 5½ x 13¼ in., Ira Spanierman, New York, 1966), but this has not been decisively confirmed.[1]

1. Information supplied by Ila Weiss, November 5, 1980; and Weiss, *Gifford*, 305–306, fig. VIII F 4, n.p.

Sanford Robinson Gifford
Sunset Over New York Bay
c. 1878, Oil on canvas
8¼ x 13 in. (20.96 x 33.02 cm.)
Signed (lower right): *S R Gifford*
Signed (on back): *S R Gifford*
(fig. 21)

PROVENANCE
[Robert Sloan Gallery, New York, 1966]
[S. Andrew Kulin, Cambridge, Mass.; William Postar, Boston, Mass., as agent]
Jo Ann and Julian Ganz, Jr., 1975

BIBLIOGRAPHY
Ila Weiss, *Sanford Robinson Gifford (1823–1880)*, (Ph.D. diss., Columbia University, 1968; reprinted with a new preface, New York and London: Garland Publishing, Inc., 1977), xxvi, xxxviii,n, 342–343; fig. IX H 3, n.p.

This work is a study for *Sunset Over New York Bay* (1878, oil on canvas, 23 x 40 in., Everson Museum of Art, Syracuse, N.Y.).

❦ Thomas Ridgeway Gould (1818–1881)

Thomas Ridgeway Gould, born in Boston in 1818, was a dry goods merchant who studied drawing and modeling in his spare time. After his business failed during the Civil War, he turned to sculpture for a living and produced portrait busts of many of Boston's leading citizens, including Ralph Waldo Emerson. In 1868 he moved to Florence, where he lived, except for brief visits to the United States, for the rest of his life.

In his Florence studio Gould turned his attention to creating idealized works, including the popular *West Wind* of 1874, of which seven replicas were eventually commissioned. During the 1870s he continued to produce ideal works and portraits busts. He died in Florence in 1881.

Thomas Ridgeway Gould
The West Wind
1874, Marble
48 in. (121.92 cm.)
Signed (lower back): *THE WEST WIND. / T. R. Gould. Inv. et Fecit. / Florence / 1874.*
(fig. 57)

PROVENANCE
[Hirschl & Adler Galleries, New York, 1978]
Jo Ann and Julian Ganz, Jr., 1978

RELATED BIBLIOGRAPHY
Edward Strahan (pseud. Earl Shinn), *The Masterpieces of the Centennial International Exhibition, Volume I, Fine Art* (Philadelphia: Gebbie & Barrie, n.d.), 296 (illus.).
William J. Clark, Jr., *Great American Sculptures* (Philadelphia: Gebbie & Barrie, Publishers, 1878), 122–124 (illus.).
Samuel G. W. Benjamin, *Art In America: A Critical and Historical Sketch* (New York: Harper & Brothers, Publisher, 1880), 154.
Lorado Taft, *The History of American Sculpture*, new edition with supplementary chapter by Adeline Adams (New York: The Macmillan Company, 1930), 189–190 (illus.).
Wayne Craven, *Sculpture in America* (New York: Thomas Y. Crowell Company, 1968), 205.
William H. Gerdts, *American Neo-Classic Sculpture: The Marble Resurrection* (New York: The Viking Press, 1973), fig. 62, pp. 84–85.

The West Wind was Gould's most famous work. This is a reduction from the original completed in 1870 (St. Louis Mercantile Library Association, St. Louis, figure 71 in. high, approx. 78 in. with base). At least seven replicas were made. Starting in 1874[1] and climaxing in 1876, when *The West Wind* was shown at the Philadelphia Centennial Exhibition, accusations were made to the effect that the work was essentially copied from one of the versions of Antonio Canova's (1757–1822) statue *Hebe*. The accusations were denied by Gould's supporters, although it is evident, by comparing *The West Wind* and *Hebe*, that Gould was influenced by Canova's work. The 1874 version of *The West*

Wind is slightly different, showing a distinct asymmetry of the drapery at the waist, and is less like *Hebe* than the original sculpture. In a letter written while the original *West Wind* was still in progress, Gould felt disinclined to "cheapen" the "singular originality" of this work "for the present by means of photography."[2] It is unlikely that Gould would not have known Canova's work, and it may have been due as much to an uneasiness over being accused of stolen ideas as it was of others stealing his own that made Gould cautious.

1. Taft, *History of American Sculpture*, 189.
2. Gould, Florence, Italy, to Alfred Stebbins, San Francisco, April 10, 1870, Archives of American Art, roll no. PAA1, frame nos. 816–817.

Seymour Joseph Guy (1824–1910)

Seymour Joseph Guy, born in Greenwich, England, in 1824, was orphaned at the age of nine. At thirteen he began to work as a sign painter, practicing painting in his free time. He later studied with London artists Ambrose Jerome, a portraitist, and the marine painter Thomas Buttersworth. In 1854 he emigrated to America and opened a studio in New York, where he began his career as a portrait painter, later turning to genre for his subject matter.

Guy, like John George Brown (q.v.), another painter of his generation who was also born in England, specialized in themes involving children. Both artists worked in the 10th Street Studio Building and must have been familiar with each other's work. Unlike Brown, whose contemporary popularity and financial success is well documented, the source of Guy's patronage is uncertain, but he appears to have had a reasonably successful career. At least one of his paintings was included in the Thomas B. Clarke collection, one of the leading collections of American paintings of the time. Guy became an associate of the National Academy of Design in 1861 and an academician in 1865 and exhibited at the academy between 1860 and 1890. He also exhibited at the Philadelphia Centennial Exposition, the Paris Exhibition of 1878, the

Boston Athenaeum, the Brooklyn Art Association, and the Maryland Historical Society. Guy died in New York City in 1910.

Seymour J. Guy
Unconscious of Danger
1865, Oil on canvas
20 x 16 in. (50.8 x 40.64 cm.)
Signed (lower right): *SJGuy / N.Y. 1865* (SJG in monogram)
(fig. 50)

PROVENANCE
Bernard H. Cone, New York
Private Collection
[Kennedy Galleries, Inc., New York, 1973]
Jo Ann and Julian Ganz, Jr., 1973

EXHIBITED
Brooklyn Art Association, Brooklyn, N.Y., *Spring Exhibition*, March 21–24, 1866, no. 186, as *Unconscious of Danger*.
Goupil's Gallery, New York, *New Pictures at Goupil's Gallery*, late 1860s, as *Unconscious of Danger*.
James Graham & Sons, New York, An Exhibition of American Genre Paintings, March 2–25, 1942, no. 15, as *Please Be Careful*, n.p., lent by Bernard H. Cone Collection.

BIBLIOGRAPHY
Clark S. Marlor, *A History of the Brooklyn Art Association with an Index of Exhibitions* (New York: James F. Carr, 1970), 212.

The following description of the work was published in *New Pictures at Goupil's Gallery:* "One of the best pictures yet painted by this rapidly-improving artist. It represents a young lad, unconscious of danger, while dreaming of the future, walking to the edge of a high ledge of rocks, while his sister is in the act of striving to bring him back. It is excellent in drawing, exquisitely finished, and tender in expression." This description suggests that the theme of this work may have been influenced by John Greenleaf Whittier's 1855 poem, *The Barefoot Boy.* Although the girl portrayed may have been Guy's seven- or eight-year-old daughter, Anna M. Guy, the artist's eldest son, Charles H. Guy, was five or six in 1865 and, therefore, probably not the model for the boy. The location appears to be the Hudson River Palisades.

Seymour J. Guy
Making Believe
1870, Oil on canvas
15 x 12 in. (38.1 x 30.48 cm.)
Signed (upper right): *SJGuy. / 1870* (SJG in monogram)
(fig. 52)

PROVENANCE
[New London, Conn., art market]
[Nathan Liverant and Son, Colchester, Conn., 1975]
Jo Ann and Julian Ganz, Jr., 1975

This work is a later version of *Making a Train* (1867, oil on canvas, 18⅛ x 24⅜ in., Philadelphia Museum of Art). The girl appears older in *Making Believe* and is probably the same model, possibly the artist's daughter, Anna M. Guy, who was twenty-two years old at the time of the June 1880 census.

Seymour J. Guy
The Pick of the Orchard (Picking Apples)
c. 1870, Oil on academy board
21⅜ x 13¼ in. (54.29 x 33.66 cm.)
Signed (lower right): *SJGuy* (SJG in monogram)
(fig. 49)

PROVENANCE
[Sandor's Antiques, Lambertville, N. J.]
Lee B. Anderson, New York
[Hirschl & Adler Galleries, New York, 1973]
Jo Ann and Julian Ganz, Jr., 1973

EXHIBITED
Lyman Allyn Museum, New London, Conn., *American Romantic Paintings of the 18th and 19th Centuries from the Collection of Lee B. Anderson*, February 26–March 26, 1961, no. 34, n.p., as *Picking Apples*.
Museum of Fine Arts, St. Petersburg, Fla., *The Good Life: An Exhibition of American Genre Painting by Artists Born During the First Four Decades of the 19th Century*, September 28–October 24, 1971; Loch Haven Art Center, Orlando, Fla., November 3–28, 1971, no. 13, as *Girl Under Apple Tree*, n.p., Lee B. Anderson Collection, New York.
Whitney Museum of American Art, New York, *18th and 19th Century American Paintings from Private Collections*, June 27–September 11, 1972, no. 26, n.p., as *Picking Apples*.

BIBLIOGRAPHY
Catalogue of Paintings by Seymour J. Guy, N.A., and Arthur Parton, N.A., to be sold by auction, Tuesday and Wednesday Evenings, February 7th and 8th at the Fifth Avenue Art Galleries . . . . New York: Ortgies & Co., Managers, 1893, probable identification (see below), p. 12.

Because of the similarity in title and size, this work probably was listed as no. 48, *The Pick of the Orchard*, 13½ x 21½ in. (width x height?), in *Catalogue of Paintings*, p. 12.

Seymour J. Guy
Story of Golden Locks
c. 1870, Oil on canvas
34 x 28⅛ in. (86.36 x 71.44 cm.)
Signed (lower left): *S. J. Guy*
(fig. 51)

PROVENANCE
[Continental Art Gallery, San Francisco]
[John C. R. Tompkins, Millbrook, N.Y., 1972]
[Tillou Gallery, Litchfield, Conn., 1972]
[Nathan Liverant and Son, Colchester, Conn.]
[Hirschl & Adler Galleries, New York, 1973]
Jo Ann and Julian Ganz, Jr., 1973

EXHIBITED
Los Angeles County Museum of Art, *American Narrative Painting*, October 1–November 17, 1974, no. 58, pp. 116, 124, 125 (illus.).

BIBLIOGRAPHY
Samuel G. W. Benjamin, *Art In America: A Critical and Historical Sketch* (New York: Harper & Brothers, Publishers, 1880); related work: p. 120 (illus.).
Edward Strahan (pseud. Earl Shinn), *The Art Treasures of America*, 3 vols. (Philadelphia: George Barrie Publisher, c.1879–1882); related work: vol. 3, p. 126.
Martha Hutson, "American Narrative Painting, The Painter's America: Rural and Urban Life, 1810–1910 Exhibition Review," *American Art Review*, 1 (November–December, 1974): 99 and cover.

This work is closely related in style and setting to *Making a Train* (1867; see Guy, *Making Believe*) and is probably from the same period. Guy's eldest child, Edith, and her two younger brothers Charles and William, who, at the time of the June 1880 census were twenty-seven, twenty, and nineteen, respectively, may have served as the models. A second version of this work entitled *A Bed-Time Story* was illustrated as an engraving probably by Frederick Juengling (1846–1889) in Benjamin, *Art*, p. 120. This is probably the work listed as *The Bedtime Story* (location unknown) in the Collection of Thomas B. Clarke, New York, in Strahan, *Treasures*, vol. 3, p. 126. Although nearly identical to *Golden Locks* in figures and composition, the girl in *The Bedtime Story* is now fully dressed and the setting is a richly furnished bedroom rather than an attic. *Golden Locks* probably reflects a more accurate model of the transient nature of the artist's household during the earlier part of his career.

John Haberle (1853–1933)

John Haberle, one of the most accomplished trompe l'oeil artists of the nineteenth century, was born in New Haven, Connecticut, in 1853 and spent most of his life there. He was employed for many years as a preparator in the paleontological museum at Yale University. Haberle studied art for a time at the National Academy in New York but apparently received most of his artistic training from his employer, the Yale paleontologist Othniel Charles Marsh. He exhibited for the first time at the National Academy of Design in 1887, and the painting, depicting an assortment of bank notes, coins, and postage stamps, was purchased for the Thomas B. Clarke collection.

Haberle's trompe l'oeil paintings of money and stamps, which include the 1889 *U.S.A.*, were all painted during a four-year period—1887 to about 1891. He may have been inspired to paint these works by the 1886 arrest of William Harnett (q.v.) for counterfeiting (it was illegal to make an exact facsimile of U. S. currency); the arrest seems to have simply goaded Haberle to produce even more exact replicas of coins and dollar bills. When *U.S.A.* was first exhibited in Chicago in 1889, an art critic of the Chicago *Inter-Ocean* alleged that the bills and stamps had simply been pasted onto the canvas; Haberle traveled to Chicago to prove that he had in fact painted the entire composition. In the mid-1890s Haberle's eyes began to trouble him, and he abandoned trompe l'oeil painting in favor of still lifes of flowers and fruit, often in outdoor settings. He died in New Haven in 1933.

John Haberle
U.S.A.
1889, Oil on canvas
8½ x 12 in. (21.59 x 30.48 cm.)
Signed (upper right): *J. HABERLE* = (drawing of a face) / *NEW HAVEN—CONN-*
(fig. 93)

PROVENANCE
Marvin Preston, Detroit, Mich., 1890 (from the artist)
Marvin Preston, Ferndale, Mich., (by inheritance, grandson)
[Sally Turner Gallery, Plainfield, N.J.]
Jo Ann and Julian Ganz, Jr., 1974

EXHIBITED
The Art Institute of Chicago, *Second Annual Exhibition of American Oil Paintings*, June–July (?), 1889.
New Britain Museum of American Art, New Britain, Conn., *John Haberle 1856–1933: Retrospective Exhibition*, January 6–28, 1962, n.p. (illus., and detail of upper right).

BIBLIOGRAPHY
The Inter-Ocean, Chicago, June (?), 1889.
The Chicago Daily News, July 3, 1889.
The Inter-Ocean, Chicago, July 7, 1889.
Alfred Frankenstein, *After the Hunt: William Harnett and Other American Still Life Painters 1870–1900*, revised ed. (Berkeley and Los Angeles: University of California Press, 1969), 117–118, plate 94, n.p.

A clipping from a New York review of *Imitation* (location unknown, no. 362 in sixth Autumn Exhibition of the National Academy of Design of 1887) is located below the bank notes. When Haberle exhibited *U.S.A.* at the Art Institute, he was accused by a local critic of masquerading a collage as an oil painting.[1] Clippings referring to this event became part of *A Bachelor's Drawer* (1890–1894, oil on canvas, 20 x 36 in., The Metropolitan Museum of Art, New York).

1. Frankenstein, *Hunt,* 117.

🐚 **George Henry Hall (1825–1913)**

George Henry Hall was considered by his contemporaries to be one of America's foremost still-life painters. He was born in 1825 in Manchester, New Hampshire, but grew up in Boston where he began to paint about 1842, without any formal instruction. In 1849 he traveled to Europe in the company of his friend Eastman

Johnson (q.v.), studying with him in the Royal Academy in Düsseldorf. Hall then went to Paris until his return to New York in 1852, at which time he began his career as a still-life painter. From 1853 until the 1890s he exhibited his paintings almost annually at the National Academy of Design, where he was elected an associate in 1853 and an academician in 1868. Hall also exhibited at galleries in Boston and Philadelphia and at the Brooklyn Art Association from 1861 to 1881. He made frequent trips abroad to Spain, Italy, and Egypt, often incorporating indigenous plants into his still lifes. Hall's still-life paintings range from complex compositions of fruit, flowers, and objets d'art to intimate studies such as his *Still Life: Pink Rose in Green Vase*. His work was praised by *The Crayon*, the leading American art journal of the 1850s and sixties, which wrote, "we never saw the beauty or color and the poetic reality of his class of subjects to better advantage." Hall died in New York City in 1913.

George Henry Hall
Still Life: Pink Rose in Green Vase
1880s, Oil on canvas
9 x 6 in. (22.86 x 15.24 cm.)
Signed (lower right): *Geo. Henry Hall*
(fig. 84)

PROVENANCE
[Hirschl & Adler Galleries, Inc., New York, 1974]
Jo Ann and Julian Ganz, Jr., 1975

The artist painted a number of floral still lifes arranged in containers he collected in Italy.

William Michael Harnett (1848–1892)

William Michael Harnett is today acknowledged to be one of America's greatest still-life painters. He was born in county Cork, Ireland, and came to Philadelphia with his family around 1849. He began his career as an engraver. In 1867 he enrolled in evening classes at the Pennsylvania Academy of the Fine Arts, and after moving to New York in 1869, attended classes at the National Academy of Design, where he exhibited his first painting in 1875, and at the Cooper Union. In 1876, Harnett returned to Philadelphia to resume his studies at the Pennsylvania Academy and began exhibiting his still lifes at academy exhibitions. Harnett went to Europe in 1880, remaining there until 1886. In London and Frankfurt Harnett studied the still-life paintings of seventeenth-century Dutch masters and then went to Munich for about four years, achieving considerable popular success. A version of his *After the Hunt*, depicting dead game and hunting accoutrements, was accepted by the Paris Salon of 1885 and had a significant influence upon late nineteenth-century still-life painting after it was shown in the United States.

In 1886 Harnett settled in New York. The paintings of his last six years include many tabletop still lifes in which objects of different form and texture are set against a paneled wall, as in *La Flûte Enchantée*. Harnett would often use the same objects in painting after painting, rearranging them to create different compositions. He died in New York City in 1892 and was buried in Philadelphia.

William Michael Harnett
La Flûte Enchantée
1887, Oil on wood panel
14 x 12 in. (35.56 x 30.48 cm.)
Signed (lower left): *WMHARNETT. / 1887.* (W over M superimposed on H)
Label (on back): *Painting by Wm. M. Harnett presented to Mr. & Mrs. Clarkson Cowl Jan. 4, 1899 by Geo. A. Hearn.*
(fig. 95)

PROVENANCE
George A. Hearn
Mr. and Mrs. Clarkson Cowl, January 4, 1899
[The Downtown Gallery, New York, 1945]
J. S. Newberry, Detroit, Mich.
Helen L. Goldman
[Kennedy Galleries, New York, 1975]
Jo Ann and Julian Ganz, Jr., 1975

ON DEPOSIT
The Detroit Institute of Arts, 1953

EXHIBITED
The Downtown Gallery, New York, *American Art: 1945 New Paintings and Sculpture by Leading American Artists, 20th Annual Exhibition*, November 6–December 1, 1945, no. 28, n.p., as *The Enchanted Flute.*

BIBLIOGRAPHY
Alfred Frankenstein, *After the Hunt: William Harnett and Other American Still Life Painters 1870–1900*, revised ed. (Berkeley and Los Angeles: University of California Press, 1969), 83, 178, cat. no. 107.

Elements identified in Frankenstein, *Hunt*, 178, include: four books, only one bearing a legible title, "Divina / Com / et / Purgat / orio / Dante / Firenze / 1503"; a Roman lamp; a Dutch jar; a meerschaum pipe; the artist's flute; a sheet music cover entitled "Opera / La Tra. . . / aria," presumably an aria from Giuseppe Verdi's *La Traviata;* a Gregorian neumes sheet; and a sheet from *The Magic Flute* entitled "La Flûte Enchantée / Chanson de Friseleur / Mozart / alle-gretto / No. 37," containing Papageno's song "Der Vogelfanger bin ich, ja," which is actually No. 2 in the opera. The number of love themes depicted here may be related to a family tradition noted in Frankenstein, *Hunt*, 83, which stated that Harnett became engaged only shortly before his death. Closely related works include: *Still Life* (1885, oil on wood panel, 13¾ x 10⁵⁄₁₆ in., The Armand Hammer Collection); *Still Life with Flute, Vase, and Roman Lamp* (1885, oil on wood panel, 13¾ x 10¼ in., Yale University Art Gallery, New Haven, Conn.); *My Gems* (1888, oil on wood panel, 18 x 14 in., National Gallery of Art, Washington, D.C.).

William Stanley Haseltine (1835–1900)

William Stanley Haseltine was born in Philadelphia in 1835 to a wealthy family. After graduating from Harvard University, he accompanied his Philadelphia painting teacher, Paul Weber, to Düsseldorf, where he studied for two years. There he met Worthington Whittredge (q.v.), Albert Bierstadt (q.v.), and Emanuel Leutze. After working in Rome for an additional three years, Haseltine returned to New York City and began to paint landscapes—primarily coastal scenes emphasizing rocks and waves—which he exhibited at the National Academy of Design, the Brooklyn Art Association, and the Century and Salmagundi Clubs in New York. In 1866 he went to Paris for two years.

In 1869 Haseltine and his family moved to Rome, where he lived, except for annual visits to the United States, for the rest of his life. He became a prominent host to American artists and visitors in Rome and exhibited his paintings in Paris and in Italy as well as in America. Haseltine helped to found the American Academy in Rome and was asked to select works by American artists living in Italy for the 1893 Columbian Exposition. After accompanying his son, the sculptor Herbert Haseltine, on a trip to the West Coast and Alaska in 1899, Haseltine returned to Rome, where he died in 1900.

William Stanley Haseltine
Rocks at Narragansett
1860s, Oil on canvas
12 x 22 in. (30.48 x 55.88 cm.)
Signed (lower right): *WSH* (in monogram)
(fig. 23)

PROVENANCE
[Victor D. Spark, New York, 1974]
Jo Ann and Julian Ganz, Jr., 1974

EXHIBITED
Los Angeles County Museum of Art, *Pertaining to The Sea*, March 23–May 2, 1976, no. 20 (illus.).

RELATED BIBLIOGRAPHY
Helen Haseltine Plowden, *William Stanley Haseltine, Sea and Landscape (1835–1900)* (London: F. Muller, Ltd., 1947), 81–82.
John Wilmerding, *A History of American Marine Painting* (Boston: The Peabody Museum of Salem, Massachusetts, and Little, Brown and Company, 1968), 203.

The painting is dated on the basis of costume, the woman's hat being particularly typical of the kind worn in the 1860s. Although Haseltine painted marine paintings throughout the 1860s, the affectionate grouping of the man and the woman suggests that it was painted shortly after either the artist's marriage to his first wife, Helen Lane, on October 9, 1860, or her death on June 11, 1864.

Martin Johnson Heade (1819–1904)

One of the major luminist artists, Martin Johnson Heade was born in 1819 in Lumberville, Pennsylvania. He studied with the painters Edward and Thomas Hicks and then traveled to Europe (probably in the early 1840s), spending two years in Rome. He at first concentrated on portraiture, producing a few genre scenes and landscapes as well. In 1859 he established a studio in New York, although he traveled almost constantly; by 1860, he had lived in eight cities and had seen much of America and Europe. By this time, his attention turned to landscape. The salt marsh became Heade's favorite subject, and he painted marsh scenes throughout his later career: in Massachusetts and Rhode Island in the 1860s; in New Jersey in the 1870s; and in Florida in the 1890s. Over one hundred of his marsh paintings are known today.

In 1863, Heade made the first of three trips to South America—perhaps inspired by the South American paintings of his friend Frederic Church (q.v.)—and began to paint forest and flower still lifes based on his travels. His interest in hummingbirds, in particular, dates from these trips, and at one point Heade planned to publish a book containing chromolithographs of his hummingbird paintings. In the 1870s, Heade started to combine hummingbirds and orchids in his works, creating sensual and exotic images which came to take precedence over his landscapes in the later stages of his career.

In 1881 Heade left New York for Washington, D.C., and four years later he moved to St. Augustine, Florida, where he died in 1904. His work was largely forgotten until the 1940s when collectors such as Maxim Karolik (who purchased more than fifty Heades) rediscovered his paintings.

Martin Johnson Heade
Twilight on Newbury Marsh
late 1860s, Charcoal and white chalk on paper
13½ x 29 in (34.3 x 73.7 cm.)
Unsigned
(fig. 8)

PROVENANCE
[Newburyport, Mass., art market]
Mr. and Mrs. William Graf, Newbury, Mass.
[Davis and Long Company, New York]
Jo Ann and Julian Ganz, Jr., 1980

BIBLIOGRAPHY
Theodore E. Stebbins, Jr., *The Life and Works of Martin Johnson Heade* (New Haven and London: Yale University Press, 1975), 56–60, 284, cat. no. 385 (illus.); related works (see below): 283–385.

This is one of a series of such drawings done by Heade, probably around 1867 or 1868.[1] The marsh is located to the east of Newbury. The view faces north with the Plum Island River separating the mainland on the left from the island and the sea on the right. Newburyport can be seen on the horizon to the left.[2] For related watercolor and drawings see Stebbins, *Heade*, cat. nos. 379–380, 382–384, 386–388, pp. 283–285.

1. Stebbins, *Heade*, 56.
2. Site identified by John Wilmerding in Stebbins, *Heade*, 60.

Martin Johnson Heade
Victorian Vase with Flowers of Devotion
c. 1870–1875, Oil on canvas
18⅛ x 10 in. (46.0 x 25.4 cm.)
Signed (lower right): *M.J.Heade*
(fig. 100)

PROVENANCE
[Hirschl & Adler Galleries, New York, 1981]
Jo Ann and Julian Ganz, Jr., 1981

This painting is closely related to a work entitled *Flowers in a Vase, with a Book and Hatpin* (c. 1865–1875, oil on canvas, 18 x 10⅛ in., Dr. and Mrs. Alick Osofsky, Hewlett Bay Park, New York).[1]

1. See Theodore E. Stebbins, Jr., *The Life and Works of Martin Johnson Heade* (New Haven and London: Yale University Press, 1975), 240, cat. no. 139 (illus.).

Martin Johnson Heade
An Amethyst Hummingbird with a White Orchid
1870s, Oil on canvas
20 x 12⅛ in. (50.8 x 30.8 cm.)
Signed (lower left): *M.J. Heade* (fragmentary)
(fig. 91)

PROVENANCE
[Art market, France]
[Nicholas Weitzner, Scarsdale, N.Y., by 1970]
Joseph D. Schwerin, New York, 1971
Jo Ann and Julian Ganz, Jr., 1974

BIBLIOGRAPHY
Theodore E. Stebbins, Jr., *The Life and Works of Martin Johnson Heade* (New Haven and London: Yale University Press, 1975), 145, cat. no. 198, plate 8; related discussion (see below): 145–147, 251.

The Amethyst hummingbird is a native of Brazil as is the Lealia Purpurata orchid, which is that country's national flower. However, it is possible that the initial sketches for the work were made in the United States.[1] The sketch, *Study of "Lealia Purpurata" and Another Orchid* (c. 1865–1875, oil on unstretched canvas, Historical Society, St. Augustine, Florida)[2] served as an exact model for this and two other vertical white orchid and hummingbird pictures: *Hummingbird with a White Orchid* (c. 1870s, oil on canvas, 20 x 10½ in., Shelburne Museum, Shelburne, Vt.);[3] *White Brazilian Orchid* (c. 1870s, oil on canvas, 20 x 12 in., Dr. and Mrs. Alick Osofsky, Hewlett Bay Park, New York).[4]

1. Stebbins, *Heade*, 145–147
2. Stebbins, *Heade*, 146–147, 243, fig. 80, cat. no. 159.
3. Stebbins, *Heade*, 251, cat. no. 197.
4. Stebbins, *Heade*, 251, cat. no. 199.

❧ Edward Lamson Henry (1841–1919)

Born in Charleston, South Carolina, in 1841, Edward Lamson Henry studied at the Pennsylvania Academy of the Fine Arts in 1858. In 1859, at the age of eighteen, he began to exhibit his work at the National Academy of Design, where he continued to exhibit for the next sixty years. Henry went to Europe in 1860, where he divided his time between Paris (studying with Suisse, Gleyre, and Courbet) and Italy. Returning to the United States in 1862, he started to paint historical and contemporary genre scenes of American life. During the Civil War he served briefly as a captain's clerk, keeping a sketchbook in which he recorded his observations that resulted in several paintings with Civil War themes.

Following the war, Henry lived in New York City, working in the famous 10th Street Studio Building. From 1869 to 1872 he produced several paintings with scenes from colonial life, a theme in Henry's work that gained increasing popularity after America celebrated its centennial. Following his marriage in 1875, Henry again went abroad and then in 1883 moved his home and studio to Cragsmoor, New York, a remote area in the Shawangunk Mountains. Henry began to include scenes and figures from Cragsmoor in his paintings, earning a reputation as a recorder of American manners, customs, architecture, and furniture. Many of his paintings were reproduced in the form of platinotypes or photogravures, sometimes colored by hand. He continued to paint up to the time of his death in Ellenville, New York, in 1919.

Edward Lamson Henry
Can They Go Too?
1877, Oil on academy board
6 x 4¹⁵⁄₁₆ in. (15.24 x 12.54 cm.)
Signed (lower left): *E L Henry. 77*
(fig. 41)

PROVENANCE
Hubbard Kirkpatrick, New York
Estate of Hubbard Kirkpatrick's sister in Anna, Illinois
Private Collection, New Canaan, Conn., 1978
[Hirschl & Adler Galleries, New York, 1978]
Jo Ann and Julian Ganz, Jr., 1978

RELATED BIBLIOGRAPHY
Elizabeth McCausland, *The Life and Work of Edward Lamson Henry N.A. 1841–1919 (New York State Museum Bulletin Number 339)* (Albany, New York: The University of the State of New York, September, 1945), 55, 128, 169, 328.

The dog in the foreground is probably modeled on one of the artist's two black and tan dogs who frequently served as models in his early work.[1] Mrs. Henry (Frances Livingston Wells) may have served as the model for the woman (see McCausland, *Henry*, cat. no. 122, *Portrait of Mrs. Henry* [1876, oil on canvas, 13¼ x 11¼ in., New York State Museum, Albany, New York], 169, fig. 41, p. 128). The importance of the dogs in this work reflects the Henrys' own strong attachment to their pets, possibly as the result of a childless marriage.

1. McCausland, *Henry*, 55, 328.

Edward Lamson Henry
Mother and Child Under a Rose Trellis
1877, Oil on academy board
6³/₁₆ x 5⅛ in. (15.72 x 13.02 cm.)
Signed (lower right): *ELHenry.77*
(fig. 42)

PROVENANCE
[S. T. Freeman, Philadelphia]
Mrs. George C. Thomas, Philadelphia
Sophia Thomas Volkmar
[Schweitzer Gallery, New York]
Private Collection, New York
[Schweitzer Gallery, New York]
Jo Ann and Julian Ganz, Jr., 1977

It was the Henrys' custom during this period to spend at least part of their summers at the home of Judge Charles P. Daly at Sag Harbor, Long Island, New York.[1] Sag Harbor, therefore, may have served as the setting for this work.

1. McCausland, *Henry*, 36, 323.

Edward Lamson Henry
Watching Mother Embroider
1878, Oil on academy board
7 x 5¾ in. (17.78 x 14.61 cm.)
Signed (lower left): *E L Henry. 78*
(fig. 40)

PROVENANCE
Charles Lalli
[Post Road Antiques, Larchmont, N.Y.]
Jo Ann and Julian Ganz, Jr., 1974

 Albert Herter (1871–1950)

Albert Herter, known primarily as a mural and portrait painter, was born in New York City in 1871, the son of Christian Herter who founded the New York design firm of Herter Brothers. He studied in New York at the Art Students League and with Carroll Beckwith and later in Paris under J. P. Laurens. His work was represented in both European and American collections, and he won honors at exhibitions both at home and abroad, including the bronze medal at the 1900 Paris Exposition and a silver medal

at the Pan-American Exposition in Buffalo in 1901. He was a member of the Society of American Artists, the American Water Color Society, and an associate member of the National Academy of Design. He was a devotee of French tapestries, and in 1908 he founded Herter Looms (first called Aubusson Looms), a business with showrooms in New York and San Francisco. Among his designs were "Gifts of the Old World," commissioned by the St. Francis Hotel in San Francisco in 1913, and a series depicting the history of New York, made for the Harriman family in 1912. Herter died in 1950 in Santa Barbara, California.

Albert Herter
Pastoral
1892, Watercolor and gouache on paper
6⁵/₁₆ x 17 in. (16.0 x 43.2 cm.), sight
Signed (lower left): *-Albert Herter-/-92-*
(fig. 73)

PROVENANCE
[Hirschl & Adler Galleries, New York, 1978]
Jo Ann and Julian Ganz, Jr., 1978

This work was possibly exhibited as no. 288 *Elfin Play* at the Twenty-Fifth Annual *Exhibition of the American Water Color Society*, New York, National Academy of Design, February 1–27, 1892, p. 16.

Albert Herter
Two Women on Stairs
1901, Watercolor and gouache on paper
15¼ x 8⁹/₁₆ in. (39.4 x 21.8 cm.), sight
Signed (lower left): *ALBERT HERTER.*
(fig. 72)

PROVENANCE
The Curtis Publishing Company, Philadelphia, 1901
Miss Florence Geckeler, McKinley, Pa., March

4, 1907, gift from the Curtis Publishing Company to its employee upon her marriage ("C. H. Ludington, Jr., Secretary and Treasurer, The Curtis Publishing Company, to Miss Florence Geckeler, March 4, 1907," Albert Herter file, Hirschl & Adler Galleries, New York)
[Hirschl & Adler Galleries, New York, 1979]
Jo Ann and Julian Ganz, Jr., 1980

BIBLIOGRAPHY
The Ladies' Home Journal, October, 1901, cover and table of contents, n.p., as *Cover Design*, 11⅝ x 6⅝ in.; related works (see below): p. 5.
George Parsons Lathrop, "Japan in American Art, with original illustrations by Albert and Adele Herter," *The Monthly Illustrator*, 5 (July, 1895); related works (see below): pp. 2–6.

Herter's American hybrid of oriental and occidental motifs had been noted in 1895.[1] In the context of *The Ladies' Home Journal*, Herter's use of drapery, especially, was much more closely related to the art photographs in the monthly series, "The Foremost Women Photographers in America," edited by Frances Benjamin Johnston, which began in the May 1901 issue of the *Journal*, than to the typical illustrations which appeared in the magazine.[2]

1. Lathrop, "Japan," especially the related *Portrait of Phillipa Picard*, 1895, p. 6 (illus.).
2. *Journal*, 5.

John William Hill was born in London in 1812 and came to the United States with his family in 1819. In 1822 his family moved from Philadelphia to New York, where Hill received his early artistic training from his father, an aquatint engraver. During the early part of his career, Hill was a topographical artist, employed first by the New York State Geological Survey and later by Smith Bros. of New York, for whom Hill drew views of American cities which were published as lithographs in the 1840s and fifties. By the mid-1850s, however, Hill began to paint landscapes and flower and bird studies in watercolor, under the influence of the English Pre-Raphaelites. He exhibited his nature studies at the National Academy of Design and the Pennsylvania Academy of the Fine Arts. He died at his home near West Nyack, New York, in 1879. In 1888 his son, the artist John Henry Hill, honored his father by publishing etchings after his father's landscapes in *An Artist's Memorial*.

John William Hill
Pineapples
after 1855, Watercolor on paper
10½ x 15⅛ in. (26.67 x 38.42 cm.), sight
Signed (lower right): *J .W. Hill.*
(fig. 88)

PROVENANCE
[Village Green Antiques, Brattleboro, Vt.]
[Post Road Antiques, Larchmont, N.Y., 1977]
Jo Ann and Julian Ganz, Jr., 1977

Born in Cincinnati, Ohio, Hirst first studied at the Cincinnati Art Academy with John Noble (1874–1934). By 1882 she had moved to New York where she studied with Agnes Dean Abbatt (1847–1917), John David Smillie (1833–1909), and Charles Courtney Curran (1861–1942). She exhibited, and probably primarily painted, floral still lifes in watercolor and oil as late as 1888. However, the return of William Michael Harnett (q.v.) to New York and his occupancy of a studio close to Hirst's between 1886 and 1889 caused a radical change in the latter's style around 1890. The loan of her studio to the landscapist William Crowthers Fitler (1857–1912) in 1889 acted as a catalyst for this change, as Hirst's future husband left the studio cluttered with books and pipes. By 1890, and probably for the rest of her active life, Hirst painted still lifes primarily, in the manner of Harnett. She probably stopped exhibiting oils after 1905, but she continued to exhibit watercolor still lifes of books and their accoutrements as late as 1936. Indeed, Hirst may have developed a specialized market for her work late in her career, as the prices of her watercolors were highest in the 1920s and early 1930s. She was a longstanding member of the New York Water Color Club and the National Association of Women Painters and Sculptors from whom she received the National Association Prize for Painting in 1931.

Claude Raguet Hirst
Still Life with Clippings
1891, Oil on canvas
9 x 13 in. (22.86 x 32.02 cm.)
Signed (lower left): *Claude Raguet Hirst / N.Y.*
Label (on back): [s]*ale* (torn) ["C]*lippings*" / *Miss Claude Raguet Hirst / 30 East 14th St. / New York.* (fig. 96)

PROVENANCE
[Hirschl & Adler Galleries, New York, 1980]
Jo Ann and Julian Ganz, Jr., 1980

Although most of the words in the newspaper are almost illegible, two words in the left column seem to read "Help Wanted," indicating that it is the classified section. It appears to be partially dated in the upper left "[two illegible words] 11 1891." Hirst moved from the studio listed on the label toward the end of 1893.

Winslow Homer (1836–1910)

Born in Boston, Winslow Homer began his artistic career in 1854 by copying sheet-music illustrations for Bufford's lithography firm in that city. In 1857, he was working as a free-lance artist, submitting illustrations to *Ballou's* and *Harper's Weekly* magazines. Two years later, Homer moved to New York, where he continued to produce illustrations for *Harper's*, soon focusing on Civil War scenes. He also began to paint in oil and submitted his Civil War paintings to the National Academy of Design in 1863 and 1864, the year he was elected an associate member. He became an academician in 1866. That same year he went to Paris and, returning to New York at the end of 1867, continued to submit engravings, principally of children and wistful young women, to *Harper's* and other magazines.

In 1873 he spent his first summer in Gloucester, Massachusetts, and the next year went to the Adirondacks. These areas, representing the themes of the sea and woods, were to figure significantly in his later work. In 1873 Homer began to paint in watercolor, a medium he was to use extensively during the remainder of his career. During the 1870s he painted a series of watercolors and oils of country schools, including the remarkable *Blackboard* of 1877.

In 1881 Homer again left for Europe, spending a year and a half in the Northumberland coastal village of Cullercoats, near the town of Tynemouth. There, working primarily in watercolor, he depicted the Northumbrians' constant battle with the sea. In November 1882 he returned to the United States and settled in Prout's Neck, Maine, where he was to live, except for occasional excursions, for the rest of his life. Along with his oil paintings and watercolors of the Maine coast, Homer continued to paint Adirondack subjects and scenes set in the Bahamas and Florida, where he spent several winters during the years 1884–1904. He exhibited his work regularly at the National Academy of Design and by the mid-1880s had achieved a reputation as a major artist—one that endures to the present day. In his late career Homer sent several of his paintings to international exhibitions, winning gold medals on at least three occasions. He died in Prout's Neck in 1910.

Winslow Homer
Blackboard
1877, Watercolor on paper
19⁷⁄₁₆ x 12³⁄₁₆ in. (49.4 x 31.0 cm.), sight
Signed (center right): *HOMER '77*
(fig. 58)

PROVENANCE
William Townsend, Boston
Estate of William Townsend, Boston
Rose Townsend, Boston
Thomas H. Townsend, Boston
[Vose Galleries, Boston, 1977]
Jo Ann and Julian Ganz, Jr., 1977

EXHIBITED
National Academy of Design, New York, *Tenth Annual Exhibition of the American Society of Painters in Water Colors*, 1877, no. 122, p. 10.
Los Angeles County Museum of Art, Installation of works by Winslow Homer, November–December, 1977.

BIBLIOGRAPHY
"The Painters in Water Colors: Pictures by American Artists in the Exhibition" (second paper), *The Evening Post*, New York, February 13, 1877, p. 1.
"The Old Cabinet," *Scribner's Monthly* 13 (April, 1877): 866.
William Howe Downes, *The Life and Works of Winslow Homer* (Boston and New York: Houghton Mifflin Company, 1911), 89, 279.
Michael Quick, "Homer in Virginia," *Los Angeles County Museum of Art Bulletin*, 24, p. 74, fig. 22.
Gordon Hendricks, *The Life and Work of Winslow Homer* (New York: Harry N. Abrams, Inc., 1979), 126 (fig. 189), 130, as *Blackboard* (or *A School Teacher*).

Homer exhibited five works at the 1877 Annual Exhibition. The other four were: 42. *Book* (Museum of Fine Arts, Springfield, Mass., as *The New Novel*); 198. *Rattlesnake* (private collection, Ohio); 280. *Lemon* (Sterling and Francine Clark Art Institute, Williamstown, Mass., as *Peeling a Lemon*); and 396. *Backgammon* (Collection Mrs. John D. Rockefeller 3rd). While respecting Homer's originality, both the *Post* and *Scribner's* were generally critical of the results of his works in that exhibition. However, the *Post* felt that *Blackboard* was "in some respects by far the best of his contributions,"[1] and *Scribner's* noted that "in the 'Book' (42), and in the 'Blackboard' (122), Homer is himself again—one of the few American painters of originality and force."[2]

1. *Post*, 1; quoted in Hendricks, *Homer*, 130.
2. *Scribner's*, 866; reference provided by Helen Cooper, Yale University Art Gallery, New Haven.

Harriet Hosmer (1830–1908)

Harriet Hosmer, the most famous of a number of women sculptors working in Rome in the mid-nineteenth century, was born and raised in Watertown, Massachusetts. Her artistic interests were encouraged by her father, a doctor, and in the late 1840s she took lessons in Boston with the sculptor Paul Stevenson. In 1850 she studied anatomy in the medical department of Washington University in St. Louis and in 1852 accompanied Charlotte Cushman, a well-known actress and lecturer, to Rome, where Hosmer studied with the English sculptor John Gibson. By 1855 she had completed her first life-sized work. Hosmer's subjects came from Italian and ancient history, literature, and fairy tales. *Puck,* among a group of her sculptures that were categorized as "conceits" or "fancy pieces," was the most famous of Hosmer's sculptures; no less than thirty replicas were created, one of which was purchased by the Prince of Wales.

Hosmer became one of Rome's leading personalities, attracting the admiration and friendship of both royalty and fellow artists. Elizabeth Barrett Browning wrote about her as follows:

She lives here all alone (at twenty-two); dines and breakfasts at the cafes precisely as a young man would; works from six o'clock in the morning till night, as a great artist must, and this with an absence of pretension and simplicity of manners which accord rather with the childish dimples in her rosy cheeks than with her broad forehead and high aims.

Hosmer's affection for the Brownings is evident from her *Clasped Hands of Robert and Elizabeth Barrett Browning.*

Throughout her career, Hosmer supported herself from the sale of her sculpture, which, until 1860, consisted entirely of "ideal" pieces. Following a visit to the United States in 1860, however, Hosmer received the first of a series of portrait commissions. By 1875 her career as a sculptor was over, although she did execute a very few pieces after this time. In 1900 she returned to the United States where she died eight years later in Watertown.

Harriet Hosmer
Clasped Hands of Robert and Elizabeth Barrett Browning
1853, Bronze
8¼ in. (21 cm.), length
Inscribed (on end of Elizabeth's hand): *Copyright*
Inscribed (on end of Robert's hand): *HANDS-of-RoBERT / AND / Elizabeth Barrett Browning / cast / By / Harriet Hosmer / Rome 1853*
(fig. 37)

PROVENANCE
Geraldine Rockefeller Dodge, Madison, N.J.
[Sotheby Parke Bernet, Inc., New York (Sale No. 3791, *The Contents of Giralda, From the Collection of the Late Geraldine Rockefeller Dodge at Madison, New Jersey,* Lot No. 1034 (illus., n.p.), October 7–11, 1975; Hirschl & Adler Galleries, New York, as agent]
Jo Ann and Julian Ganz, Jr., 1975

BIBLIOGRAPHY
Nathaniel Hawthorne, *The Marble Faun; or, the Romance of Monte Beni,* 2 vols. (Boston: Ticknor and Fields, 1860), 1, p. 154.
Harriet Hosmer to Mrs. Edward Ripley, September 27, c. 1895, Wellesley College Library, Wellesley, Mass.
Ruth Bradford, "The Life and Works of Harriet Hosmer, The American Sculptor," *New England Magazine,* 45 (November, 1911): 268.
Harriet Hosmer, *Letters and Memories,* Cornelia Carr, ed. (New York: Moffat, Yard and Company, 1912), 92 (illus., n.p.).
Travellers in Arcadia: American Artists in Italy 1830–1875, The Detroit Institute of Arts, January 9–February 18, 1951; and The Toledo Museum of Art, March 4–25, 1951, cat. no. 56, pp. 41 (illus.)–42.
Sarah Wingate Taylor, "Harriet and The Browning Hands," *Yankee,* 21 (October, 1957): 45 (illus.), 46–47.
Susan Van Rensselaer, "Harriet Hosmer," *Antiques,* 84 (October, 1963): 426, 428 (illus.).
William H. Gerdts, *Women Artists of America 1707–1964* (Newark, N.J.: The Newark Museum, April 2–May 16, 1965), 24.
Margaret Wendell LaBarre, "Harriet Hosmer: Her Era and Art," (M.A. thesis, University of Illinois, 1966), 148–152, 247–248ff. (On microfilm: Archives of American Art, roll no. 1045).
Wayne Craven, *Sculpture In America* (New York: Thomas Y. Crowell, 1968), 327.
William H. Gerdts, "Marble and Nudity," *Art in America,* 59 (May–June, 1971), 67.
———, and others, *The White Marmorean Flock: Nineteenth Century American Women Neoclassical Sculptors* (Poughkeepsie, N.Y.: Vassar College Art Gallery, April 4–30, 1972), 6, cat. nos. 2a, 2b (illus., n.p.).
———, *American Neo-Classic Sculpture: The Marble Resurrection* (New York: The Viking Press, 1973), 141 (fig. 74).
Art at Auction, The Year at Sotheby Parke Bernet, 1975–6 (New York: Rizzoli International and Sotheby Parke Bernet Publications, Ltd., New Jersey, 1976), 118.
Josephine Withers, "Artistic Women and Women Artists," *Art Journal,* 35 (Summer, 1976): 335 (illus.), 336.
William H. Gerdts, "The *Medusa* of Harriet Hosmer," *Bulletin of The Detroit Institute of Arts,* 56, no. 2 (1978): 98, 99 (fig. 2), 107.

At Elizabeth Browning's insistence, Hosmer did the casting herself rather than have an assistant do it.[1] The result was described by Hawthorne as "symbolizing the individuality and heroic union of two high poetic lives!"[2]

1. Hosmer, *Letters,* 92
2. Hawthorne, *The Marble Faun,* vol. 1, 154.

Harriet Hosmer
Puck
after 1854, Marble
31 in. (78.74 cm.)
Inscribed (on lower back): *H. HOSMER / ROME*
(fig. 36)

PROVENANCE
Estate of R. A. Carter, Los Angeles
[Sotheby Parke Bernet, Los Angeles (Sale No. 254, *Fine Nineteenth and Twentieth Century European and American Paintings, Drawings and Sculpture*, Lot No. 149, illus.), June 18, 1979]
Jo Ann and Julian Ganz, Jr., 1979

BIBLIOGRAPHY
Ellet, Mrs., *Women Artists In All Ages and All Countries* (New York: Harper & Brothers, 1859), 367–369.
Nathaniel Hawthorne, *Passages from the French and Italian Note-Books of Nathaniel Hawthorne*, 2 vols. (Boston: James R. Osgood, 1872), 1, p. 157; 2, p. 230.
Art Journal (American Edition), new series, 1 (1875): 317 (illus.).
William J. Clark, Jr., *Great American Sculptures* (Philadelphia: Gebbie & Barrie, Publishers, 1878; reprinted, New York and London: Garland Publishing, Inc., 1977), 139.
Ruth Bradford, "The Life and Works of Harriet Hosmer, The American Sculptor," *New England Magazine*, 45 (November, 1911): 267.
Harriet Hosmer, *Letters and Memories*, Cornelia Carr, ed. (New York: Moffat, Yard and Company, 1912), 36, 40, 72, 76, 78, 79, 94, 123.

Lorado Taft, *The History of American Sculpture*, new edition with a supplementary chapter by Adeline Adams (New York: The Macmillan Company, 1930), 205.
Albert Ten Eyck Gardner, *Yankee Stonecutters: The First American School of Sculpture 1800–1850* (New York: Published for The Metropolitan Museum of Art by Columbia University Press, 1945), 67.
Susan Wingate Taylor, "Harriet and The Browning Hands," *Yankee*, 21 (October 1957): 44 (illus.).
Susan Van Rennselaer, "Harriet Hosmer," *Antiques*, 84 (October 1963): 425–426.
William H. Gerdts, *Women Artists of America 1707–1964* (Newark, N.J.: The Newark Museum, April 2–May 16, 1965), 12 (illus.), 13.
Margaret Wendell LaBarre, "Harriet Hosmer: Her Era and Art," (M.A. thesis, University of Illinois, 1966), 197–201, 256–258ff. (On microfilm: Archives of American Art, roll no. 1045).
Wayne Craven, *Sculpture In America* (New York: Thomas Y. Crowell, 1968), 273, 328, 329, 344 (fig. 9.10).
Lilian M. C. Randall, "An American Abroad: Visits to Sculptors' Studios in the 1860s," *The Journal of the Walters Art Gallery*, 33–34 (1970–1971): 48–49.
William H. Gerdts and others, *The White Marmorean Flock: Nineteenth Century American Women Neoclassical Sculptors* (Poughkeepsie, N.Y.: Vassar College Art Gallery, April 4–30, 1972), 4, 5, cat. no. 5 (illus., n.p.).
———, *American Neo-Classic Sculpture: The Marble Resurrection* (New York: The Viking Press, 1973), 136 (fig. 166).

Puck was first designed in the summer of 1854, but because of its popularity, at least thirty replicas were produced over a period of years. The figure sits on what is probably a toadstool and holds a beetle in his right hand while resting his left hand on a lizard. Although it has been suggested that the statue has symbolic content,[1] this may not have been intended by the sculptor.[2] Hosmer later created a companion piece, *Will-o'-the-Wisp* in 1866.

1. See LaBarre, *Hosmer*, 200.
2. See Hosmer, *Letters*, 79.

David Johnson (1827–1908)

David Johnson was born in New York City in 1827, the brother of the portraitist Joseph Hoffman Johnson. His only formal training as an artist consisted of a few lessons from Jasper F. Cropsey (q.v.), and Johnson, unlike most of his artistic contemporaries, never traveled abroad. Nonetheless he became a successful and well-respected landscape painter. He spent his career in New York City but went on frequent sketching trips to New England and upstate New York and, on at least one occasion (1860), to Virginia. In 1861 he was elected an academician of the National Academy of Design and in 1876 received a medal at the Philadelphia Centennial Exhibition. He was also one of the founders of the Artists' Fund Society in 1859.

Johnson enjoyed his greatest success in the late 1860s and seventies, exhibiting many paintings of Hudson River, Adirondack, and New England views. Particularly well known for his detailed depiction of rocks and trees in the Pre-Raphaelite manner, he was an excellent draftsman whose precision is reflected in his paintings as well as his drawings. Although the quality of Johnson's later work remained high, he seems to have produced only a small number of paintings after 1880. In 1904 he moved to Walden, Orange County, New York, where he died in 1908.

David Johnson
The Natural Bridge of Virginia
1860, Oil on canvas
24 x 20 in. (60.96 x 50.8 cm.)
Signed (lower right): *D. Johnson. 1860*
Signed (on the stretcher): *The Natural Bridge of Virginia, / David Johnson 1860*
(fig. 3)

PROVENANCE
[Ortgies & Co., New York (*Paintings in Oil, by David Johnson, N.A. To be sold by Auction . . . at Fifth Avenue Art Galleries*) February 13–14, 1890]
Charles F. Gunther, Chicago
Y.M.C.A., Chicago
[Sally Turner Gallery, Plainfield, N.J., 1974]
Jo Ann and Julian Ganz, Jr., 1975

BIBLIOGRAPHY

John I. H. Baur, " '. . . the exact brushwork of Mr. David Johnson,' An American Landscape Patinter, 1827–1908," *The American Art Journal*, 12 (Autumn 1980): 46 (fig. 23), 48.

An undated oval engraving (Hirschl & Adler Galleries, New York) inscribed "Natural Bridge, Virginia. / Engraved expressly for the Ladies Repository by S. V. Hunt from the original Painting by David Johnson in the possession of S. P. Avery" varies somewhat in figures and composition. Another version, *Natural Bridge, Virginia* (1860, oil on canvas, 14¼ x 22¼ in., Reynolda House, Winston-Salem, N.C.) shows the bridge in the middle distance.

ꕤ (Jonathan) Eastman Johnson (1824–1906)

Eastman Johnson, one of America's best-known figure painters, was born in 1824 in Lovell, Maine, and first showed artistic talent drawing crayon portraits of his family and friends. After a brief apprenticeship at Bufford's lithography shop in Boston, Johnson began his artistic career as a portraitist in 1842 in Augusta, Maine, again working in crayon and charcoal. He continued his career in Washington, D.C. (1845–1846) and Boston (1846–1849), with growing success as a portrait draftsman. By the summer of 1849 he had resolved to go to Europe for further study and spent his first two years in Düsseldorf, where he shared a studio with Emanuel Leutze. From there he went to The Hague, where he remained for three and a half years, and in 1855 to Paris, where he studied briefly with Thomas Couture. The death of Johnson's mother forced his return to the United States in 1855 and shortly thereafter he began exhibiting genre paintings at the National Academy of Design, to which he was elected an associate in 1859 and an academician in 1860.

Johnson's narrative paintings encompassed many subjects. In 1856 and 1857, he studied the Chippewa Indians in Wisconsin, painting Indian portraits. During the Civil War, Johnson depicted anecdotal scenes of Union soldiers' camps. In New York, where he had established a studio, Eastman Johnson painted several prominent families in the well-appointed interiors of their Victorian homes. He also visited New England, especially Maine and Nantucket (where he spent part of the year), and recorded events from rural life such as maple sugaring, corn husking, and cranberry picking. In the 1870s, he began to paint genre scenes of women and children, of which *Bo Peep* is a fine example. After 1880, Johnson turned to portraiture almost exclusively. He died in New York City in 1906.

Eastman Johnson
Bo Peep (The Peep)
1872, Oil on academy board
21⅜ x 25⅝ in. (54.29 x 65.09 cm.)
Signed (lower left): *E. Johnson 1872*
Label (attached to back): "*Bo Peep*" / (c/o or to) *Alfred Booth* (illegible) *llet Road* / (illegible) *Park* (fig. 39)

PROVENANCE
[Düsseldorf, Germany, art market]
Walter Zehnder, Wallisellen, Switzerland
[Galerie Peyer, Zurich, Switzerland]
Jacobo Blum, Caracas, Venezuela, 1969
[Hirschl & Adler Galleries, New York, 1970]
Howard Garfinkle, Miami, Fla., 1972
[Kennedy Galleries, Inc., New York]
Jo Ann and Julian Ganz, Jr., 1978

EXHIBITED
Royal Academy of Arts, London, *One Hundred and Fifth Royal Academy Exhibition*, 1873, no. 1074 as *Bo-peep* in Algernon Graves, *The Royal*

Academy of Arts, A Complete Dictionary of Contributors and their work from its foundation in 1769 to 1904 (London: Henry Graves and Co., Ltd. and George Bell and Sons, 1906), vol. 4, p. 252 (possible exhibition: see below).

National Academy of Design, New York, *Forty-Ninth Annual Exhibition*, 1874, p. 25, no. 371 as *Bo Peep* (possible exhibition: see below).

Whitney Museum of American Art, New York, *Eastman Johnson*, March 28–May 14, 1972; The Detroit Institute of Arts, June 7–July 22, 1972; Cincinnati Art Museum, August 15–September 30, 1972; Milwaukee Art Center, October 20–December 3, 1972, xxi (cat. no. 68), 76, 78 (illus.), 79 as *The Peep*.

Hirschl & Adler Galleries, New York, *Faces and Places: Changing Images of 19th Century America*, December 5, 1972–January 6, 1973, cat. no. 57 (illus., n.p.) as *The Peep*.

BIBLIOGRAPHY

James Grant Wilson and John Fiske, eds., *Appletons' Cyclopaedia of American Biography* (New York: D. Appleton and Company, 1888; republished, Detroit, Mich.: Gale Research Company, 1968), vol. 3, p. 492, as *Bo-Peep*, exhibited at the Royal Academy.

Clara Erskine Clement (Waters) and Laurence Hutton, *Artists of the Nineteenth Century and their Works*, seventh edition, revised, 2 vols. (Boston and New York: Houghton, Mifflin and Company, 1894), vol. 2, p. 12, as *Bo-Peep*, H. Richmond Collection, exhibited at the National Academy of Design, 1874.

Kennedy and Company, New York, *Exhibition of Charcoal Drawings by Eastman Johnson,* June, 1920, p. 13 (appended list of known paintings) as *Bo-Peep.*

Kennedy Galleries, New York, *Rare American Masterpieces of the 18th, 19th, and 20th Centuries Volume II* (New York: Kennedy Galleries, 1974), cat. no. 22 (illus., n.p.) as *Bo-Peep.*

A replica of this work (*Bo Peep,* 1872, oil on paper board mounted on panel, 22⅛ x 26½ in., Amon Carter Museum, Fort Worth, Texas) could also have been the work exhibited at either the Royal Academy or the National Academy. Further, it is not known which of the two versions is referred to in Clement and Hutton, *Artists;* Wilson and Fiske, *Appletons';* and Kennedy and Company, *Drawings.*

Francis Coates Jones (1857–1932)

Francis Coates Jones was born in Baltimore, Maryland, the younger brother of landscape painter H. Bolton Jones. In 1876 the brothers went abroad, visiting studios in London and Brittany, which sparked Francis's interest in art. During the next four years he studied at the Ecole des Beaux-Arts and at the Académie Julian under Bouguereau and Lefebvre and traveled extensively throughout Europe. He began showing his work at the National Academy of Design in 1877. After returning to America in 1881 Jones worked briefly in his brother's studio in New York, becoming a member of the Society of American Artists in 1882 and exhibiting at the Brooklyn Art Association. By 1884, following an extended European tour, he had settled permanently in New York. In 1885 Jones won the National Academy's Thomas B. Clarke prize and became an associate member. He was made an academician in 1894, taught at the academy and served as its treasurer for twenty-two years. Working as an illustrator, muralist, and easel painter, Jones appears to have been well known in artistic circles, was the recipient of several awards, and served as a trustee of The Metropolitan Museum of Art from 1917 to 1930. He died in New York City in 1932.

Francis Coates Jones
Woman in Classic Dress
1890s, Pastel on paper
16¾ x 13¾ in. (42.5 x 34.9 cm.), sight
Signed (lower right): *FRANCIS C JONES*
(fig. 67)

PROVENANCE
[Sotheby Parke Bernet, Inc., New York (Sale No. 4338, *Fine Americana,* Lot No. 279) January 30–February 2, 1980; Hirschl & Adler Galleries, New York, as agent]
Jo Ann and Julian Ganz, Jr., 1980

The bravura handling of the medium in this work suggests the influence of William Merritt Chase (1849–1916). See, for example, Chase, *At the Window,* (c. 1890, pastel on paper, 18½ x 11 in., The Brooklyn Museum).[1]

1. Dianne H. Pilgrim, "The Revival of Pastels in Nineteenth-Century America: The Society of Painters in Pastel," *The American Art Journal,* 10 (November 1978): 56, fig. 15.

Francis Coates Jones
Lady and Lyre
c. 1900–1910, Pastel on paper
12½ x 15 in. (31.75 x 38.1 cm.), sight
Signed (lower left): *FRANCIS C JONES*
(fig. 66)

PROVENANCE
[Sotheby Parke Bernet, Inc., New York (Sale No. 4236, *American 19th & 20th Century Paintings, Drawings, Watercolors & Sculpture,* Lot. No. 115, illus., n.p.) April 20, 1979; Hirschl & Adler Galleries, New York, as agent]
Jo Ann and Julian Ganz, Jr., 1979

This is possibly related to *The Song* (c. 1905, oil on canvas, 24⅜ x 40⅜ in., Wichita Art Museum, Wichita, Kansas), but not necessarily a study. Jones was an original member of the Society of American Painters in Pastel and had, therefore, been working in pastel at least as early as the 1880s.

John Frederick Kensett (1816–1872)

Born in 1816 in Cheshire, Connecticut, John F. Kensett began his artistic career by working for more than a decade as an engraver of business items and bank notes, a trade he learned in his father's firm. He traveled through Europe in 1840, in the company of painters John Casilear, Asher B. Durand, and Thomas Rossiter. He then settled in Paris, alternating between painting landscapes and engraving to support himself. Late in 1847, after spending two years in London and an additional twenty months in Germany, Switzerland, and Italy, Kensett returned to New York City.

Shortly after his arrival, Kensett began exhibiting his paintings at the National Academy of Design and quickly established his reputation as one of America's leading landscape painters. Following his return from Europe his output as an artist was consistent in both its style and subject matter, treating familiar outdoor scenes in a quiet manner which offered a contrast to the dramatic landscapes of Albert Bierstadt (q.v.) and Frederic Edwin Church (q.v.). Although Kensett traveled west in 1870 with fellow artists Worthington Whittredge (q.v.) and Sanford Gifford (q.v.) and made several painting tours of Europe, most of his paintings have as their subject the mountains and coastal regions of New York and New England. As a founding trustee of The Metropolitan Museum of Art, Kensett was an influential figure in the New York art world. He died in New York in 1872.

John F. Kensett
Lake George
1858, Oil on canvas
24⅛ x 36¼ in. (61.28 x 92.08 cm.)
Signed (lower right): *JF.K.58.* (in monogram)
(fig. 13)

PROVENANCE
Judge Coxe, Hicksville, N.Y.
Mrs. Julia F. Wotman, Encino, Calif.
[M. Knoedler & Co., Inc., New York, 1966]
Theodore E. Stebbins, Jr., Branford, Conn., 1969
[Kennedy Galleries, Inc., New York, 1969]
Jo Ann and Julian Ganz, Jr., 1969

EXHIBITED
Kennedy Galleries, Inc., New York, *Exhibition of Nineteenth Century American Landscape Painting*, May 1–28, 1969, no. 27.

Los Angeles County Museum of Art, *Chosen Works of American Art 1850–1924 from the Collection of Jo Ann and Julian Ganz, Jr.*, October 1–November 16, 1969, no. 7 (illus.), n.p.
Santa Barbara Museum of Art, Santa Barbara, Calif., *American Paintings, Watercolors and Drawings from the Collection of Jo Ann and Julian Ganz, Jr.*, June 23–July 22, 1973, no. 45 (illus.), n.p.

BIBLIOGRAPHY
Los Angeles County Museum of Art, *Members' Calendar*, October, 1969, p. 4.
Donelson F. Hoopes, "The Jo Ann and Julian Ganz, Jr. Collection," *American Art Review*, 1 (September–October, 1973), 48 (illus.), 49.
Theodore E. Stebbins, Jr., "Luminism in Context: A New View," in John Wilmerding, *American Light: The Luminist Movement 1850–1875* (Washington: National Gallery of Art, 1980), 212, fig. 228.

Because of its identical title and near-identical size, this may be the work listed as 68. *Lake George*, 24 x 36, p. 13 in *Catalogue of the Entire Collection of Paintings Belonging to the Late Mr. A. M. Cozzens To be sold by Auction at the Clinton Hall Art Galleries & Book Sale Rooms . . . May 22, 1868, . . . Leavitt, Strebeigh & Co., . . . New York.* The Cozzens *Lake George* had been exhibited as no. 234 *Lake George*, p. 17 at the *Forty-First Annual Exhibition of the National Academy of Design*, New York, in 1866.

 John Crookshanks King (1806–1882)

John Crookshanks King was born in 1806 in Scotland and came to the United States in 1829. After working as a machinist in New Orleans and Louisville, he settled in Cincinnati where he met Hiram Powers (q.v.) and the art patron Nicholas Longworth, both of whom encouraged him to become a sculptor. By 1837 King had abandoned his career as a machinist and moved back to New Orleans to work there as a sculptor. With the hope of increasing patronage, King moved to Boston in 1843 where he exhibited several of his portrait busts in the 1841 exhibition

of the Boston Athenaeum. King depended upon portrait commissions for his livelihood and did not attempt ideal pieces or "fancy" sculpture. He enjoyed success modeling busts of some of the leading Boston citizens, but by 1860 his popularity as a sculptor seems to have faded, and little work emerged from his studio after that date. He died in Boston in 1882.

John Crookshanks King
Cat on a Cushion
mid-19th century, Marble
15 in. (38.1 cm.)
Inscribed (on center back): *J C KING*
(fig. 33)

PROVENANCE
[Terry DeLapp, Los Angeles]
Jo Ann and Julian Ganz, Jr., 1976

The only animal to receive significant attention among American neoclassic sculptors was the dog. King may have been influenced by this trend, as his work does suggest knowledge of the best-known of the dog sculptures, Horatio Greenough's (1805–1852) *St. Bernard Dog* (c. 1844, marble, Perkins Family Lot, Mount Auburn Cemetery, Cambridge, Massachusetts).[1]

1. See William H. Gerdts, *American Neo-Classic Sculpture: The Marble Resurrection* (New York: The Viking Press, 1973), 142, fig. 178.

❧ George Cochran Lambdin (1830–1896)

George Cochran Lambdin, the son of the well-known portrait painter James Reid Lambdin, was born in Pittsburgh in 1830 but spent most of his youth in Philadelphia. Lambdin studied art with his father and in 1848 exhibited three genre scenes at the Pennsylvania Academy, to which he would be elected an academician in 1863. In 1855–1856 Lambdin studied in Paris and Munich and in 1863 is thought to have studied with William Trost Richards (q.v.). Lambdin moved from Philadelphia to New York in 1868 and was elected a member of the National Academy of Design. Two years later, after another trip to Europe, Lambdin returned to Philadelphia where he lived for the remainder of his life. He died in Germantown, Pennsylvania, in 1896.

In his early career, Lambdin painted and exhibited portraits, genre and Civil War scenes, and flower pictures, but after 1870 he devoted almost all his attention to depicting flowers. These paintings were quite popular, as is evidenced by the many chromolithographs of his work which were published and distributed. Lambdin was a skillful gardener; his paintings of roses growing against a wall are probably copied directly from the garden at his Germantown home. With a reputation as a painter of flowers which exceeded that of either Hall (q.v.) or Heade (q.v.), Lambdin was probably the best-known flower painter of his generation, rivaled only by John La Farge.

George C. Lambdin
Lilies
1872, Oil on wood panel
22 x 17½ in. (55.88 x 44.45 cm.)
Signed (lower left): *Geo. C. Lambdin. 1872.*
(fig. 85)

PROVENANCE
Private Estate, New York State
[Ira Spanierman, New York, 1978]
[Hirschl & Adler Galleries, Inc., New York, 1979]
Jo Ann and Julian Ganz, Jr., 1979

The vase also appears in *Flowers in a Vase* (1875, oil on canvas, private collection, New York), plate XI in William H. Gerdts and Russell Burke, *American Still-Life Painting* (New York: Praeger Publishers, 1971). Although there is a difference of two years, the work may have been the one placed on sale by Rufus Ellis Moore as no. 231 *Lilies* at the Spring Exhibition of the Brooklyn Art Association, Brooklyn, New York, April 27–May 9, 1874 (see Brown, *Picnic Party in the Woods*, q.v.).

George C. Lambdin
A Bouquet of Roses
1876, Oil on wood panel
19¼ x 15¼ in. (48.9 x 38.74 cm.)
Signed (lower right): *Geo. C. Lambdin. 76.*

Signed (on back): *A Bouquet of Roses/Geo. C. Lambdin/Germantown/Philad/1876.*
(fig. 86)

PROVENANCE
[Hirschl & Adler Galleries, New York, 1980]
Jo Ann and Julian Ganz, Jr., 1980

George C. Lambdin
Roses on a Wall (Roses and Butterfly)
1877, Oil on canvas
20¼ x 16½ in. (51.44 x 41.91 cm.)
Signed (lower center): *Geo. C. Lambdin/77*
Signed (on back, before relining): *Roses on a Wall/Geo.C. Lambdin*
(fig. 89)

PROVENANCE
[Kennedy Galleries, New York]
Theodore E. Stebbins, Jr., Branford, Conn.
[Kennedy Galleries, New York]
[Paul Magriel, New York]
[Coe Kerr Gallery, New York]
Jo Ann and Julian Ganz, Jr., 1973

EXHIBITED (as *Roses and Butterfly*)
Coe Kerr Gallery, New York, *150 Years of American Still Life Painting*, April 27–May 16, 1970, no. 28, p. 21 (illus.).
Santa Barbara Museum of Art, Santa Barbara, Calif., *American Paintings, Watercolors and Drawings from the Collection of Jo Ann and Julian Ganz, Jr.*, June 23–July 22, 1973, no. 46 (illus.).

The Hunt Institute for Botanical Documentation, Carnegie-Mellon University, Pittsburgh, *American Cornucopia: 19th Century Still Lifes and Studies*, no. 38, pp. 8, 25, 27 (illus.).

BIBLIOGRAPHY
Margie Carlin, *The Pittsburgh Press Roto*, May 16, 1976, p. 38 (illus.), as *Roses and Butterfly*.

The combination of yellow and pink roses was a favorite of Lambdin's, suggesting his interest in rose cultivation. While pink hybrid roses were first produced in the nineteenth century, attempts to produce the first yellow hybrid from pink and yellow roses were unsuccessful until 1900. Because the subject of this painting was a repeated motif in Lambdin's work, it is not certain whether this is the work exhibited as no. 248 *Roses on a Wall* at the Spring Exhibition of the Brooklyn Art Association, Brooklyn, New York, April 21–May 3, 1879.

Fitz Hugh Lane (1804–1865)

Fitz Hugh Lane, born in Gloucester, Massachusetts, in 1804 and partially crippled in early childhood, began his artistic career as an apprentice at Pendleton's lithography shop in Boston. During his years with Pendleton, Lane made small sketches of the Boston harbor and environs which were incorporated into sheet music covers. In the early 1840s he formed a lithographic firm with J.W.A. Scott, a marine painter, and began to publish large lithographs of New England coastal scenes, first with Scott and later on his own. Influenced in part by Robert Salmon, whose works Lane studied, and perhaps by the European seascapes which he saw exhibited at the Boston Athenaeum, he began to paint in oil in addition to producing lithographs.

In 1849, after the dissolution of his lithography firm, Lane devoted his full attention to marine painting. He returned to Gloucester and began a series of annual visits to the Maine coast, visiting the area from 1848 to 1855. These trips strengthed Lane's already distinctive style. *Twilight on the Kennebec*, one of the number of images of dawn or dusk which he painted, comes from this period and was shown at the American Art Union in 1849. From this time on, Lane's paintings are characterized by a feeling of expansiveness, of stillness, and of time suspended. Prior to Lane, emotion in marine painting was usually expressed through the turmoil of stormy seas. Lane brought a new meditativeness to the recording of the environment and a sensitivity to the qualities of light and atmosphere that made him a leader among the group of American painters we now call luminists.

In addition to traveling to Maine, Lane also made trips during the 1850s to New York, Baltimore, San Juan, and possibly New Brunswick and Nova Scotia. He exhibited his paintings at the American Art Union and at the Boston Athenaeum. Lane's works enjoyed considerable popularity, and he influenced many of the painters working in the Gloucester area. He died there in 1865.

Fitz Hugh Lane
Boston Harbor, Sunset
1850–1855, Oil on canvas
24 x 39¼ in. (60.96 x 99.7 cm.)
Unsigned
(Old note attached to back of canvas found in 1962): *Lane of Boston Ma. . ., Boston Harbor.*
(fig. 7)

PROVENANCE
Mrs. Malcolm E. Smith (Helen LeR. Miller) and Mrs. William Hoffman (Katherine C. Miller), Rhinebeck, N.Y.
[Parke-Bernet Galleries, Inc., New York (Sale No. 2103, *Early American Cabinetwork Paintings Glass and Decorative Objects*, Lot No. 185, pp. 36–37, illus.) April 14, 1962]
[Kennedy Galleries, New York]
Mr. and Mrs. Bronson Trevor, New York
[Hirschl & Adler Galleries, New York, 1976]
Jo Ann and Julian Ganz, Jr., 1976

EXHIBITED
The Metropolitan Museum of Art, New York, *Three Centuries of American Painting*, April 9–October 17, 1965, Collection Mr. and Mrs. Bronson Trevor, unnumbered checklist.

BIBLIOGRAPHY
John Wilmerding, *Fitz Hugh Lane 1804–1865: American Marine Painter* (Salem, Mass.: The Essex Institute, 1964), 55, no. 21.
Stuart P. Feld, "Loan Collection," *The Metropolitan Museum of Art Bulletin*, 23 (April 1965): 289 (illus.).
John Wilmerding, *Fitz Hugh Lane* (New York: Praeger Publishers, 1971), 75.

This work is closely related to *Boston Harbor At Sunset* (1850–1855, oil on canvas, 26 x 42 in., Museum of Fine Arts, Boston). The Massachusetts State House Dome of Charles Bulfinch (1763–1844) can be seen in the distance.

George Willoughby Maynard (1843–1923)

George Willoughby Maynard was known principally as a mural painter. Born in 1843 in Washington, D.C., he studied at the National Academy of Design and in 1869 accompanied Francis Davis Millet (q.v.) to Antwerp, where he studied under Jan Van Lerius at the Royal Academy. After his return to the United States in 1874, Maynard, along with Augustus Saint-Gaudens, Millet, and Francis Lathrop, worked as an assistant to John La Farge on the interior of Trinity Church in Boston. In 1877 he again went to Europe, making a special study of mural painting.

Maynard painted murals for many of the nation's leading institutions, including the Library of Congress and the Columbia University Library, and was one of the artists who took part in the decoration of buildings at the 1893 Columbian Exposition. He was made an associate of the National Academy in 1881 and an academician in 1885; he was also a member of the Society of American Artists, the Brooklyn Art Association, and the American Water Color Society. He died in 1923 in New York.

George W. Maynard
A Geographer
1880, Watercolor on paper
13⁵⁄₁₆ x 19⁵⁄₈ in. (33.8 x 49.9 cm.), sight
Signed (lower right): *Geo. W Maynard/1880*
(fig. 59)

PROVENANCE
[Bernard Black Gallery, New York]
Joan Patterson Roberts, New Canaan, Conn.
[Sotheby Parke Bernet, New York (Sale No. 4116, *Fine Americana*, Lot No. 608, as *The Geography Student*), April 27–29, 1978; Hirschl and Adler Galleries, New York, as agent]
Jo Ann and Julian Ganz, Jr., 1978

EXHIBITED
Bernard Black Gallery, New York, *Americans Since 1860*, November, 1964, no. 6, as *The Geography Student*.

Probably exhibited at the *Fourteenth Annual Exhibition of the American Water Color Society*, National Academy of Design, New York, 1881 as no. 471, *A Geographer*, p. 30. It is closely related to *Treasure Trove*, 18 x 14 in., which was included in the *Sixteenth Annual Exhibition of the American Water Color Society*, National Academy of Design, New York, 1883, as no. 20, p. 6 (illus., n.p.), in both theme and composition.

 Jervis McEntee (1828–1891)

Born in 1828 in Rondout, New York, Jervis McEntee was first exposed to art and literature through the instruction of Henry Pickering, a gentleman from New York City who boarded with the McEntee family for a time. In 1850 McEntee went to New York and studied with Frederic Church. That year, he began to exhibit paintings at the National Academy of Design. By 1852, however, he had returned to Rondout and was engaged in the flour and feed business for the next three years, although he continued to send works annually to the academy exhibitions. A magazine account of 1860 noted that his New York studio was filled with landscapes, many of them autumn scenes of the Catskills and Adirondacks.

In 1868–1869 McEntee and his wife traveled in England and France and in Italy and Switzerland where they joined the painter Sanford Gifford (q.v.). Several of the Italian scenes McEntee sketched were turned into oil paintings, and a few of these were shown at the Brooklyn Art Association and at the National Academy of Design, to which McEntee had been elected an associate in 1861. Although the artist did a number of fine sketches throughout his European travels, he continued to concentrate on American woodland scenes in his finished works. In 1876 he exhibited ten works, three of which were awarded commendations for "excellence in landscapes" at the Centennial Exhibition in Philadelphia.

McEntee died in Rondout in 1891 after fighting the effects of Bright's disease.

Jervis McEntee
View on the Hudson River
early 1850s, Oil on canvas
6 x 11³⁄₈ in. (15.24 x 28.89 cm.)
Signed (lower left): *JME.* (in monogram)
(fig. 22)

PROVENANCE
[Hamilton Gallery, New York, 1969]
[Hirschl & Adler Galleries, New York, 1969]
Jo Ann and Julian Ganz, Jr., 1969

EXHIBITED
Hirschl & Adler Galleries, New York, *The American Scene: A Survey of the Life and Landscape of the 19th Century*, October 29–November 22, 1969, no. 67, p. 55 (illus.).
Santa Barbara Museum of Art, Santa Barbara, Calif., *American Paintings, Watercolors and Drawings from the Collection of Jo Ann and Julian Ganz, Jr.*, June 23–July 22, 1973, no. 47 (illus.), n.p.

Stylistically, this work appears to be from the beginning of McEntee's career, painted in the early 1850s, possibly in the vicinity of Rondout (now Kingston), New York.

 Francis Davis Millet (1846–1912)

Francis Davis Millet, known primarily for his mural decorations and historical genre paintings, was born in Mattapoisett, Massachusetts, in 1846. After graduating from Harvard in 1869, Millet studied lithography with Dominique Fabronius. In 1871, he went abroad and attended Antwerp Academy under Nicholas DeKeyser and Jan Van Lerius, winning a series of academy prizes. He returned to America in 1875 and began to exhibit at the National Academy of Design the following year. In 1876 he was chief assistant to John La Farge on the murals in Boston's Trinity Church. In 1877 Millet went to Europe and served as a correspondent and artist covering the Russo-Turkish War. After 1884 Millet divided his time between Broadway, England—a center for American expatriate artists—and New York. His paintings, especially those with classical subjects, were clearly influenced by the British academic artists, and examples of his work now hang in the Tate Gallery, London. Millet served in a number of prominent administrative positions, including trustee of The Metropolitan Museum of Art, director of decoration for the 1893 Columbian Exposition, and vice-chairman of the United States Commission of Fine Arts. He served as secretary and director of the American Academy in Rome and occupied that position until 1912 when he was lost at sea in the Titanic disaster.

Francis D. Millet
The Poppy Field (Poppies)
1884, Oil on wood panel
16¼ x 9¾ in. (41.28 x 24.77 cm.)
Signed (lower left): *F. D. Millet 1884*
(fig. 75)

PROVENANCE
Private Collection, Boston
The Massachusetts Horticultural Society, Boston
[Boston, art market]
[Graham Williford, New York]
Jo Ann and Julian Ganz, Jr., 1975

EXHIBITED
American Art Galleries, New York, *Special Exhibition of Representative American Painting, Mostly Fresh Pictures contributed by the Artists,* commencing January 17, 1884, p. 11, no. 65, as *The Poppy Field.*

BIBLIOGRAPHY
Undated clipping, *New York Daily News,* Millet Scrapbook II, n.p., American Academy of Arts and Letters, New York.
H. Barbara Weinberg, "The Career of Francis Davis Millet," *Archives of American Art Journal,* 17, no. 1 (1977): 7 (fig. 8)–8, as *Poppies.*

Francis D. Millet
After the Festival
1888, Oil on canvas
20 x 16⅛ in. (50.8 x 41.0 cm.)
Signed (lower left): *F. D. Millet/1888*
(fig. 76)

PROVENANCE
William T. Evans, New York
[American Art Galleries, New York (*American Paintings Belonging to William T. Evans,* no. 13) January 31–February 2, 1900]
[Hirschl & Adler Galleries, New York, 1978]
Jo Ann and Julian Ganz, Jr., 1978

Louis C. Moeller (1855–1930)

Louis Moeller was born in New York City in 1855, the son of Charles Moeller, a decorative painter. After taking drawing classes at the National Academy of Design, Moeller studied for six years in Munich under Frank Duveneck

and the German painter Wilhelm von Diez. Upon returning to New York in 1884, Moeller began exhibiting small genre paintings, one of which won him the National Academy's Hallgarten prize that year. He was elected an associate of the academy in 1884 and became a full academician in 1894. His popularity was such that the important American collector Thomas B. Clarke owned at least a dozen of his paintings. Moeller maintained his New York studio while living in Mount Vernon and Wakefield, New York, and later in Weehawken, New Jersey. Prevented by illness from painting in his later years, Moeller died in Weehawken in 1930.

Louis C. Moeller
The Evening News
1880s, Oil on canvas
6 x 6½ in. (15.24 x 16.51 cm.)
Signed (upper right): *Louis Moeller*
(fig. 62)

PROVENANCE
[Hamilton Gallery, New York]
Jo Ann and Julian Ganz, Jr., 1971

EXHIBITED
Santa Barbara Museum of Art, Santa Barbara, Calif., *American Paintings, Watercolors and Drawings from the Collection of Jo Ann and Julian Ganz, Jr.,* June 23–July 22, 1973, no. 50 (illus.), n.p.

Reading was a favorite subject of Moeller's. The simplicity of this painting's background suggests that it may have been a study for a more elaborate work.

Henry Siddons Mowbray (1858–1928)

Born Harry Siddons in Alexandria, Egypt, he was adopted as a child by an aunt and uncle named Mowbray following his parents' early deaths. Mowbray briefly attended West Point and then in 1877 studied with Alfred C. Howland, a New York landscape painter then living in Williamstown, Massachusetts. In 1878 Mowbray left for Paris and the Atelier Bonnat. While there he came to know Jean-Léon Gérôme, whose exotic, oriental themes, as well as crisp, meticulous style, had a great influence upon his work.

Returning to New York in 1885, Mowbray continued to paint neoclassic allegories and harem scenes. He attracted the attention of art patron Thomas B. Clarke, who purchased several of his paintings, and in 1888, the National Academy of Design awarded Mowbray the Thomas B. Clarke prize and elected him an associate member. In 1889 Mowbray received his first mural commission from Clarke, and after 1897, he abandoned easel painting to concentrate on murals, sometimes collaborating with the architect Charles McKim. Mowbray taught at the Art Students League and helped to found the American Academy in Rome, serving as its director from 1902 to 1904. In 1921 President Wilson appointed him to the National Commission of Fine Arts, and he served in that capacity until his death in Washington, Connecticut, in 1928.

Henry Siddons Mowbray
Studio Lunch
c. 1880–1883, Oil on canvas
8⁵⁄₁₆ x 10⁷⁄₁₆ in. (21.11 x 26.51 cm.)
Signed (lower right): *H. SIDDONS MOWBRAY.*
(fig. 63)

PROVENANCE
[Terry DeLapp, Los Angeles, 1973]
Jo Ann and Julian Ganz, Jr., 1973

RELATED BIBLIOGRAPHY
H. Siddons Mowbray, *H. Siddons Mowbray, Mural Painter 1858–1928*, Herbert F. Sherwood, ed. (Stamford, Conn.: Privately printed by Florence Millard Mowbray, 1928), 16–44.

Gwendolyn Owens, "H. Siddons Mowbray, Easel Painter," *Art and Antiques*, 3 (July–August, 1980):82–89.

Photographs of Mowbray suggest that this may be a portrait of the artist and his model in his Paris studio dating from the early 1880s, for it is a stylistically early work. The drawing on the wall appears to be of the model holding a fan similar to the one on the wall above. This fan and the jugs suggest a Spanish influence, the result of Mowbray's trip to Spain in early 1880.

Joseph Mozier (1812–1870)

Joseph Mozier, born in Burlington, Vermont, in 1812, started his career as a merchant in New York City. In 1845, having decided to become a sculptor, he traveled to Europe for several years of study in Florence and finally settled in Rome, where he remained until his death. Most of his sculptures are ideal figures that depict historical and allegorical subjects and also reflect the increasing interest in literary themes. His *Il Penseroso* was displayed at the 1876 Centennial Exhibit in Philadelphia, and *Undine* won the grand prize in the 1867 Rome Art Exhibition. He died in 1870 at Faido, Switzerland.

Joseph Mozier
Undine
c. 1867, Marble
55 in. (139.7 cm.)
Inscribed (on back): *J. MOZIER. Sc: ROME. 186*
(fig. 55)

PROVENANCE
[Italian art market]
Mr. Clothier, Forest Tavern, near Natural Bridge, Va., early 1900s
Mr. Zollman, Roanoke, Va., c. 1941
Mr. and Mrs. Marshall L. Harris, Roanoke, c. 1941
Jo Ann and Julian Ganz, Jr., 1974; [W. L. Whitwell, Roanoke, as agent]

RELATED BIBLIOGRAPHY
Lorado Taft, *The History of American Sculpture*, new edition with a supplementary chapter by Adeline Adams (New York: The Macmillan Company, 1930), 109.
Adeline Adams, "Joseph Mozier," *Dictionary of American Biography*, Dumas Malone, ed. (New York: Charles Scribners' Sons, 1943), vol. 13, p. 302.
Albert Ten Eyck Gardner, *Yankee Stonecutters: The First American School of Sculpture 1800–1850* (New York: Published for The Metropolitan Museum of Art by Columbia University Press, 1945), 69.

William H. Gerdts, "American Neoclassic Sculpture," *The Shaping of Art and Architecture in Nineteenth-Century America* (New York: The Metropolitan Museum of Art, 1972), 46, 54 (fig. 8).

————, *American Neo-Classic Sculpture: The Marble Resurrection* (New York: The Viking Press, 1973), 42, 44, 88 (fig. 70), 89.

A slightly larger replica of *Undine* (height, 64 in.), dated 1866, is in the collection of the University of Dayton, Ohio.

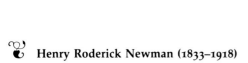

Henry Roderick Newman (1833–1918)

Henry Roderick Newman, an architecture and flower painter, was born in Easton, New York, in 1833. During the 1860s he worked as an artist in New York City but spent much of his time in Stockbridge, Massachusetts, and in the Green Mountains of Vermont. In 1869 he traveled to France to work under Thomas Couture and in 1870 settled in Florence, where he spent the rest of his life. Newman came into contact with the Brownings and Ruskin in Florence and is known to have been influenced by Pre-Raphaelite criticism and philosophy. He died in Florence in 1918.

Henry Roderick Newman
Italy (Grape Vines and Roses: An Italian View)
1883, Watercolor on paper
39½ x 26⅜ in. (100.33 x 66.99 cm.), sight
Signed (lower right): *Henry Roderick Newman/ 1883*
(fig. 90)

PROVENANCE

Mrs. John J. Donaldson, New York, commissioned from the artist, c. 1882
[Virgil L. Holmes, Parsippany, N.J.]
Jo Ann and Julian Ganz, Jr., 1973

EXHIBITED (as *Grape Vines and Roses: An Italian View*)

Los Angeles County Museum of Art, *Pertaining to the Sea*, March 23–May 2, 1976, no. 36, n.p.

American Federation of Arts, *American Master Drawings and Watercolors: A History of Works on Paper from Colonial Times to the Present*, Minneapolis Institute of Arts, September 1–October 26, 1976; Whitney Museum of American Art, New York, November 23, 1976 –January 23, 1977; The Fine Arts Museums of San Francisco, California Palace of the Legion of Honor, February 19–April 17, 1977 (see bibliography).

BIBLIOGRAPHY

Theodore E. Stebbins, Jr., *American Master Drawings and Watercolors: A History of Works on Paper from Colonial Times to the Present* (New York: Harper & Row, Publishers, 1976), 172, 173 (fig. 137), 426, as *Grape Vines and Roses: An Italian View*.

H[arry] Buxton Forman, "An American Studio in Florence," *The Manhattan*, 3 (June, 1884): 536 as *Italy*:

In the autumn [of 1882] he began a great picture in water-color which he called "Italy." This piece, a commission for Mrs. J. J. Donaldson, is, to a certain extent, an ideal composition, though in all essential particulars realistic. It was executed from faithful studies made at San Terenzio in the Gulf of Spezia—the loveliest spot in the whole Riviera del Levante, famous for its connection with the wanderings of the mighty and sombre exile Dante, and the tragic fate of another antipodal poet and exile, Percy Bysshe Shelley. This sumptuous "Italy" of Mr. Newman tells, in the glowing language of line and color, the story of "unearthly beauty" which weighed so depressively on the heart of Mary Shelley, during the whole visit which was fraught for her with such a dire birth of calamity. . . . The castle of Lerici forms a picturesque central object; to the right stand the ruins of the convent at which Dante left the manuscript of the "Inferno" when he fled into France; and between the convent and the horizon line is the point at which Shelley's Torbay-rigged Don Juan was last seen before the sudden squall came up on that fatal 8th of July, 1822, and overwhelmed the frail bark with her precious freight of potential poetry and her actual burden of

"Love and life and light and deity."

To the same region of work as this "Italy" belongs a remarkable drawing of the Casa Magni, Shelley's abiding-place at the time of his death.

The watercolor of *Casa Magni, San Terenzio* (1879, etched by Arthur Evershed, 1880) was commissioned by Forman to serve as the frontispiece for vol. 4 of *The Prose Works of Percy Bysshe Shelley*, Harry Buxton Forman, ed. (London: Reeves and Turner, 1880), which contained Shelley's *Letters from Italy 1818–1822*. The work depicts the house surrounded by turbulent waters suggestive of Shelley's death. Mrs. Donaldson could certainly have been aware of *Casa Magni* in commissioning *Italy*.

Rhoda Holmes Nicholls (1854–1930)

Rhoda Holmes Nicholls was born in 1854 in Coventry, England, and came to the United States in 1884 after her marriage to Burr H. Nicholls, an American painter. She had studied at the Bloomsbury School of Art in London and in Rome and was already a successful artist by the time of her marriage. Living in New York City during the remainder of her career, she exhibited her works regularly at leading American exhibitions, including the Brooklyn Art Association and the National Academy of Design. She was especially well known for her watercolor painting and was an associate of the American Water Color Society. For several years she worked with William Merritt Chase and was in charge of the watercolor division of his art school at Shinnecock Hills. She also taught at the Art Students League and conducted summer classes at Gloucester and Provincetown, Massachusetts, or at Kennebunkport, Maine.

A special exhibition of her watercolors was held at the Corcoran Gallery of Art in 1924. She died at the age of seventy-six in Stamford, Connecticut, in 1930.

Rhoda Holmes Nicholls
After the Ball
c. 1885, Watercolor on paper
13¹⁵/₁₆ x 21 in. (35.4 x 53.3 cm.), sight
Signed (lower left): *Rhoda/Holmes/Nicholls*
(fig. 64)

PROVENANCE
[Hirschl & Adler Galleries, New York, 1972]
Jo Ann and Julian Ganz, Jr., 1975

RELATED BIBLIOGRAPHY
Frances M. Benson, "Five Women Artists in New York,"*Essays on American Art and Artists* (Boston: American Art Company, Publishers, 1895), 9–10.

The chest, with a small child staring at it, is depicted in no. 19, *A Daughter of Eve*, p. 6 (illus., n.p.) in American Art Galleries, New York, *Illustrated Catalogue of the Prize Fund Exhibition*, commencing April 20, 1885. This suggests that *After the Ball* came from the same period. The artist had been in Venice before her arrival in America, and the Venetian scene leaning to the left of the chest and the mask suggest her connection to the city which she had only recently left.

 Helen Searle Pattison (1830–1884)

Helen Searle Pattison was born in 1830 in Burlington, Vermont. Around 1860 she became the pupil of Johann Wilhelm Preyer, a painter of still lifes, and began to paint still lifes herself, which she exhibited at the National Academy of Design and abroad. In 1876 she married the artist James William Pattison, and for six years they lived near Paris. Returning to the United States in 1882, she and her husband eventually settled in Jacksonville, Illinois, where he was head of the School of Fine Arts. She died in Jacksonville in 1884.

Helen Searle Pattison
Still Life: Plums, Peach and Grapes
August–September, 1868, Oil on canvas
8½ x 10¾ in. (21.59 x 27.31 cm.)
Inscribed (lower left, center and right): ⁸/₈68
⁸/₁₀68 ⁸/₁₁68 ⁹/₂₃68
(fig. 80)

PROVENANCE
Estate of the artist
Penelope Pattison Allen Chapman (by inheritance, granddaughter)
[Hirschl & Adler Galleries, New York, 1975]
Jo Ann and Julian Ganz, Jr., 1975

 Raphaelle Peale (1774–1825)

Raphaelle Peale, one of the first painters in America to be known primarily for his still-life paintings, was born in Annapolis, Maryland, in 1774. One of the sons of painter and naturalist

Charles Willson Peale, Raphaelle was trained as an artist by his father and first received professional recognition in 1795, when he entered thirteen paintings in the Columbianum exhibition. In the early part of his career, he painted mainly portraits and miniatures, probably learning the latter art from his uncle, James Peale. Much of Raphaelle's time was also spent working with his father on the natural history exhibits in the Peale Museum in Philadelphia.

In 1803, Raphaelle Peale made a tour of the South and New England, tracing silhouettes with the use of a new invention, the physiognotrace, and experiencing his only period of financial success. At the first exhibition of the Pennsylvania Academy of the Fine Arts in 1811, Peale exhibited two miniatures, but in 1812 he exhibited three still lifes along with a miniature. Thereafter he concentrated upon still-life painting.

In 1825, Peale, who had created still lifes of such sensitivity and balance, died in Philadelphia, after suffering the effects of years of gout and alcoholism.

Raphaelle Peale
A Dessert
August 5, 1814, Oil on wood panel
13⅜ x 19 in. (33.97 x 48.26 cm.)
Signed (lower right): *Raphaelle Peale Aug:⁻ 5th 1814/Philad:°*
Inscribed (on back): *Fullerton*
(fig. 77)

PROVENANCE
James Fullerton, Boston
Oswald J. Arnold, Chicago and Minneapolis
Charlotte Arnold, Minneapolis (by inheritance, sister)
Descendants of Charlotte Arnold, San Diego, Calif.
[Terry DeLapp, Los Angeles, 1975]
Jo Ann and Julian Ganz, Jr., 1976

EXHIBITED
Boston Athenaeum, *Annual Exhibition*, 1828, no. 151 as *A Desert* [sic], J. Fullerton Collection.

EXTENDED LOAN
The Minneapolis Institute of Arts, November 9, 1949–August 28, 1951.

❧ John Frederick Peto (1854–1907)

Born in Philadelphia in 1854, the son of a gilder and picture framer, Peto was raised by his grandmother. In 1878, he enrolled in the Pennsylvania Academy of the Fine Arts, where he first met trompe l'oeil painter and fellow student William Harnett (q.v.), whose work he admired. Peto opened a studio in Philadelphia about 1880 and exhibited still-life paintings with the Pennsylvania Society of Arts and at the Pennsylvania Academy from 1879 until 1887. He produced intricate rack pictures, such as *Office Board for Christian Faser*, for local businessmen and also reportedly worked as a portraitist (both in oil and photography) as a means of support.

Growing increasingly reclusive, Peto in 1889 settled in Island Heights, New Jersey, where he played cornet at religious camp meetings. He continued to paint still lifes, selling his paintings for as little as three or four dollars to friends or summer visitors to the area. Peto's tabletop arrangements of everyday (and often worn) objects—mugs, newspapers, pipes, books, and candlesticks—in muted colors reflect the introspective mood of America at the end of the nineteenth century.

Many of Peto's paintings were later given the forged signature of the better-known William Harnett. Peto died in Island Heights, New Jersey, in 1907.

John F. Peto
Office Board for Christian Faser
1881, Oil on canvas
24 x 20 in. (60.96 x 50.8 cm.)
Unsigned
(fig. 97)

PROVENANCE
John W. Barnes, New York
Mrs. John W. Barnes, Silvermine, Conn.
[Hirschl & Adler Galleries, New York, 1971]
Jo Ann and Julian Ganz, Jr., 1971

EXHIBITED
The Brooklyn Museum, Brooklyn, N.Y., *John F. Peto*, April 11–May 21, 1950; Smith College Museum of Art, Northampton, Mass., March 1–24, 1950; California Palace of the Legion of Honor, San Francisco, June 10–July 19, 1950, no. 2, pp. 18, 27, 45, with the John W. Barnes Collection.
Williams College, Williamstown, Mass., *An Exhibition of Works of Art Lent by the Alumni of Williams College*, May 5–June 16, 1962, p. 29, no. 64, with the John W. Barnes Collection.
La Jolla Museum of Art, La Jolla, Calif., *The Reminiscent Object: Paintings by William Michael Harnett, John Frederick Petro, and John Haberle*, July 11–September 19, 1965; Santa Barbara Museum of Art, Santa Barbara, Calif., September 28–October 31, 1965, no. 24 (illus.), n.p.

Santa Barbara Museum of Art, Santa Barbara, Calif., *American Paintings, Watercolors and Drawings from the Collection of Jo Ann and Julian Ganz, Jr.*, June 23–July 22, 1973, no. 52 (illus.), n.p.

BIBLIOGRAPHY
Alfred Frankenstein, *After the Hunt: William Harnett And Other American Still Life Painters 1870–1900*, revised edition (Berkeley and Los Angeles: University of California Press, 1969), 103, 108, pl. 83 (n.p.).
Santa Barbara Museum of Art, *Bulletin*, June, 1973 (illus., n.p.).
Henry J. Seldis, "Collecting an Adventure for Jo Ann and Julian Ganz," *Calendar*, Los Angeles Times, July 8, 1973, p. 60 (illus.).
Donelson F. Hoopes, "The Jo Ann and Julian Ganz, Jr., Collection," *American Art Review*, 1 (September–October, 1973): 56 (illus.).

Painted for Christian Faser, who sold mirrors and picture frames at Faser's Art Gallery, 824 Arch Street, Philadelphia, this work is dated on the basis of the 1881 *Public Ledger Almanac* depicted in it. The *Almanac* used this cover between 1873 and 1898, changing only the colors from year to year. It was distributed free to subscribers of the Philadelphia *Public Ledger* and, thus, had a wide circulation in the community. Peto used the almanac cover with its genre depictions of the four seasons frequently in his rack paintings.[1]

1. See Frankenstein, *Hunt*, 108.

John F. Peto
Old Companions
1904, Oil on canvas
22 x 30 in. (55.88 x 76.2 cm.)
Signed (upper right): *J. Peto / 1904*
Signed (on back): *J. F. Peto, Island / Heights, N.J. 1904*
(fig. 98)

PROVENANCE
Estate of the artist
Mrs. George (Helen Peto) Smiley, Island Heights, N.J. (daughter of the artist)
[Sally Turner Gallery, Plainfield, N.J., as agent, 1966]
The Hon. and Mrs. J. William Middendorf II, New York

[Sotheby Parke Bernet, New York, (Sale No. 3348, *Traditional and Western American Paintings, Drawings, Watercolors and Sculpture and Illustrations*, Lot. No. 55) April 19–20, 1972]
[Meredith Long & Co., Houston, Texas, 1972]
Jo Ann and Julian Ganz, Jr., 1973

EXHIBITED

The Brooklyn Museum, Brooklyn, N.Y., *John F. Peto*, April 11–May 21, 1950; Smith College Museum of Art, Northampton, Mass., March 1–March 24, 1950; California Palace of the Legion of Honor, San Francisco, June 10–July 9, 1950, pp. 27, 42 (fig. 20), 49, as no. 44 *Books on a Shelf*, Collection of Mrs. George (Helen Peto) Smiley.

The Pennsylvania Academy of the Fine Arts, Philadelphia, *The One Hundred and Fiftieth Anniversary Exhibition*, January 15–March 13, 1955, pp. 109 (illus.), 113, no. 176, Collection of Mrs. (George) Helen Peto Smiley.

Florence, Italy; Madrid, Spain; Innsbruck, Austria; Ghent, Belgium, 1955, *Exhibition Commemorating the One Hundred and Fiftieth Anniversary of the Pennsylvania Academy of the Fine Arts*, no. 64.

The Metropolitan Museum of Art, New York, *American Paintings & Historical Prints from the Middendorf Collection*, October 4–November 26, 1967; The Baltimore Museum of Art, July 9–September 24, 1967, no. 45, pp. 66, 67 (illus.).

Everson Museum of Art, Syracuse, N.Y., *Portraiture and Still Life from the Collection of Mr. and Mrs. J. William Middendorf II*, 1969.

University Art Museum, Berkeley, Calif., *The Reality of Appearance: The Trompe L'Oeil Tradition In American Painting*, July 15–August 31, 1970; National Gallery of Art, Washington, D.C., March 21–May 3, 1970; Whitney Museum of American Art, New York, May 19–July 5, 1970; California Palace of the Legion of Honor, San Francisco, July 15–August 31, 1970; The Detroit Institute of Arts, September 15–October 31, 1970, no. 64, pp. 20, 21 (illus.), 104, 105 (illus.), Collection of Mr. and Mrs. J. William Middendorf II, New York.

Santa Barbara Museum of Art, Santa Barbara, Calif., *American Paintings, Watercolors and Drawings from the Collection of Jo Ann and Julian Ganz, Jr.*, June 23–July 22, 1973, no. 55 (illus.), n.p.

Los Angeles County Museum of Art, *American Paintings from Los Angeles Collections*, May 7–June 30, 1974, checklist, n.p.

BIBLIOGRAPHY

Belle Krasne, "Peto's Harnetts and Peto's Petos," *The Art Digest*, 24 (May 1, 1950): 13 (illus.) as *Books on a Shelf*.

Erle Loran, "Scheduled for San Francisco," *Art News*, 49 (Summer, 1950): 34 (illus.), as *Shelf of Books*, Collection of Mrs. G. (Helen Peto) Smiley.

Fine Art Reproductions of Old & Modern Masters (Greenwich, Conn.: New York Graphic Society, 1961), 25 (illus.), Collection of (Mrs. George) Helen Peto Smiley.

Alfred Frankenstein, *After the Hunt: William Harnett and Other American Still Life Painters 1870–1900*, revised edition (Berkeley and Los Angeles: University of California Press, 1969), 107, pl. 88 (n.p.), (in Index, p. 198, listed as *Books on a Shelf*), Collection of Mr. and Mrs. J. William Middendorf, New York.

———, "Exhibition Preview: The Reality of Appearance," *Art in America*, 58 (March–April, 1970): 94 (illus.), Collection of Mr. and Mrs. J. William Middendorf II, New York.

William H. Gerdts and Russell Burke, *American Still-Life Painting* (New York: Praeger Publishers, 1971), 144, 146, 147 (fig. 10–12).

Stuart P. Feld, "The Nineteenth-Century Artist and His Posthumous Public," in *The Shaping of Art and Architecture in Nineteenth-Century America* (New York: The Metropolitan Museum of Art, 1972), 121, 131 (fig. 2), Collection of Ambassador and Mrs. J. William Middendorf II.

Donelson F. Hoopes, "The Jo Ann and Julian Ganz, Jr., Collection," *American Art Review*, 1 (September–October 1973): 50, 57 (illus.).

Los Angeles County Museum of Art, *Members Calendar*, 12 (May, 1974), (illus., n.p.).

Art Week, West Coast Art News, Oakland, Calif., May 25, 1974, p. 5 (illus.).

Henry J. Seldis, "Palette of the American Experience," *Calendar*, Los Angeles Times, June 2, 1974, p. 64 (illus.).

Hiram Powers (1805–1873)

Hiram Powers was born in Woodstock, Vermont, in 1805 and moved to Cincinnati with his family in 1818. His early sculpture brought him to the attention of Cincinnati art patron Nicholas Longworth, whose financial support enabled Powers to move in 1834 to Washington, D.C., where he produced busts of President Jackson, John Quincy Adams, Chief Justice Marshall, and other notables. Another patron, Colonel John Preston, offered to finance a trip to Italy for Powers, and in 1837 the sculptor departed for Florence, where he was to spend the rest of his life. In Florence, Powers quickly made friends with the American expatriate sculptor Horatio Greenough, and following Greenough's death in 1853, Powers came to be regarded as the artistic leader of the many American sculptors then residing in the city.

Powers's fame outside Italy was established in the 1840s with his *Greek Slave*, which was exhibited in London in 1845 and in the United States in 1847–49, and made Powers one of the most acclaimed sculptors of his day. The *Greek Slave* was the first life-sized statue by an American sculptor of a totally nude female figure to be placed on exhibition, but Powers convincingly defended the virtue of his creation. Powers modeled several other ideal statues and busts during his career—including his *Proserpine*—but continued to model portrait busts for individual clients as well. He died in Florence in 1873, very successful and highly regarded as an artist.

Hiram Powers
Loulie's Hand
c. 1839, Marble
3 in. (7.62 cm.)
Unsigned
(fig. 32)

PROVENANCE
The artist to his wife, Florence, Italy, Christmas, 1839
Mrs. Bernardo (Christina Michahalles) Seeber, Rome, Italy (by inheritance, great-granddaughter of the artist)
Jo Ann and Julian Ganz, Jr., 1976 (through the courtesy of Mr. and Mrs. Arthur Manella)

BIBLIOGRAPHY
Nathaniel Hawthorne, *The Marble Faun: or, the Romance of Monte Beni*, 2 vols. (Boston: Ticknor and Fields, 1860), 1, p. 154.
———, *Passages from the French and Italian Note-Books*, 2 vols. (Boston: James R. Osgood and Company, 1872), 2, pp. 25–26.
Sylvia E. Chase, *White Silence: Greenough, Powers, and Crawford, American Sculptors in Nineteenth-Century Italy* (Coral Gables, Fla.: University of Miami Press, 1972), 234.
William H. Gerdts, *American Neo-Classic Sculpture: The Marble Resurrection* (New York: The Viking Press, 1973), 30, 140, 141 (fig. 175).

Because of the work's provenance, it is assumed that this is the first replica of *Loulie's Hand* and, therefore, the work described by Hawthorne upon his visit to Powers's studio on June 13, 1858:

One piece of sculpture Powers exhibited, however, which was very exquisite, and such as I never saw before. Opening a desk, he took out something carefully enclosed between two layers of cotton wool, on removing which there appeared a little baby's hand most delicately represented in the whitest marble; all the dimples where the knuckles were to be, all the creases in the plump flesh, every infantine wrinkle of the soft skin being lovingly recorded. "The critics condemn minute representation," said Powers; "but you may look at this through a microscope and see if it injures the general effect." Nature herself never made a prettier or truer little hand. It was the hand of his daughter,—"Luly's [sic] hand," Powers called it,—the same that gave my own such a frank and friendly grasp when I first met "Luly." The sculptor made it only for himself and for his wife, but so many people, he said, had insisted on having a copy, that there are now forty scattered about the world. At sixty years, Luly ought to have her hand sculptured again, and give it to her grandchildren with the baby's hand of five months old. The baby-hand that had done nothing, and felt only its mother's kiss; the old lady's hand that had exchanged the love-pressure, worn the marriage-ring, closed dead eyes,—done a lifetime's work, in short. The sentiment is rather obvious, but true nevertheless.[1]

1. Hawthorne, *Passages*, vol. 2, 25–26.

Hiram Powers
Proserpine
1844, Marble
25 in. (63.5 cm.)
Inscribed (on lower back): *H. POWERS / Sculp / 1844.*
(fig. 30)

PROVENANCE
The Hon. and Mrs. William Starr Miller, New York City and Rhinebeck, N.Y., 1848
Mrs. William W. Hoffman (grandniece)
[Hobart House, Haddam, Conn., 1962]
Jo Ann and Julian Ganz, Jr., 1975

BIBLIOGRAPHY
Charles Edwards Lester, *The Artist, The Merchant, and The Statesman of the age of the Medici, and of our own times*, 2 vols. (New York: Paine & Burgess, 1845), 1, pp. 16, 17.
Regine (Mrs. William Starr) Miller, *Excerpts from an Italian Diary*, typescript, Jo Ann and Julian Ganz, Jr. Collection, entries for February 8 and 15, 1848.
Henry T. Tuckerman, *Book of the Artist: American Artist Life* (New York: G. P. Putnam & Son; London: Sampson Low & Co., 1867), 282, 286.
Nathaniel Hawthorne, *Passages from the French and Italian Note-Books*, 2 vols. (Boston: James R. Osgood and Company, 1872), 2, pp. 22, 23.
William J. Clark, Jr., *Great American Sculptures* (Philadelphia: Gebbie & Barrie, Publishers, 1878; reprinted, New York & London: Garland Publishing, Inc., 1977), 50.
Samuel G. W. Benjamin, *Art in America: A Critical and Historical Sketch* (New York: Harper & Brothers, Publishers, 1880), 140.
Lorado Taft, *The History of American Sculpture*, new edition with a supplementary chapter by Adeline Adams (New York: The Macmillan Company, 1930), 60, 61 (fig. 6), 67, 68.
Albert TenEyck Gardner, *Yankee Stonecutters: The First American School of Sculpture 1800–1850* (New York: Published for The Metropolitan Museum of Art by Columbia University Press, 1945), 12, 15.

Samuel A. Roberson and William H. Gerdts, "The Greek Slave," *The Museum*, new series, 17 (Winter–Spring, 1965): 3.

Wayne Craven, *Sculpture In America* (New York: Thomas Y. Crowell, 1968), 115.

Sylvia E. Crane, *White Silence: Greenough, Powers, and Crawford, American Sculptors in Nineteenth Century Italy* (Coral Gables, Fla.: University of Miami Press, 1972), 188 (illus.), 192, 199, 222, 223, 224, 237.

William H. Gerdts, *American Neo-Classic Sculpture: The Marble Resurrection* (New York: The Viking Press, 1973), 31, 52, 93 (fig. 81).

Richard P. Wunder, *Hiram Powers: Vermont Sculptor* (Taftsville, Vt.: The Countryman Press, 1974), 1 (fig. 1), 18 (figs. 8, 9), 19 (figs. 10, 11), 20, 33.

Wayne Craven, "Images of a Nation in Wood, Marble and Bronze: American Sculpture from 1776 to 1900," in *200 Years of American Art* (New York: Whitney Museum of American Art, 1976), 38 (pl. 7), 41, 298.

Powers created three versions of *Proserpine*, daughter of the goddess of agriculture, Ceres, who was abducted by the god of the underworld, Pluto, and condemned to spend part of the year in Hades, returning to earth every spring. As the first version, done on commission for Edward L. Carey of Philadelphia, neared completion in 1843, Powers replaced its complex base of a basket of spring flowers with the wreath of acanthus leaves, symbol of immortality, on the Ganz replica, to make the piece more salable. Edward Everett, then United States Minister to Great Britain, had convinced Powers to send this replica to the Royal Academy spring exhibition in London, but a discoloration had appeared on the right shoulder during cutting. Although Powers began another replica of the second version (1844, Honolulu Academy of Arts), it was not finished in time for the exhibition. The Ganz replica was retained by the artist until it was sold to Mr. Miller, who had seen the Carey version while in Florence in 1840.[1] A later version of the bust replaced the wreath with an even more simplified molding. *Proserpine* was Powers's most popular piece, and over one hundred replicas were created.

1. Information supplied by Richard P. Wunder, Orwell, Vermont.

Hiram Powers
Bust of The Greek Slave
after 1845, Marble
25 in. (63.5 cm.)
Inscribed (on lower back): *H. POWERS*
(fig. 31)

PROVENANCE

[Christie, Manson & Woods, Ltd., London (*Paintings and Drawings, Bronzes and Prints, Particularly of American, Australian, Canadian, New Zealand, Indian and South African Interest*, Lot No. 61, pp. 14, 61 (Pl. 8)), October 10, 1975]
[Hirschl & Adler Galleries, New York, 1975]
Jo Ann and Julian Ganz, Jr., 1976

BIBLIOGRAPHY

Regine (Mrs. William Starr) Miller, *Excerpts from an Italian Diary*, typescript, Jo Ann and Julian Ganz, Jr. Collection, entry for February 8, 1848.

Samuel A. Roberson and William H. Gerdts, "The Greek Slave," *The Museum* (Newark), new series, 17 (Winter–Spring, 1965): 30 (fig. 24), 32.

Samuel A. Roberson, "A Note on the Technical Creation of The Greek Slave," *The Museum* (Newark), new series, 17 (Winter–Spring, 1965) 30 (fig. 24), 32.

Wayne Craven, *Sculpture In America* (New York: Thomas Y. Crowell, 1968), 115, 116.

Sylvia E. Crane, *White Silence: Greenough, Powers and Crawford, American Sculptors in Nineteenth Century Italy* (Coral Gables, Fla.: University of Miami Press, 1972), 213 (illus.), 237, 331.

William H. Gerdts, *American Neo-Classic Sculpture: The Marble Resurrection* (New York: The Viking Press, 1973), 32, 52 (fig. 2), 53 (fig. 3).

Richard P. Wunder, "The Irascible Hiram Powers," *The American Art Journal*, 4 (November, 1972): 10 (fig. 1).

Wayne Craven, "Images of a Nation in Wood, Marble and Bronze: American Sculpture from 1776 to 1900," in *200 Years of American Sculpture* (New York: Whitney Museum of American Art, 1976), 298.

In 1843 Powers began the first of his full-length versions of the *Greek Slave*. The earliest busts of the work date from 1845–50. They were available in full-size, of which this version is an example, and reduced-size, which were one third smaller. The former was considered by the artist as a complement to his bust of *Proserpine* (q.v.).[1]

1. Information supplied by Richard P. Wunder, Orwell, Vermont, and Miller, *Diary*, Feb. 8, 1848, Florence, Studio of Hiram Powers: "the head [sic] of the Greek Slave & Proserpine are beautiful."

William Trost Richards (1833–1905)

William Trost Richards, born in Philadelphia in 1833, was first employed as a designer of ornamental metalwork. By 1850 he had begun to study with Paul Weber, a German portrait and landscape painter who also taught William Stanley Haseltine (q.v.). Richards exhibited at the Pennsylvania Academy of the Fine Arts in 1852. In 1855 he went to Europe for a year, visiting Paris, Florence, and Düsseldorf.

Returning to the United States in 1856, Richards began painting scenes in the Adirondacks and Pennsylvania countryside. In the late 1850s and early 1860s he produced a series of drawings and paintings of individual plants, observed and rendered with Ruskinian detail. In 1863 he became a member of the Association for the Advancement of Truth in Art, a society that advocated the Pre-Raphaelite style. Between

1864 and 1866, Richards completed a series of charcoal and pencil drawings of woodland landscapes whose large scale was unprecedented in his work; *Landscape with Brook* is one example.

Late in 1866, Richards again traveled abroad, visiting Paris, Italy, and Germany. During the 1870s he devoted himself to depicting American coastal subjects, traveling along the Atlantic coast from New Jersey to Maine until he finally made Newport his permanent summer home in 1874. During the 1880s and nineties, following a two-year stay in England (1878–1880), Richards continued to paint both marine subjects and landscapes, exhibiting his work regularly at the Pennsylvania Academy and the National Academy of Design. In 1905 he was awarded the Pennsylvania Academy's gold medal of honor, and he died in Newport in November of that year.

BIBLIOGRAPHY

Linda S. Ferber, *William Trost Richards: American Landscape & Marine Painter 1833–1905* (Brooklyn, New York: The Brooklyn Museum, 1973); related works: pp. 28, 29 (fig. 7), 64, 65 (cat. no. 36).

———, *William Trost Richards (1833–1905): American Landscape and Marine Painter* (Ph.D. diss., Columbia University, 1980; New York & London: Garland Publishing, Inc., 1980), related works: pp. 147–150, 424, 491 (fig. 112), 492 (figs. 113–114), 493 (fig. 115).

It is possible that this drawing, like the others in the series of monumental, highly detailed drawings of the 1860s, may have been considered a finished cartoon, complete in itself, but available as an oil painting upon commission.[1]

1. Ferber, *Richards,* 149.

William Trost Richards
Landscape with Brook
1865, Charcoal and white chalk on paper
37¼ x 50¾ in. (94.6 x 128.9 cm.), sight
Signed (lower right): *Wᵐ T. RICHARDS. 1865*
(fig. 4)

PROVENANCE
Private Collection, Brooklyn, N.Y.
[Hirschl & Adler Galleries, New York, 1976]
Jo Ann and Julian Ganz, Jr., 1977

William Trost Richards
At Atlantic City
1877, Oil on canvas
24¼ x 20¼ in. (61.6 x 51.44 cm.)
Signed (lower left): *Wᵐ T. RICHARDS. 1877 / Philᵃ- - -*
(fig. 5)

PROVENANCE
Stryker family, Philadelphia
[Bernard & S. Dean Levy, Inc., New York, 1975]
Jo Ann and Julian Ganz, Jr., 1975

EXHIBITED

Los Angeles County Museum of Art, *Pertaining to the Sea,* March 23–May 2, 1976, no. 46, n.p.

BIBLIOGRAPHY

Linda S. Ferber, *William Trost Richards (1833–1905): American Landscape and Marine Painter* (Ph.D. diss., Columbia University, 1980; New York & London: Garland Publishing, Inc., 1980), 245–248, 257, 430 (related work), 431, 536 (related work: fig. 201), 538 (figs. 205, 206).

This work is closely related to *At Atlantic City* (c. 1873, oil on canvas, location unknown).[1] The publication of the c. 1873 work, then in the collection of Joseph Ferrel of Philadelphia, in [George William Sheldon], "American Painters.—William Trost Richards," *The Art Journal,* new series, 3 (August, 1877): 242 (illus.), 244, may have resulted in the 1877 work's commission, or sale, if it were already extant. If the work were painted before the article appeared, it could be *Pine Trees & Sea,* a work mentioned in a letter from Allen D. Vorce, art dealer, Hartford, Connecticut, to Richards of August 13, 1877: "We have not been able to dispose of 'Pine trees and sea'. In ordinary times it would sell as it is liked as well as anything we ever had of yours."[2] A study, *New Jersey Pines: Study for At Atlantic City (Delaware Capes)* (n.d., pencil on paper, unsigned), is in the collection of Mrs. J. B. Conant of New York.[3]

1. Ferber, *Richards,* 245, 430, 536 (fig. 201).
2. Archives of American Art, cited in Ferber, *Richards,* 257n.
3. Ferber, *Richards,* 431, 538 (fig. 206).

William Henry Rinehart (1825–1874)

William Henry Rinehart was born near Union Bridge, Maryland, in 1825, the son of a farmer. He began working as a stonecutter while studying art at the night school of the Maryland Institute. In 1855, encouraged by medals won at institute exhibitions and with the support of art patron William T. Walters, Rinehart went abroad for two years to study in Florence. He returned to Baltimore briefly in 1857 but in 1858 went to Rome where he lived, with the exception of short intervals, until his death in 1874.

Despite his decision to live in Italy, most of Rinehart's sculpture was designed for, and purchased by, Americans—particularly prominent Baltimoreans. Most of his commissions, especially during the late stages of his career, were for portrait busts, but Rinehart was also interested in modeling ideal sculpture which took its subject matter from mythology or history. In addition, Rinehart modeled many statues for cemeteries and public squares, most of them in the vicinity of Baltimore. He left his estate in trust to provide for the education of young sculptors.

William Henry Rinehart
Harriet Newcomer
1868, Marble
47 in. (119.4 cm.) (height)
Inscribed (on back): *WM. H. RINEHART / SCULP^T ROMA. 1868*
(fig. 101)

PROVENANCE
Benjamin F. Newcomer, Baltimore
Mrs. Henry B. Gilpin, his daughter, "Scaleby," Boyce, Va.
Kenneth Gilpin, "Scaleby," Boyce, Va.
Estate of Kenneth N. Gilpin, "Scaleby," Boyce, Va.

[Christie, Manson & Woods, International Inc., New York (*The Contents of Scaleby, Boyce, Virginia, The Property of the Estate of Kenneth N. Gilpin*, Sale "GILPIN-5052," Lot. no. 133, p. 21 (illus.)), June 16, 1981]
Jo Ann and Julian Ganz, Jr., 1981

BIBLIOGRAPHY
William Henry Rinehart, *Libro Maestro* (the artist's account book for 1862–1874), p. 116 (1866), in the library of the Peabody Institute, Baltimore
William Sener Rusk, *William Henry Rinehart, Sculptor* (Baltimore: Norman T.A. Munder, Publisher, 1939), 65–66, pl. 9 (n.p.)
Marvin Chauncey Ross and Anna Wells Rutledge, *A Catalogue of the Work of William Henry Rinehart, Maryland Sculptor, 1825–1874* (Baltimore: The Walters Art Gallery, 1948), cat. no. 115, p. 60, pl. 23 (n.p.).

Harriet Newcomer, later Mrs. Henry B. Gilpin (1861–1942), was a daughter of Benjamin F. Newcomer who served as one of the artist's executors and as a trustee of the Rinehart Bequest.

Although the head of "Hattie" Newcomer was modeled in Baltimore in 1866, when she would have been six or seven years old, the lifesize marble sculpture was not completed until 1868 in Rome.

William Henry Rinehart
Hero
1868, Marble
26½ in. (67.31 cm.)
Inscribed (on lower back): *WM. H. RINEHART. SCULP$^t_ø$ / ROMAE. 1868*
(fig. 56)

PROVENANCE
Phipps Estate, Old Westbury, N.Y.
Pratt Estate, Old Westbury, N.Y.
Schultz Estate, Old Westbury, N.Y.
[Hirschl & Adler Galleries, New York, 1978]
Jo Ann and Julian Ganz, Jr., 1978

BIBLIOGRAPHY
Lorado Taft, *The History of American Sculpture*, new edition with a supplementary chapter by Adeline Adams (New York: The Macmillan Company, 1930), 175.

William Sener Rusk, *William Henry Rinehart, Sculptor* (Baltimore: Norman T. A. Munder, Publisher, 1939), xi, 16, 55, 56, pl. 2 (n.p.).
Marvin Chauncey Ross and Anna Wells Rutledge, *A Catalogue of the Work of William Henry Rinehart, Maryland Sculptor, 1825–1874* (Baltimore: The Walters Art Gallery, 1948), 13, 14, 25–26, pl. 7 (cat. no. 17a, n.p.).
Wayne Craven, *Sculpture In America* (New York: Thomas Y. Crowell, 1968), 290, 293.
William H. Gerdts, "American Neoclassic Sculpture," in *The Shaping of Art and Architecture in Nineteenth-Century America* (New York: The Metropolitan Museum of Art, 1972), 45, 46, 48, 52 (fig. 4).
———, *American Neo-Classic Sculpture: The Marble Resurrection* (New York: The Viking Press, 1973), 20, 38–39.
———, *The Great American Nude: A History in Art* (New York: Praeger Publishers, 1974), 94, 96 (fig. 5-19).
———, "Images of a Nation in Wood, Marble and Bronze: American Sculpture from 1776 to 1900," in *200 Years of American Sculpture* (New York: Whitney Museum of American Art, 1976), 43, 44, 58 (pl. 11).

Based on the legend of Hero and Leander, the statue depicts Hero, a priestess of Aphrodite, guiding her lover, Leander, who swam to her every night across the Hellespont, now called the Dardanelles. One stormy night Hero's lamp blew out and Leander was drowned, whereupon she threw herself into the sea. Interest in the subject was rekindled by Lord Byron's swim across the Hellespont earlier in the century. The composition of the work was based upon Heinrich von Dannecker's (1758–1841) famous neoclassic statue *Ariadne on the Panther* (1814, marble, destroyed World War II). The artist conceived statues of both Hero and Leander around 1858, but they could be purchased separately, and Hero, the more popular work, was generally acquired by itself.

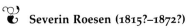

Severin Roesen (1815?–1872?)

Severin Roesen is today recognized as one of the most accomplished of America's still-life painters. Little is known about his youth and early career as an artist; he was probably born in or near Cologne, Germany, c. 1815, and may have been trained as a porcelain and enamel painter. In 1848, when many Germans were immigrating to the United States, Roesen came to New York with his family. He exhibited eleven still-life paintings at the American Art Union between 1848 and its closing sale in 1852 and exhibited with the Pennsylvania Academy of the Fine Arts in 1863.

About 1858 Roesen settled in Williamsport, Pennsylvania, where he continued to paint elaborate arrangements of flowers and fruit. Influenced by Dutch and German still life, his paintings are filled with meticulous details and display the variety and bounty of nature.

Roesen disappeared around 1872 and probably died soon thereafter. His place of death has been variously reported as Philadelphia, New York, and Williamsport.

Severin Roesen
Flower Still-Life with Bird's Nest
1853, Oil on canvas
40 x 32 in. (101.6 x 81.28 cm.)
Signed (lower right): *S.Roesen / 1853.*
(fig. 83)

PROVENANCE
[William Postar, Boston, 1974]
Jo Ann and Julian Ganz, Jr., 1974

BIBLIOGRAPHY
Lois Goldreich Marcus, *Severin Roesen: A Chronology* (Williamsport, Pennsylvania, 1976), 21, 28 (fig. 18).

The composition, which includes day lilies, lilacs, peonies, tulips, daisies, roses, iris, morning glories, primroses, blue bells, nasturtium, and a crown imperial at its peak is generally based upon the seventeenth-century Dutch still-life tradition. What are presumably poppy buds are depicted in a state of momentary bloom, accentuating an overall image of fecundity created by an arrangement of flowers which do not necessarily bloom at the same time.

Randolph Rogers (1825–1892)

Born in Waterloo, New York, in 1825, Randolph Rogers spent his youth in Michigan. He moved to New York around 1847 and became a dry-goods clerk, but his talent for sculpting figures was noticed by his employer, who in 1848 provided funds for Rogers's formal instruction in Italy. After studying with the sculptor Lorenzo Bartolini in Florence, Rogers moved to Rome in 1851, where he established a studio and worked until his death in 1892.

Like most other American sculptors then living in Rome, Rogers executed most of his works on commission. Portraits in marble and literary subjects such as the popular *Nydia, Blind Girl of Pompeii* constitute the largest proportion of his work, but Rogers was also successful in winning civic commissions, and he designed many monuments in the United States—notably a set of doors for the U.S. Capitol, depicting the life of Christopher Columbus, and the sculpture for the Washington Monument in Richmond. Rogers enjoyed considerable success as a sculptor, and his studio was one of the busiest in Rome. Before his death, he shipped the casts of most of his works to the University of Michigan.

Randolph Rogers
Ruth Gleaning
after 1867, Marble
35½ in. (90.17 cm.)
Inscribed (on lower back): *Randolph Rogers, Rome.*
(fig. 35)

PROVENANCE
Estate of Mrs. P. Hanson Hiss, Jr., New Canaan, Conn.
[Forge Antiques, Bedford Hills, N.Y.]
[Northern Westchester Auction Galleries, Jefferson Valley, N.Y.]
[Post Road Antiques, Larchmont, N.Y., 1975]
Jo Ann and Julian Ganz, Jr., 1975

BIBLIOGRAPHY
Henry T. Tuckerman, *Book of the Artists: American Artist Life* (New York: G. P. Putnam & Son; London: Sampson Low & Co., 1867), 592.
Edward Strahan (pseud. Earl Shinn), *The Masterpieces of the Centennial International Exhibition, Volume I: Fine Art* (Philadelphia: Gebbie & Barrie, c. 1876–1878; republished, New York & London: Garland Publishing, Inc., 1977), 56 (illus.), 127–128, 298.
William J. Clark, Jr., *Great American Sculptures* (Philadelphia: Gebbie & Barrie, Publishers, 1878; republished, New York & London: Garland Publishing, Inc., 1977), 75–76, 77–78.
Martin L. D'Ooge, *Catalogue of the Gallery of Art and Archaeology in the University of Michigan* (Ann Arbor, Michigan: University of Michigan, 189?), nos. 140, 141, p. 22.

Lorado Taft, *The History of American Sculpture*, new edition with a supplementary chapter by Adeline Adams (New York: The Macmillan Company, 1930), 160, 161–162.

Albert TenEyck Gardner, *Yankee Stonecutters: The First American School of Sculpture 1800–1850* (New York: Published for The Metropolitan Museum of Art by Columbia University Press, 1945), 71, 75.

———, *American Sculpture: A Catalogue of the Collection of The Metropolitan Museum of Art* (New York: The Metropolitan Museum of Art, 1965), 25–26 (illus.).

Wayne Craven, *Sculpture In America* (New York: Thomas Y. Crowell Company, 1968), 313, 314, 316.

Millard F. Rogers, Jr., "Nydia, popular Victorian image," *Antiques*, 97 (March 1970): 376.

———, *Randolph Rogers: American Sculptor in Rome* (Amherst, Mass.: The University of Massachusetts Press, 1971), 15–19 (fig. 2, p. 16), 197–199.

William H. Gerdts, *American Neo-Classic Sculpture: The Marble Resurrection* (New York: The Viking Press, 1973), 34, 47, 69 (fig. 30).

———, *The Great American Nude: A History in Art* (New York: Praeger Publishers, 1974), 91.

200 Hundred Years of American Sculpture (New York: Whitney Museum of American Art, 1976), 304.

The work illustrates the *Book of Ruth* 2:13. Ruth kneels before Boaz, grateful for his permission to glean in his fields: "Then she said, Let me find favour in thy sight my lord; for that thou hast comforted me, and for that thou has spoken friendly unto thine handmaid, though I be not like unto one of thine handmaidens." *Ruth* was first modeled in 1853 in a full-sized version approximately 45¾ inches high. The earliest known reduction dates from c. 1867.[1]

1. Information supplied by Millard F. Rogers, Jr., director, Cincinnati Art Museum, Cincinnati, Ohio.

ℜ John Singer Sargent (1856–1925)

John Singer Sargent, son of a New England doctor and his Philadelphian wife, was born in 1856 in Florence, where his expatriate American parents spent part of each year. After beginning to sketch and paint in watercolors, encouraged by his mother who was herself an amateur artist, Sargent received formal artistic training in Rome as early as 1868 and was enrolled in the Academia delle Belle Arte in Florence in 1870. In 1874, after his family moved to Paris, Sargent studied with the French portraitist Carolus-Duran. Trips to Spain in 1879, where he studied the paintings of Velázquez, and to Holland in 1880, where he studied Hals, had an important influence on his work. In 1880 and 1882 Sargent visited Venice, where a number of his American friends had settled. Sargent transferred his studio to London in 1886 and in 1887 traveled to Boston, where his reputation had been growing steadily. His second visit to America in 1890 brought him forty portrait commissions, and during the 1890s he became a tremendously successful painter of portraits. About this time he also began to work on the murals which he executed for the Boston Public Library, working on them for the next twenty-five years. Sargent was elected an academician in 1897 at both the National Academy of Design and the Royal Academy in London, as well as becoming a French Legion of Honor officer.

With the exception of some commissioned charcoal drawings, Sargent left his work in portraiture in 1909 and devoted his full attention to landscapes and genre scenes. He frequently used watercolor, a medium which he employed from time to time throughout his career and developed fully in his late period. The last ten years of his life were spent in Boston and London, where he died in 1925. In December of that year the Museum of Fine Arts, Boston, held a memorial exhibition in which 113 of Sargent's works were shown.

John Singer Sargent
The Sulphur Match
1882, Oil on canvas
23 x 16¼ in. (58.42 x 41.28 cm.)
Signed (upper right): *John S. Sargent / Venice 1882*
(fig. 60)

PROVENANCE
Louis Curtis, Brookline, Mass.
Mrs. Louis Curtis, Brookline, Mass.
The Hon. Laurence Curtis, Brookline, Mass.
[Hirschl & Adler Galleries, New York, 1975]
Jo Ann and Julian Ganz, Jr., 1976

EXHIBITED
Copley Gallery, Boston, *Loan Exhibition*, January, 1917.
Grand Central Art Galleries, New York, *Retrospective Exhibition of Important Works of John Singer Sargent*, February 23–March 22, 1924, no. 37, pp. 37, 47 (illus.), Louis Curtis Collection.

Museum of Fine Arts, Boston, *Memorial Exhibition of the Works of the Late John Singer Sargent*, November 3–December 27, 1925, no. 16, p. 4, illus. (n. p.), Louis Curtis Collection.

The Metropolitan Museum of Art, New York, *Memorial Exhibition of the Work of John Singer Sargent*, January 4–February 14, 1926, no. 8, p. 4, illus. (n.p.), Mrs. Louis Curtis Collection.

Corcoran Gallery of Art, Washington, D.C., *The Private World of John Singer Sargent*, April 18–June 14, 1964; Cleveland Museum of Art, Cleveland, Ohio, July 7–August 16, 1964; Worcester Art Museum, September 17–November 1, 1964; Munson-Williams-Proctor Institute, Utica, N.Y., November 15, 1964–January 3, 1965, no. 18, n.p., Mrs. Louis Curtis Collection.

BIBLIOGRAPHY

Nathaniel Pousette-Dart, *Distinguished American Artists: John Singer Sargent* (New York: Frederick A. Stokes Company, 1924), illus. (n.p.).

Leila Mechlin, "The Sargent Exhibition, Grand Central Art Galleries, New York," *The American Magazine of Art*, 15 (April, 1924): 189 (illus.).

Rose V. S. Berry, "John Singer Sargent: Some of his American Work," *Art and Archaeology*, 18 (September 1924): 96 (illus.), 97, 100.

Obituary, *New York Evening Post*, April 15, 1925.

William Howe Downes, *John S. Sargent, His Life and Work* (Boston: Little, Brown, and Company, 1925), 132, illus. (n.p.), as *The Sulphur Match* (*Cigarette*).

The Hon. Evan Charteris, K.C., *John Sargent* (New York: Charles Scribner's Sons, 1927), 282.

Charles Merrill Mount, *John Singer Sargent, A Biography* (New York: W. W. Norton & Company, Inc., 1955), 444, no. K825.

Richard Ormond, *John Singer Sargent, Paintings-Drawings-Watercolors* (New York: Harper & Row, Publishers, 1970), 29.

James Normile, "In Praise of Women," *Architectural Digest*, 32 (May-June 1976): 69 (illus.), 155.

At the time of the Grand Central Art Galleries exhibition in 1924, it was suggested by several familiar with the Frank Duveneck (1848–1919) Munich circle of artists that the man depicted was the artist J. Frank Currier (1843–1909).[1] It is possible that Currier was in Venice during one or both of Sargent's trips to Venice in 1880 and 1882. Duveneck's portrait of Currier (c. 1879, oil on canvas, 24½ x 21, Art Institute of Chicago), in which Currier wears a similar hat to that depicted in the Sargent, appears to be of the same man. The woman depicted is Sargent's favorite model, Gigia Viani.[2] While in Venice, Sargent stayed with his relatives, the Daniel Sargent Curtis family in their home in the Palazzo Barbaro.[3]

1. Berry, *Sargent*, 97, 100.
2. Ormond, *Sargent*, 29.
3. Mount, *Sargent*, 71.

Julian Scott (1846–1901)

Julian Scott, known primarily for his paintings of the American West and of the Civil War, was born at Johnson, Vermont, in 1846. During the Civil War he enlisted in the army and later served as a colonel on the staff of General Smith, and many of his later paintings draw upon his experiences in the Civil War. Following the war, he studied at the National Academy of Design in New York City and finished his studies in Paris. In 1870 he was elected an associate of the academy. In 1890 Scott was hired, together with Gilbert Gaul, Peter Moran, and Walter Shirlaw, to do illustrations for a special report for the Eleventh Census on *Indians Taxed and Indians Not Taxed*, and he spent several years studying Indians in the Indian territories and in the Southwest. He died in Plainfield, New Jersey, in 1901.

Julian Scott
Horseman, Anadarco, Oklahoma
1890, Oil on canvas
12½ x 10¹⁄₁₆ in. (31.75 x 25.56 cm.)
Signed (lower right): *JScott* (JS in monogram) / *Anadarco, I.T. 1890*
(I.T.: Indian Territory)
(fig. 70)

PROVENANCE
Thomas Donaldson, Philadelphia

The Hon. John Wanamaker, Philadelphia, 1901

The University Museum, University of Pennsylvania, Philadelphia, gift from Mr. Wanamaker, 1901

[Hirschl & Adler Galleries, New York, 1971]

Private Collection, 1972

[Hirschl & Adler Galleries, 1976]

Jo Ann and Julian Ganz, Jr., 1976

EXHIBITED
Hirschl & Adler Galleries, New York, *Faces and Places: Changing Images of 19th Century America*, December 5, 1972–January 6, 1973, no. 83 (illus., n.p.).

The umbrella was used by Indians during this period as an indication of rank, especially that of chief.[1] Traditional power structures among the western tribes were, however, changing when Scott painted this work, a point stressed by the *Report on Indians Taxed and Indians Not Taxed in The United States* (*Except Alaska*) *at the Eleventh Census: 1890* (Washington, Government Printing Office, 1894), p. 531:

In 1878 the [Federal Government] agency for the Kiowa, Comanche, and Apache reservation was removed from Fort Sill to Anadarko, on the Washita river, and there these tribes are now associated with the Wichitas and affiliated bands. This removal has been salutary in every way; the influence of the peaceful and loyal Wichitas over the wilder bands is excellent; large camps have been broken up dissipating the influence of the chiefs and establishing heads of families. Instead of a single encampment of the whole band, one now finds never more than 2 or 3 lodges in a group, oftener but the single family, which in some cases is removed 15 miles from the agency.

The image of *Horseman, Anadarco, Oklahoma*, however, was not included in the *Report*.

1. For a photographic illustration see Freeman Tilden, *Following the Frontier* (New York: Alfred A. Knopf, 1964), 128 (illus.), 130.

Aaron Draper Shattuck (1832–1928)

Aaron Draper Shattuck was born in Francestown, New Hampshire, in 1832, and began his artistic training in Boston, where he studied with Alexander Ransom in 1851. Moving with Ransom to New York in 1852, Shattuck enrolled in antique and life classes at the National Academy of Design where he was elected an associate in 1856 and an academician in 1861. He remained a portraitist until about 1854, when he made his first sketching tour of the White Mountains and turned to painting landscapes. During the summer Shattuck traveled to New Hampshire, Maine, or upper New York, returning to New York City in the winter. Unlike many of his contemporaries, he never studied in Europe.

Shattuck exhibited regularly at the National Academy, the Brooklyn Art Association, and occasionally at the Boston Athenaeum and the Pennsylvania Academy of the Fine Arts. His handling of detail, in particular, set his work apart from that of his contemporaries. Henry T. Tuckerman wrote that Shattuck was "one of the first of our landscape painters to render foregrounds with care and fidelity." He showed a preference for small-scale canvases, and his choice of subject matter tended toward quiet, intimate scenes. The artist had several interests in addition to painting. He invented and patented a metal stretcher key, made violins, and raised sheep. After a serious illness in 1888, Shattuck abandoned painting but lived comfortably on his farm in Granby, Connecticut, until his death in 1928.

Aaron Draper Shattuck
Leaf Study with Yellow Swallow Tail
c. 1859, Oil on canvas
18 x 13 in. (45.72 x 33.02 cm.), arched top
Unsigned
(fig. 6)

PROVENANCE
Estate of the artist
Eugene and Katherine S. Emigh (by inheritance, the artist's granddaughter)
[Hirschl & Adler Galleries, New York, 1973]
Jo Ann and Julian Ganz, Jr., 1973

EXHIBITED
The New Britain Museum of American Art, New Britain, Conn., *Aaron Draper Shattuck, N.A., 1832–1928: A Retrospective Exhibition*, March 17–April 26, 1970, no. 13 (illus., n.p.), Katherine and Eugene Emigh Collection.
Santa Barbara Museum of Art, Santa Barbara, Calif., *American Paintings, Watercolors and Drawings from the Collection of Jo Ann and Julian Ganz, Jr.*, June 23–July 22, 1973, no. 66, n.p.
National Collection of Fine Arts, Smithsonian Institution, Washington, D.C., *America as Art*, April 30–November 7, 1976, checklist, no. 141.

BIBLIOGRAPHY
Joshua C. Taylor, *America as Art* (Washington, D.C.: Published for the National Collection of Fine Arts by the Smithsonian Institution Press, 1976), 120 (illus.). (Published in conjunction with the exhibition of the same name.)

Charles B. Ferguson, "Aaron Draper Shattuck, White Mountain School Painter," *American Art Review*, 3 (May–June 1976): 72–74 (illus., p. 73).
Joshua C. Taylor, *The Fine Arts In America* (Chicago and London: The University of Chicago Press, 1979), 97 (illus.).
Linda S. Ferber, *William Trost Richards (1833–1905): American Landscape and Marine Painter* (Ph.D. diss., Columbia University, 1980; New York & London: Garland Publishing, Inc., 1980), 139, 423, 486 (fig. 101).

Although Shattuck has not been documented as being involved in the English Pre-Raphaelite movement, the detailed depiction of nature in this work does suggest the influence of John Ruskin.[1] He appears to have been admired by William Trost Richards (q.v.) for this quality.[2]

1. Ferguson, *Shattuck*, 72, 74.
2. Ferber, *Richards*, 139.

Francis Augustus Silva (1835–1886)

Francis Augustus Silva was born in New York City in 1835. According to family tradition, his grandfather was a Frenchman who had been a portrait painter in Lisbon. Silva was apprenticed to a sign painter in New York, but became so successful that he set up his own studio there in 1858. In 1861 he enlisted in the New York State Militia and served in the Civil War. Following his marriage in 1868, Silva settled in New York to begin his career as a professional artist. He exhibited yearly at the National Academy of Design from 1868 until 1886 and at the Brooklyn Art Association from 1869 to 1885. He was elected a member of the American Water Color Society in 1872 and of the Artists' Fund Society in 1873.

Silva, whom John Baur has called "one of the most sensitive luminists," became known for his quiet marine paintings with subtle manipulations of light and atmosphere. Living in Brooklyn where he could see the ships he loved to paint, Silva took frequent trips up and down the eastern seabord from New Jersey to Massachusetts, painting scenes of Narragansett Bay as well as the Hudson. His only time abroad seems to have been in 1879 when he visited Venice.

Although he continued to maintain his studio in New York, Silva moved to New Jersey in 1880, and it is New Jersey landscapes and seascapes that were to be his primary themes from that point on. Silva died of double pneumonia in New York in 1886.

Francis A. Silva
Sunrise at Tappan Zee (Sunrise)
1874, Oil on canvas
20¹⁄₁₆ x 36⅛ in. (50.96 x 91.76 cm.)
Signed (lower right): *F. A. Silva / 74*
(fig. 9)

PROVENANCE
[William Schaus, New York]
[Hirschl & Adler Galleries, New York, 1975]
Jo Ann and Julian Ganz, Jr., 1975

EXHIBITED
Los Angeles County Museum of Art, *Pertaining to the Sea*, March 23–May 2, 1976, no. 52 (illus.), n.p., as *Sunrise*.

BIBLIOGRAPHY
John I. H. Baur, "Francis A. Silva: Beyond Luminism," *The Magazine Antiques*, 118 (November, 1980): 1024 (fig. 8), 1025; related works: pp. 1019 (pl. 1), 1021 (fig. 4), 1023 (fig. 6).

The compositional motif of this work was a repeated one for Silva thoughout the early 1870s.[1]

1. See Baur, "Silva," pp. 1019 (pl. 1), 1021 (fig. 4), 1023 (fig. 6) and an unidentified catalogue illustration (*Francis A. Silva File*, Hirschl & Adler Galleries, New York), no. 67, *Seining on Tappan Zee, Nyack, N.Y.*, 1872, oil on canvas, 20 x 36 in., location unknown, which is closely related to *Sunrise at Tappan Zee* (*Sunrise*).

Lilly Martin Spencer (1822–1902)

Born in England of French immigrant parents, Lilly Martin Spencer was raised in Marietta, Ohio. Her success in drawing charcoal portraits of family and friends prompted her to begin painting in oil. Her first exhibition in Marietta in 1841 attracted the attention of art patron Nicholas Longworth of Cincinnati, who offered to send her to Europe for formal training. Instead, she chose to remain in Cincinnati, painting domestic genre scenes, portraits, and scenes inspired by poems and ballads. She studied briefly with John Insco Williams in Cincinnati and in 1848 moved to New York City. There she began to concentrate almost exclusively on painting contemporary scenes from domestic life, selling her paintings through the American Art Union until it was dissolved in 1852. She took drawing lessons at the National Academy of Design, where she was elected an academician in 1850 and also exhibited at the Brooklyn Art Association during the 1860s and seventies. While pursuing her career as an artist, Spencer was also a wife and mother. She is said to have had thirteen children, eight of whom lived to maturity and often appear as subjects in her work. In the later part of her career, Spencer seems to have concentrated on portraiture and still life. She continued painting until her death in 1902 in New York City.

Lilly Martin Spencer
Mother and Child
1858, Oil on academy board
16 x 12 in. (40.64 x 30.48 cm.), arched top
Signed (lower right): *Lilly M. Spencer / 1858*
(fig. 38)

PROVENANCE
[Hamilton Gallery, New York]
Jo Ann and Julian Ganz, Jr., 1974

EXHIBITED
Los Angeles County Museum of Art, *American Narrative Painting*, October 1–November 17, 1974, no. 54, pp. 18, 116, 117 (illus.).

BIBLIOGRAPHY
Robin Bolton-Smith and William H. Truettner, *Lilly Martin Spencer 1822–1902: The Joys of Sentiment* (Washington, D.C.: Published for the National Collection of Fine Arts by the Smithsonian Institution Press, 1973); related works: 51 (fig. 31), 52 (fig. 32), 152, 169–170, 211.
Martha Hutson, "American Narrative Painting; The Painter's America: Rural and Urban Life, 1810–1910," *American Art Review*, 1 (November–December 1974): 106–107 (illus.).

The work probably depicts the artist and her son Charles and is a variant of *"This Little Pig Went to Market"* (1857, oil on academy board with arched top, 16 x 12 in., Campus Martius Museum, Marietta, Ohio).[1] It may have served as a pendant to *Listening to Father's Watch* (1857, oil on academy board, 16 x 11⅞ in., The Currier

Gallery of Art, Manchester, N.H.),[2] which depicted the artist's husband Benjamin Rush Spencer and her son William Henry. The chair also appears in the posthumous portrait of *Nicholas Longworth Ward* (1858–1860, oil on canvas, 50½ x 40⅛ in., The Newark Museum).[3]

1. Bolton-Smith, *Spencer*, 52 (fig. 32), 169–70.
2. Bolton-Smith, *Spencer*, 51 (fig. 31), 152.
3. Bolton-Smith, *Spencer*, 57 (fig. 35), 211.

Thomas Sully (1783–1872)

Thomas Sully was born at Horncastle, England and emigrated to Charleston, South Carolina, with his parents in 1792. His first instruction in painting came from his schoolmate Charles Fraser, his brother Lawrence, and his brother-in-law Jean Belzons, and Sully, like them, began his career as a miniaturist. From 1801 until he settled in Philadelphia in 1807, Sully traveled widely in the United States, spending time in Richmond, Norfolk, New York, and Boston. During this period he began to paint oil portraits and received advice from some of the nation's leading artists—notably John Trumbull and Gilbert Stuart. In 1809 several Philadelphia art patrons provided Sully with funds for further study in England. He carried letters of introduction to Benjamin West, who encouraged him to seek advice from a portrait painter. Sully turned to Sir Thomas Lawrence for guidance and after a year in London, returned to Philadelphia in 1810. In 1838, at the height of his career, he again visited England where he painted a portrait of Queen Victoria.

Following the death of Charles Willson Peale in 1827, Sully's position as Philadelphia's leading portrait painter was unquestioned, and he maintained that position throughout his long career. The register in which Sully recorded information about his commissions lists over 2,600 paintings. He was active in the affairs of the Pennsylvania Academy, having become an academician in 1812, and was invited to become its president in 1843—an honor which he declined. During his career he traveled frequently to other cities to paint portraits and maintained

particularly close ties with friends in Charleston. In addition to his portraits, he painted historical compositions, landscapes, so-called fancy pictures, and copies after old masters. He died in Philadelphia, in 1872, in his nintieth year.

Thomas Sully
Portrait of the Misses Mary & Emily McEuen
1823, Oil on canvas
44¼ x 34¼ in. (112.4 x 87 cm.)
Signed (lower center, on folio): *Sketches from nature / TS 1823.* (TS in monogram)
Inscribed (on a label affixed to the stretcher): *Presented by Elizabeth M. Smith / to / her Sisters / =Mary & Emily McEuen= / =Dec. 25th 1823=*
(fig. 29)

PROVENANCE

Mary and Emily McEuen, Philadelphia, 1823
Mrs. William M. (Mary McEuen) Boyce, Philadelphia, by 1839
Oliver Boyce Judson, Philadelphia (grandson)
[M. Knoedler and Company, New York, 1940]
[Macbeth Gallery, New York]
Bartlett Arkell, New York
Mrs. Louise R. Arkell, New York
Mrs. Stephen A. Wilson, New York (daughter of Mrs. Arkell)
[Hirschl & Adler Galleries, New York, 1976]
Jo Ann and Julian Ganz, Jr., 1976

EXHIBITED

M. Knoedler & Co., New York, *American Painting in the 18th, 19th, and 20th Centuries,* August–September 6, 1940, no. 23, typescript, n.p., as *Mrs. Boyce and Mrs. Smith.*
Hirschl & Adler Galleries, New York, *The American Experience,* October 27–November 27, 1976, no. 19 (illus.), n.p.

BIBLIOGRAPHY

Thomas Sully, *Original Thomas Sully Register,* manuscript, Historical Society of Pennsylvania, Philadelphia, page for 1823.
Charles Henry Hart, ed., *A Register of Portraits by Thomas Sully (1801–1871)* (Philadelphia: Charles Henry Hart, 1909), no. 1108 (p. 111).
Edward Biddle and Mantle Fielding, *The Life and Works of Thomas Sully,* (Philadelphia: Wickersham Press, 1921), no. 1151 (p. 219); related works: nos. 1616, 1618 (p. 276).

D.B., "New Exhibitions of the Month," *The Art News,* 38 (August 17, 1940): 13 (illus.) as *Mrs. Boyce and Mrs. Smith of Philadelphia.*
Wolfgang Born, *Still-Life Painting In America* (New York: Oxford University Press, 1947), 20, pl. 47, as *Portrait of Mrs. Boyd* [*sic*] *and Mrs. Smith.*

The work was painted between November 3 and December 18, 1823 for Mrs. Charles Willis Smith, née Elizabeth McEuen, presumably as a Christmas gift for her sisters. In turn, Mary and Emily commissioned a portrait of Elizabeth from Sully.[1] This work was begun on November 24 and finished on December 19, 1823. Emily was married to Elizabeth's brother-in-law, James Brown Smith, on February 17, 1825. The double portrait probably remained with Mary, since a replica of Emily's portrait was painted for her by Sully in June 1825.[2] It was, in any case, inherited by Mary upon Emily's death in 1839. The flowers in the vase cannot all be readily identified but include roses, a tulip, and morning glories. These flowers may have been included for their symbolic meanings derived from the newly popular, but never precise, "language of flowers." As symbols of beauty, the roses probably refer to the portrayed sisters' beauty. The tulip, as a symbol of the declaration of love, could refer to the three sisters' love for each other, which, of course, was the reason for the portrait's commission. The morning glory, which in one of its forms symbolized the fulfilled hope of an engaged woman, might have referred to Emily's marriage plans. The oil sketch for the *Portrait* (c. 1823, oil on canvas, 6¼ x 5¼ in., private collection) included only the word "Sketches" on the folio that Emily holds, and an unclearly defined still-life.

1. Biddle, *Sully*, no. 1616.
2. Biddle, *Sully*, no. 1618.

Charles Frederick Ulrich (1858–1908)

Born in New York City in 1858, the son of a photographer, Charles Ulrich first studied art at the National Academy of Design. In 1875 at the age of seventeen, he commenced study at the Munich Academy under Ludwig Löfftz and Wilhelm Lindenschmidt. Returning to this country sometime between 1879 and 1882, Ulrich began to exhibit at the Brooklyn Art Association and the National Academy of Design, to which he was elected an associate in 1883. He also became a member of the Society of American Artists and the Society of Painters in Pastel. Ulrich's choice of subjects, which included immigrants as well as craftsmen at work, was unusual for his time, but his paintings were highly regarded. In 1884 he was the first recipient of the National Academy's Thomas B. Clarke prize for figure painting, and in 1886 a group of gentlemen gave his painting *Glass Blowers at Murano* to The Metropolitan Museum of Art. Much of Ulrich's career from the 1880s on was spent abroad: in Holland, Venice, Paris, and Rome; he died in Berlin in 1908. He was chiefly responsible for organizing the American section of the 1888 Munich exhibition, and he received an honorable mention at the Paris Exposition of 1889 and a medal at the Columbian Exposition in Chicago in 1893. Today no more than a dozen works identified as having been painted by Ulrich exist in American collections.

Charles F. Ulrich
An Etcher in His Studio
c. 1882, Oil on wood panel
12 x 8¾ in. (30.48 x 22.23 cm.)
Signed (lower right): *C·F·Ulrich.*
(fig. 61)

PROVENANCE
[Herbert Roman and Schweitzer Gallery, New York, 1975]
Jo Ann and Julian Ganz, Jr., 1975

In 1882 Ulrich exhibited the *Wood Engraver* (1882, oil on wood panel, 18½ x 10 in., location unknown) at the Fifty-Seventh Annual Exhibition of the National Academy of Design, New York, p. 26, no. 477. Because of its success, he exhibited *An Amateur Etcher* (1882, oil on wood panel?, 12 x 15 in., location unknown) in 1883 at the Fifty-Eighth Annual Exhibition of the National Academy of Design, p. 24, no. 420. The 1882 works were both portraits of young ladies. It is possible that *An Etcher in His Studio* dates from the same period and was conceived as a pendant depicting a professional to its counterparts showing amateurs.

 ### Elihu Vedder (1836–1923)

Elihu Vedder, one of the most visionary American painters of the nineteenth century, was born in New York City in 1836. He studied drawing briefly with Tompkins Harrison Matteson, a genre painter, and in 1856 he went to Europe. Vedder spent eight months in Paris and then traveled to Italy, spending most of his time in Florence, where he remained until late in 1860. Vedder returned to New York in 1861 and began to exhibit paintings—including Italian and American landscapes, paintings based on biblical themes, and paintings depicting exotic subjects, such as stories from the Arabian Nights—at the National Academy of Design. In addition to these subjects Vedder drew upon classical mythology and Eastern religion as themes for his later paintings.

In 1864 Vedder was made an associate of the academy and the next year an academician. He returned to Paris at the end of 1865, where he remained for one year before going to Rome; it was during this time that he painted the *Girl with a Lute*. In 1866 Vedder established a studio in Rome, where he remained until his death in 1923.

Despite his residence abroad, most of Vedder's patronage came from the United States, and after 1879 he made frequent trips to New York. In addition to easel paintings, he produced book illustrations and mural paintings—notably his illustrations for *The Rubáiyát of Omar Khayyam* (1884), which established his fame in the United States, and his mural paintings of the 1890s in the Walker Art Gallery of Bowdoin College and in the Library of Congress.

Elihu Vedder
Girl with a Lute
1866, Oil on wood panel
16 x 9 in. (40.64 x 22.86 cm.)
Signed (lower right): *V. Paris-66*
Signed (on back): *Elihu Vedder / Paris-1866*
(fig. 54)

PROVENANCE
[Barry & Co., Paris, 1866]
Private Collection, Boston
Mr. and Mrs. Lawrence A. Fleischman, Detroit
[Kennedy Galleries, Inc., New York]

Mr. and Mrs. Jacob M. Kaplan, New York
[Berry-Hill Galleries, New York, 1974]
Jo Ann and Julian Ganz, Jr., 1974

EXHIBITED

Smithsonian Institution Traveling Exhibition Service, Smithsonian Institution, Washington, D.C., *Paintings and Drawings by Elihu Vedder*, 1966, no. 90, as *Standing Girl with Musical Instrument*, Kennedy Galleries, New York.

Whitney Museum of American Art, New York, *18th and 19th Century American Paintings from Private Collections*, June 27–September 11, 1972, no. 71, n.p., as *Young Woman with a Lute*, Mr. and Mrs. Jacob M. Kaplan Collection.

National Collection of Fine Arts, Smithsonian Institution, Washington, D.C., *Perceptions and Evocations: The Art of Elihu Vedder*, October 13, 1978–February 4, 1979; The Brooklyn Museum, April 28–July 9, 1979, no. 47, n.p.

BIBLIOGRAPHY

Elihu Vedder, *The Digressions of V. Written for His Own Fun and That of His Friends* (Boston and New York: Houghton Mifflin Company, 1910), 303–304.

John P. Simoni, "Imagination, Symbolism Shown in Vedder Work," *The Wichita Eagle and Beacon*, February 12, 1967 (illus.).

Alfred Frankenstein, "Old Castles and Empty Tracks," *San Francisco Sunday Examiner and Chronicle*, April 30, 1967, p. 37.

Regina Soria, *Elihu Vedder: American Visionary Artist in Rome (1836–1923)* (Rutherford, New Jersey: Fairleigh Dickinson University Press, 1970), 50, 289 (cat. no. 78), pl. 13 (n.p.).

———, Joshua C. Taylor, Jane Dillenberger, Richard Murray, *Perceptions and Evocations: The Art of Elihu Vedder* (Washington: Published for the National Collection of Fine Arts by the Smithsonian Institution Press, 1979), 21, 76 (fig. 70), 77, 78, 99, 101, 172, 173 (fig. 207) (published in conjunction with the exhibition of the same name).

The sale of this work provided one of the major sources of funds for Vedder's removal to Rome in 1866:

But soon there arose a strong wind that was to bear me southward, as poorly provisioned as before, but with the feeling that once back in Italy I should be more at home, and that things would come out right in the end. At that time there was a man in Paris who contemplated tampering with pictures. He had founded a firm [Barry & Co.], and the firm bought from me a little picture, — "Girl with a Lute," — painted because I bought a lute and wished to justify my extravagance. I got for it two hundred dollars, but it was sold afterwards in Boston for seven hundred and fifty dollars; thus all were happy.[1]

1. Vedder, *Digressions*, 303.

John Ferguson Weir (1841–1926)

Son of the artist Robert W. Weir and brother of the artist Julian Alden Weir, John Ferguson Weir was born in 1841 at West Point, New York. He received his early artistic training from his father who was drawing instructor at the U.S. Military Academy and in 1861 moved to New York City where he took a studio in the 10th Street Studio Building. Three years later, upon first exhibiting his work at the National Academy of Design, he was elected an associate; he became an academician in 1866 with the exhibition of one of the first American industrial paintings, *The Gun Foundry* (Putnam County Historical Society, Cold Spring, N.Y.). Weir spent a year in Europe and in 1869 assumed the position of director of the Yale School of Fine Arts—a position he held

until 1913. While at Yale he acted not only as an administrator but as a lecturer on aesthetic principles and art history, as well as a teacher of painting and design. Although much of his time was devoted to administration of the Yale school, he continued to paint landscapes, academic portraits, and genre scenes and to produce sculpture such as the bronze statutes of President Woolsey and Professor Silliman of Yale. In 1876 Weir was chosen to be commissioner of the art exhibition at the Centennial Exhibition in Philadelphia. He died in 1926 in Providence, Rhode Island.

John Ferguson Weir

An Artist's Studio
January, 1864, Oil on canvas
25½ x 30½ in. (64.77 x 77.47 cm.)
Signed (lower left): *J. F. Weir. / January 1864* (fig. 53)

PROVENANCE

Cyrus Butler, New York, 1864
Mrs. Alice Clark Read, Lexington, Mass.
Mrs. Ruth Read Young, Bronxville, N.Y.
[Sotheby Parke Bernet, New York (Sale No. 4038, *American 19th & 20th Century Paintings, Drawings, Watercolors & Sculpture*, Lot No. 19 (illus., n.p.) as *The Artist's Studio*) October 27, 1977; Hirschl & Adler Galleries, New York, as agent]
Jo Ann and Julian Ganz, Jr., 1977

EXHIBITED

Athenaeum Club, New York, *A Reception given to meet the artists in New York*, 1864.

Brooklyn and Long Island Fair In Aid of the United States Sanitary Commission, Brooklyn, New York, February 22, 1864, no. 114, *The Studio*, with the artist, n.p.

National Academy of Design, New York, *Thirty-Ninth Annual Exhibition*, 1864, p. 18, no. 236, Cyrus Butler Collection.

Second Annual Exhibition of the Yale School of Fine Arts, Yale College, New Haven, Conn., June 8, 1870—close of summer term, p. 6, no. 72, Cyrus Butler Collection.

Young Men's Association, Troy, N.Y., *Loan Exhibition of One Hundred and Forty Ancient and Modern Paintings Loaned by the Hon. Thomas B. Carroll*, Season 1878–1879; possibly exhibited as no. 128, *The Artist's Studio*.

BIBLIOGRAPHY

Henry T. Tuckerman, *Book of the Artists: American Artist Life* (New York: G. P. Putnam & Son; London: Sampson Low & Co., 1867), 623, Collection of Cyrus Butler, Esq., N.Y.

Clara Erskine Clement (Waters) and Laurence Hutton, *Artists of the Nineteenth Century and their Works,* seventh edition, revised, 2 vols. (Boston and New York: Houghton, Mifflin and Company, 1894), 2, p. 343.

Irene Weir, *Robert W. Weir, Artist* (New York: House of Field-Doubleday, Inc., Publishers, 1947), 114, 140.

John Ferguson Weir, *The Recollections of John Ferguson Weir, Director of the Yale School of the Fine Arts 1869–1913,* Theodore Sizer, ed. (New York: The New-York Historical Society and New Haven: The Associates in the Fine Arts at Yale University, 1957), 46–47.

Betsy Fahlman, "John Ferguson Weir: Painter of Romantic and Industrial Icons," *Archives of American Art Journal,* 20, no. 2 (1980):2, 8n.

The work depicts the artist's father, Robert Walter Weir (1803–1889), Professor of Drawing at the United States Military Academy from 1834 to 1876, in his West Point studio. Identifiable works include, on the back wall to the left, two studies for Robert Weir's masterwork, *The Embarkation of the Pilgrims* (1843, oil on canvas, c. 14 x 20 feet, The Capitol, Washington, D.C.). The top study is a detail of Miles Standish and his wife, Rose; the bottom, a detail of Mr. Robinson, Pastor of the Congregation, Mrs. Brad-

ford and Mrs. Carver. On the easel is another of Robert Weir's major works, *Taking the Veil* (1863, oil on canvas, 49½ x 39¾ in., Yale University Art Gallery, New Haven, Conn.). On the right wall is one of several versions of the father's popular *Santa Claus, or St. Nicholas* (original version: 1837, oil on wood panel, 30 x 24⅜ in., New-York Historical Society, New York). One of the earliest depictions of the modern image of Santa Claus, it was based on Clement Moore's recently published poem, *The Night Before Christmas.* Along with *An Artist's Studio,* John Weir exhibited *Christmas Eve* (no. 131, p. 12) at the 1864 National Academy of Design Annual Exhibition, certainly as a further homage to his father's work. At the same exhibition, Robert Weir exhibited *Evening of the Crucifixion* (no. 195, p. 16), and this may be the work propped on the cabinet. On top of the cabinet is a replica of Shobal Vail Clevenger's 1839–40 bust of the artist Washington Allston (1779–1843). The bust and cabinet also appear in John Weir's *The Artist's Studio* (1864, oil on wood panel, 15¼ x 12¼ in., Yale University Art Gallery, New Haven, Conn.). *An Artist's Studio* was a major success when it was exhibited in the 1864 Academy Annual and resulted in the artist's election as an associate of the academy in the same year. In the catalogue to the 1864 Academy Annual, p. 18, the following unsigned poem was included in the work's entry:

I well remember how the light, the pale pure north light, fell
On all within that lofty room, and clothed with mystic spell
A massive oaken cabinet, and many a curious chair—
Bright armor of the olden time, and relics quaint and rare.

I marked them well,—the gathered books, the painter's treasures all:
Here was the resting-place of day, whatever might befall;
The inner shrine of one whose brow the stamp of genius bore,
And who the laurels of his fame with childlike meekness wore.

* * *

Oh, many a slowly-waning hour this silent room alone
Had seen the dreaming artist sit, like statue carved in stone;

Absorbed in patient watchfulness of all that Fancy brought,
Gleamings of gladness or of gloom from out the fields of thought.

* * *

🐚 Edwin Whitefield (1816–1892)

Edwin Whitefield was born in East Lulworth, Dorset, England, in 1816, but by 1838 he had immigrated to this country with the intention of making his living as an artist. He first lived in Albany, New York, and then in several towns along the Hudson River from 1842 to 1853, sketching views of American cities and residences to be reproduced in lithographic form and producing book illustrations of flowers. In subsequent years Whitefield lived in Canada, Minnesota, Chicago, and in the Boston area, where he settled permanently after 1866.

In 1845 Whitefield made illustrations for Emma C. Embury's *American Wild Flowers in their Native Haunts* (issued in the form of hand-colored lithographs), as well as some illustrations for Dr. A.B. Strong's *The American Flora, or History of Plants and Wild Flowers,* published in 1849–1851.

Edwin Whitefield
Formal Still Life

1840s, Watercolor on paper
5¼ x 6 in. (13.3 x 15.2 cm.), sight
Signed (lower center): *E. Whitefield*
(fig. 81)

PROVENANCE
[Childs Gallery, Boston]
Jo Ann and Julian Ganz, Jr., 1973

The placement and size of the signature suggest that this work was done as a model for a lithograph, possibly with an accompanying poem or description.

Edwin Whitefield
Blue and Yellow Violets in a Landscape
1855, Watercolor and pencil on paper
6¾ x 6¼ in. (17.2 x 15.9 cm.), sight
Signed (upper right): *E. Whitefield 1855*
(fig. 87)

PROVENANCE
[Childs Gallery, Boston]
Jo Ann and Julian Ganz, Jr., 1973

With its tinted wildflower in the extreme foreground against a background with a lake or river view in pencil, this work is in the tradition of the artist's illustrations for Emma C. Embury, *American Wild Flowers In Their Native Haunts— with twenty plates of plants, carefully colored after nature; and landscape views of their localities from drawings on the spot by E. Whitefield* (New York: D. Appleton & Company, 1845). However, this later work exhibits a greater attempt at the integration of the two elements.

ꭗ (Thomas) Worthington Whittredge (1820–1910)

Born in 1820 in Springfield, Ohio, Worthington Whittredge first worked as a house and sign painter and photographer. He started painting portraits in Cincinnati but soon turned to landscapes, one of which was accepted in 1846 for exhibition by the National Academy of Design. In 1849 Whittredge left for Europe. After traveling through Belgium and France, he went to Düsseldorf, where he remained for almost four years, studying under Andreas Achenbach. While there he befriended Emanuel Leutze and posed for several of the figures in Leutze's famous *Washington Crossing the Delaware*. In 1856 Whittredge took a sketching trip through Switzerland and Italy and settled in Rome, where he remained for another four years. Returning to the United States, he settled in New York City. Although he drew his subject matter from various locales, including the coasts of New England and the shores of the Hudson, he was particularly attracted to the quiet woodland interiors of the Catskill Mountains. In 1866 Whittredge made his first trip West, accompanying an army expedition. He later made two other western trips, one in 1870 with Sanford Gifford (q.v.) and John Kensett (q.v.), and the other in 1871. In 1874 Whittredge was elected president of the National Academy of Design and served in that capacity until early 1877. He died in Summit, New Jersey, in 1910, at the age of ninety.

T. Worthington Whittredge
Indian Encampment on the Platte River
c. 1870–1872, Oil on canvas
14¼ x 21¾ in. (36.2 x 55.25 cm.)
Signed (lower left): *W.Whittredge.*
(fig. 27)

PROVENANCE
The Hon. and Mrs. J. William Middendorf II, New York
[Kennedy Galleries, Inc., New York, 1964]
Private Collection
Mrs. Norman B. Woolworth, New York
[Coe Kerr Gallery, Inc., New York, c. 1969]
Edward McLaughlin, New York, 1969
[Coe Kerr Gallery, Inc., New York, 1975]
Jo Ann and Julian Ganz, Jr., 1975

This work is most likely a result of Whittredge's second western trip in 1870. The figures on the right are closely related to a similar grouping in *Crossing the Ford, Platte River, Colorado* (1870, oil on canvas, 41 x 68½ in., The Century Association, New York). The Ganz painting, however, is nearly identical in composition to *On the Plains, Colorado* (1872, oil on canvas, 30 x 50 in., St. Johnsbury Atheneum, St. Johnsbury, Vt.) and probably is the original version from which the larger painting is derived. The painting has been dated by Anthony F. Janson, senior curator, Indianapolis Museum of Art.

Index